The Secular Pilgrims of
Victorian Fiction

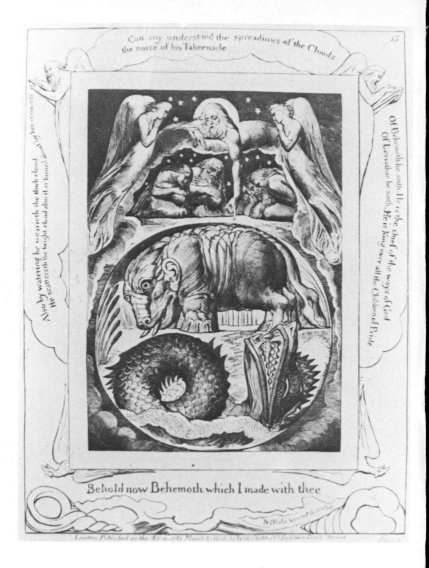

Can any understand the spreadings of the Clouds
the noise of his Tabernacle

Also by watering he wearieth the thick cloud
He scattereth the bright cloud also it is turned about by his counsels

Of Behemoth he saith He is the chief of the ways of God
Of Leviathan he saith, He is King over all the Children of Pride

Behold now Behemoth which I made with thee

WBlake invenit & sculpsit

London Published as the Act directs March 8, 1825 by Wm Blake N3 Fountain Court Strand

The Secular Pilgrims of Victorian Fiction

The novel as book of life

Barry V. Qualls

Cambridge University Press

Cambridge

London   New York   New Rochelle

Melbourne   Sydney

Published by the Press Syndicate of the University of Cambridge
The Pitt Building, Trumpington Street, Cambridge CB2 1RP
32 East 57th Street, New York, NY 10022, USA
296 Beaconsfield Parade, Middle Park, Melbourne 3206, Australia

First published 1982

Printed in Great Britain at the
University Press, Cambridge

Library of Congress catalogue card number: 82–1165

British Library cataloguing in publication data
Qualls, Barry V.
The secular pilgrims of Victorian fiction.
1. English fiction – 19th century – History and
criticism
I. Title
823'.8'09   PR871
ISBN 0 521 24409 9 hard covers
ISBN 0 521 27201 7 paperback

To
Jamima D. Qualls
and
Margaret B. Faverty

In Memoriam
Frederic E. Faverty

So dark and abstruse, without lamp or authentic finger-post, is the course of pious genius towards the Eternal Kingdoms grown. No fixed highway more; the old spiritual highways and recognized paths to the Eternal, now all torn up and flung in heaps . . . surely a tragic pilgrimage for all mortals; Darkness, and the mere shadow of Death, enveloping all things from pole to pole; and in the raging gulf-currents, offering us will-o'-wisps for load-stars, – intimating that there are no stars, nor ever were, except certain Old-Jew ones which have now gone out.

(Carlyle, *Life of Sterling*)

Contents

Illustrations

Preface

In 1833 Carlyle wrote to James Fraser that his Clothes-Volume was "put together in the fashion of a kind of Didactic Novel," with an Editor for "the main Actor in the business."[1] That Editor's task in *Sartor Resartus* is the task of the novelists – and of their narrators – who are my concern in the following pages. This concern focuses on the "double plot" which Bulwer Lytton found "a striking characteristic of the art of our century." This "duality of purpose" he defined as the combining of "an interior symbolical signification with an obvious popular interest in character and incident."[2] This "moral signification" has its sources in the religious tradition that created the nineteenth-century English Sunday: in the old emblem books and in *Pilgrim's Progress*, in the intense typological reading of scripture, and in the work of the spiritual biographers and autobiographers. Bunyan and the emblem writers saw "symbolical signification" in every natural fact, for the Bible revealed that everything declared the glory of God.

The status of the Word as the place of revelation was not, of course, so certain or so certainly secure in the nineteenth century. But Victorian novelists, who took their responsibilities as artists very seriously indeed, were determined that their words could still lead "Christian" of the latter day to the Celestial City – even as they and their readers wondered, as did Little Nell, if *Pilgrim's Progress* "was true in every word, and where those distant countries with the curious names might be." The novelists had always before them the work of the Romantics, German and English, who had stressed the prophetic visionary role of the artist; had redefined God, man, and nature; and had transmuted the spiritual biography into the *Bildungsroman*.

I take the seventeenth-century religious writings, popularly represented by Bunyan and Francis Quarles, and the Romantic revisionings of those inherited ideas and forms as the significant context in which Carlyle and the novelists of this study – and indeed most Victorian writers – worked. Next to these religious and Romantic representations of a world elsewhere I have set Carlyle.

Neither Puritan nor Romantic – but, like Blake, simply biblical – he is the nexus where the inherited religious tradition at once challenges and is incorporated into Romanticism. I use his work, especially *Sartor Resartus* and the *Latter-Day Pamphlets*, as a source for a language to describe and define Victorian fiction as the Victorians wrote it and their readers read it. *Sartor* offers that pattern of experience which Victorian novelists adopted or developed on their own for expressing "religious" possibilities in a secular age. The *Pamphlets* provide a "realistic" picture of a world without any religious or romance suggestion of "rescue," and without any notion that words might recall the unseen as well as the easily visible. I do not claim that the novelists were necessarily influenced by Carlyle: Dickens clearly was; Charlotte Brontë read nothing until after *Jane Eyre*; George Eliot reviewed his work (and George Henry Lewes dedicated his biography of Goethe to him). But Carlyle provides a clear emblematic picture for the struggles with traditions and with language which mark the careers of these popular novelists. Carlyle's "progress" is an emblem itself for the pilgrimage of the Victorian mind – and so it is used in the following pages.

In the chapters devoted to the individual novelists, Carlyle joins Bunyan and Quarles as contextual material. To focus the novelists' preoccupations – and mine – I have selected from the religious tradition emblems which the Romantics also found essential: the mirror, the prison, the labyrinth, the dunghill, the rescue of the shipwrecked pilgrim, and the conception of life as an embattled progress. And I have charted the responses of the novelists to the issues these emblems raise – about the self and about language – in a secular world. Each of these novelists felt that the focus of the Victorian Everyman must be on the world of "human interest and business," of ordinary life. Each, no matter how strong the pull of the "realistic" impulse, necessarily had recourse to the "double plot" of Bulwer's description – a plot where romance might also become Romance. Carlyle insisted in 1837 that "Romance exists . . . in Reality alone." And Bulwer added in 1842 that in literature a romance was "a truth for those who can comprehend it, and an extravagance for those who cannot."[3] To experience this Romance within reality, to know that the supernatural was in the natural, required only the "gift of seeing through other organs than the eyes."[4] This gift Caryle and the novelists were determined to give.

My focus is thus on the biblical romances, the "secular scriptures," these novelists wrote – those "little imitation[s]" of "the
ways of Providence" (Dickens' definition of art) which they offered
as at once novels and guidebooks for their readers. And these
readers constituted for them an inextricable part of their texts – as
had readers also for Bunyan. The "moral consequences of the
activities of reading and writing"[5] and the moral nature of language
itself were preoccupying concerns for authors and readers who
would have their texts be more than mere entertainments.

I have chosen novelists we all know well because I want to
establish a context for seeing anew what is familiar. I want the reader
to experience these novels as the Victorians experienced them: as
representations of and visionary responses to life as it was – as both
novels and books of life. My aim has never been to be all-inclusive. I
wanted to examine English writers dealing with the changing
conditions of language and noting the effects of this change on
English life. I have tended to give special attention to the beginning
and end of a career so as to chart how these writers dealt with the
increasing secularization of their world and the increasing
despiritualization of language. Thus I omit *Romola*; and I give little
attention to Dickens' obvious *Bildungsromane*, *David Copperfield*
and *Great Expectations*, because my emphasis is on his continuing
exploration of this form within the context of wider English social
concerns. And I do not treat Thackeray with the emphasis *Vanity
Fair* would seem, for my purposes, to demand. Thackeray's
emblematic language calls attention to itself as "mere *words*" (the
phrase is Carlyle's); his fiction announces its fictionality and the
fictionality of all myths which his characters – and his readers –
would use to order their lives. He can not sustain, he will not try to
sustain, the impulse towards "secular scripture" that characterizes
the other novelists.

Victorian novelists wrote and readers read with the "double plot"
a part of their spiritual heritage. Readers and writers and protagonists saw in "each man's life a strange emblem of every man's" (as
Carlyle said of Sterling). They found in *words* new, and sometimes
old, revelations. "Bunyan takes it for granted," William Hale White
wrote,

that the life of a man who is redeemed by the grace of God is a pilgrimage to
a better world. This, of course, is the leading thought in his book, and it is
one which we find most difficult to make our own. We can follow him
through all the incidents of his journey; we know the Valley of Humiliation,

the Valley of the Shadow, and Doubting Castle, but we are not sure, as he was sure, that the wayfarer will reach a celestial home at last. Upon this subject most of us hesitate to speak. We may hope and we may even believe, but an unmistakable instinct warns us to be silent. Perhaps, however, without disobeying it, we may be permitted to say almost in a whisper, that a man who has passed from youth to age cannot naturally rest in the sad conviction that what he has learned is to go for nothing, and that in no sense is there any continuance for him. Our faith may have no demonstrable foundation, and yet it may be a refuge for us. Our lives are shaped by so-called dreams.[6]

And these "so-called dreams," founded in the Bible and Bunyan, redefined by the Romantics, and then transmuted by Carlyle, shaped the Victorian novel into a new *scola cordis*.

This book had its origins in my childhood hearing of the Bible and Dickens and Arthurian legends; in my ninth-grade excitement about Tennyson and *Vanity Fair* – thank you, Rozale Smith; in my reading in graduate school of George Levine; and in the teaching there of Frederic E. Faverty – the most gentle and urgent of teaching voices. William Keach, Sheila Emerson, Thomas Van Laan, John Clubbe, Janet Larson, and especially Daniel Howard have given these pages careful scrutiny and have asked telling, and not always welcome, questions. Even more has been done by John M. Warner, whose attention to argument and loathing of Carlylese have served as continual calls to reflection (though he shares no responsibility for Carlylean convulsions that remain). I cannot imagine this book without his guidance, nor without the guidance of two colleagues at Rutgers: Bridget Lyons helped me to see the significance of emblems in Victorian literature; George Levine's continuing studies of the novelists gave stimulus and encouragement – as did his talk. The Rutgers Research Council and the Rutgers College Faculty Academic Study Program provided leaves that allowed time to shape this study. The Editors of *Studies in the Novel* kindly granted permission to use, in revised form, an article on *Our Mutual Friend* that originally appeared there. Mary Rueshoff and Linda Kozusko assisted with enthusiasm in the preparation of the manuscript. Larry Qualls offered suggestive readings of these pages and provided the photographs. And Dr Andrew Brown of Cambridge University Press gave help that made me wish I had enjoyed his learning and counsel at the outset of the writing.

Finally I acknowledge with gratitude those whose provisions ("part of the meaning, part of the mind") have for the past decade

kept me mostly out of Gehenna: Bridget Gellert Lyons and Robert
B. Lyons, William Keach and Sheila Emerson, John M. Warner –
and the voice of Eleanor Steber.

Note on texts and abbreviations

The following abbreviations are used within the text for works to which frequent reference is made; abbreviations indicate edition, volume and, in the case of the novelists, volume or book, chapter, and page numbers.

Carlyle

C	*The Works of Thomas Carlyle*. Ed. H. D. Traill. Centenary Edition. 30 vols. New York: Charles Scribner's Sons, 1896–1901.
FR	*The French Revolution*. Vols. II, III, IV of *Works*.
H	*On Heroes, Hero-Worship, and the Heroic in History*. Vol. 5 of *Works*.
LDP	*Latter-Day Pamphlets*. Vol. XX of *Works*.
PP	*Past and Present*. Ed. Richard D. Altick. Boston: Houghton Mifflin, 1965.
SR	*Sartor Resartus*. Ed. Charles Frederick Harrold. New York: Odyssey, 1937.

Charlotte Brontë

JE	*Jane Eyre*. Ed. Jane Jack and Margaret Smith. Oxford: Clarendon, 1969.
P	*The Professor*. Everyman's Library. London: Dent, 1969.
S	*Shirley*. Ed. Herbert Rosengarten and Margaret Smith. Oxford: Clarendon, 1979.
V	*Villette*. Ed. Mark Lilly. Penguin, 1979.

Charles Dickens

BH	*Bleak House*. Ed. George Ford and Sylvere Monod. New York: Norton, 1977.
DS	*Dombey and Son*. Ed. Alan Horsman. Oxford: Clarendon, 1974.

GE   *Great Expectations*. Ed. Angus Calder. Penguin, 1965.
LD   *Little Dorrit*. Ed. Harvey Peter Sucksmith. Oxford: Clarendon, 1979.
MC   *Martin Chuzzlewit*. Ed. P. N. Furbank. Penguin, 1968.
OCS   *The Old Curiosity Shop*. Ed. Angus Easson. Penguin, 1972.
OMF   *Our Mutual Friend*. Ed. Stephen Gill. Penguin, 1971.

George Eliot

AB   *Adam Bede*. Ed. John Paterson. Boston: Houghton Mifflin, 1968.
DD   *Daniel Deronda*. Ed. Barbara Hardy. Penguin, 1967.
FH   *Felix Holt, the Radical*. Ed. Fred C. Thomson. Oxford: Clarendon, 1980.
GEL   *The George Eliot Letters*. Ed. Gordon S. Haight. 9 vols. New Haven: Yale University Press, 1954–78.
Mid   *Middlemarch*. Ed. Gordon S. Haight. Boston: Houghton Mifflin, 1956.
MF   *The Mill on the Floss*. Ed. Gordon S. Haight. Oxford: Clarendon, 1980.
Scenes *Scenes of Clerical Life*. Ed. David Lodge. Penguin, 1973.
SM   *Silas Marner*. Ed. Q. D. Leavis. Penguin, 1967.

John Bunyan

B   *Grace Abounding to the Chief of Sinners* and *The Pilgrim's Progress*. Ed. Roger Sharrock. London: Oxford, 1966.

Francis Quarles

Quarles *Emblems, Divine and Moral*. London: William Tegg, 1866.

Introduction

The WORD made novel

Peruse this little Book; and thou wilt see
What thy heart is, and what it ought to be.
                                    (*Scola Cordis*)

Would'st read thy self, and read thou know'st not what
And yet know whether thou art blest or not,
By reading the same lines? O then come hither,
And lay my Book, thy Head and Heart together.
                            (Bunyan, *Pilgrim's Progress*)

Forward with us, courageous reader; be it towards failure, or towards
success! . . . Can many readers discern, as through a glass darkly, in huge
wavering outlines, some primeval rudiments of Man's Being, what is
changeable from what is unchangeable?
                            (Carlyle, *Sartor Resartus*)

Your homes the scene, yourselves the actors, here!
                                    (Dickens)[1]

I group the *Scola Cordis*, Bunyan, and Carlyle with Dickens
because the texts provide the emblematic context for the Victorian
novels inaugurated by Disraeli and Bulwer Lytton and Dickens and
terminated by *Jude the Obscure.* Quarles, Bunyan, and then Carlyle
offer us visions and revisions of the relationship between words and
reader, of the way authors expected their books to be used and
readers wanted to use them. Dickens, Thackeray, Charlotte Brontë,
and George Eliot shared this sense of writing as a *scola cordis*. The
novel, Carlyle declared, should provide "doctrine," "reproof,"
"edification," "healing," "guidance," "a divine awakening voice"
for "the heroic that is in all men" ("Scott": XXIX: 76, 83). The
importance of narrative, he wrote in his essay "On History," lies in
its linearity. It "travels towards one, or towards successive points,"
and in so doing offers a patterning of events which allows man to
"unite himself in clear conscious relation . . . with the whole
Future and the whole Past."[2] Narrative assures us of some
knowable order. We may lack the Heavenly City as our goal, but
"Art also and Literature" remain "intimately blended with Re-

I

ligion" because their concern is "our inward world" and the ways it connects itself with the life around us (XXVII: 88–9, 83, 94). Language's concern is with our souls.

Carlyle's ideas here reflect the verbal tradition sanctioned by Calvin, Knox, and a thousand Puritan autobiographers and preachers. Meditating upon God's Word and on the lives of his creatures had been central to the life of the English since the English and Scottish Puritans found the printed word a chief means of reforming and edifying fallen man. Bunyan looked for "a concurrance and agreement in the Scriptures" to validate his own progress (B: 63). Christian's daughter Mercy begged of the shepherds a looking-glass which "would present a man, one way, with his own Feature exactly; and . . . an other way . . . would shew the very Face and Similitude of the Prince of Pilgrims himself . . . to one where they have a mind to see him." Bunyan's marginal gloss offers a succinct comment on this "glass": "It was the Word of God" (B: 378). And this Word was the *scola cordis*. As U. Milo Kaufmann has shown, in his study of Bunyan and Puritan meditation, observing carefully one's own life or that of another was seen as "a second scripture by which to understand the written Word."[3] Meditation allowed the believer to discover God's workings in his life; it offered a heavenly ordained pattern to experience. And for the Puritan, Sacvan Bercovitch notes, casting the trials and rewards of one's life into a scriptural framework was "the safest way also to regulate conscience."

And to this end, every Puritan biographer wrote, in one degree or another, as though he were bringing the scriptures up to date through his subject's life. The result is a conventionalized rhetoric that blurs the difference between metaphor and experience, between one sect and another, even between traditionally distinct genres.[4]

This meditational, autobiographical impulse, as Ian Watt suggested, played a central role in the development of the novel. The self-consciousness which meditation suggests, the constant asking of "Who am I?" and "What shall I do?" is inextricably bound to consciousness of one's self as a time-locked being whose birth-to-death progress in history will mean everything in the end. *Telos*, the union with God, is only reached through historical being. Religious literature and early novels share a preoccupation with this image of life as an embattled journey and with this idea that words present "a just History of Fact; neither is there any Appearance of Fiction in it" (as the "Editor" of *Robinson Crusoe* declares).[5]

Any reader of the Victorian novel will quickly call to mind its focus on these central questions and its use of the same imagery to discuss them. But there is of course a major difference. A Puritan setting up a pulpit in nineteenth-century England would have found himself *in partibus infidelium*, no matter what the Methodists and other evangelicals had been doing in the way of revival. The idea of time as a seedfield for progress in holiness, the assumption that meditation involved measuring oneself by values quite external to and above one – these traditions had been under constant assault from the philosophical and scientific and industrial forces that made the age so "new." The Judeo-Christian sense of time as beginning at a known point and promising a definite end was being subverted by the work of geologists like Lyell and then biologists like Darwin. Their studies threw many Victorians *in medias res* and challenged even more their hope that there was some power controlling events. The "sum of man's misery," Carlyle wrote in "Characteristics," is "that he feel himself crushed under the Juggernaut wheels, and know that Juggernaut is no divinity, but a dead mechanical idol." Carlyle readily admitted that we have to go back to Adam in Paradise to find a time when "the body had not yet become the prison-house of the soul." But, he asserted, "meditation," by which we discover "what vital force is in us," can only further entrap when we believe in no reality except that which can be seen and quantified (XXVIII: 4–5, 29).

In "Characteristics" Carlyle identified the Romantics as artists who challenged scientific rationalism head-on, not by abandoning God and nature but by giving them new, human-centered meanings. He judged the efforts of most of them to create a new spiritual life a failure (the "False" was destroyed, but "the New appears not in its stead"), but his emphasis on them calls our attention to a source of ideas and images almost as important as the seventeenth-century religious tradition in shaping the Victorian novel. Wordsworth, for Victorians the representative Romantic poet (in 1828 Carlyle compared his work to Goethe's – XXVI: 208), offered ideas of God and nature and the child that broke with traditional religious ideas. And his notation of the "savage torpor" of contemporary city-centered life sets up those contrasts of past and present, country and city, which became cultural clichés of the period.

The Romantics, as M. H. Abrams has taught us in his *Natural Supernaturalism*, transformed the God inherited by the Victorians.

3

They may keep the images of the popular religious tradition – the pilgrim outcast, the wilderness journey (they travel and search, as "pilgrims of eternity," as energetically as any Christian – and more desperately, since their goal is so ill-defined and uncertain); and they may continue to practice a similar self-scrutiny (to such extremes that self-consciousness becomes a road to psychic paralysis). But their sense of God has changed utterly: from the being outside and beyond man, ordering all life, God comes down to nature and retreats to the world within, to the inner life where He – or the experience of "God" – comes to stand for order, creativity, imagination. The Romantics, Abrams writes, assimilated and reinterpreted traditional religious ideas "as constitutive elements in a world view founded on secular premises."

Much of what distinguishes writers I call "Romantic" derives from the fact that they undertook, whatever their religious creed or lack of creed, to save traditional concepts, schemes, and values which had been based on the relation of the Creator to his creature and creation, but to reformulate them within the prevailing two-term system of subject and object, ego and non-ego, the human mind or consciousness and its transactions with nature.[6]

In the place of Eden, the fall, and possible redemption, the Romantics erected, as Geoffrey Hartman has suggested, an analogous structure of Nature, self-consciousness and imaginative freedom.[7] They envisioned a process towards perfected wholeness rather than the teleological movement of Christian history.

These Romantic relocations of Judeo-Christian topography have signal implications for the Victorians' sense of space and time and human personality, and especially for their presentation of that iconographic figure that stands so often at the center of their fictions, the orphan. Fully to understand this Victorian archetype we must note its figuration in the Romantic and the religious traditions. The Romantics elevate the child to natural godhead because he seems so much closer to the supreme center of being, the realm of timelessness which characterizes the wholeness of Nature in contrast to the dynamic history-controlling God of the Judeo-Christian idea, or the Great Clockmaker of the eighteenth-century deists.[8] Wordsworth's child finds his birth and first begetting in life:

> No outcast he, bewildered and depressed:
> Along his infant veins are interfused
> The gravitation and the filial bond
> Of nature that connect him with the world.
> (*Prelude*: II: 232–5)

4

Child and Nature are one. But as self-consciousness develops, this human figure finds himself enclosed in a "prison-house," more and more outcast from that natural world.

The child of the religious tradition, on the other hand, is born in this "prison-house." Bunyan's sense of his youth, and of all of his "natural life," is that of a child who "had but few Equals . . . both for cursing, swearing, lying and blaspheming the holy Name of God" (B: 7–8). Hannah More's later question (in her *Strictures on Female Education*, 1799) does not suggest much softening: "Is it not a fundamental error to consider children as innocent beings, whose little weaknesses may, perhaps, want some correction, rather than as beings who bring into the world a corrupt nature and evil disposition, which it should be the great end of education to rectify?"[9] Puritan and evangelical Christianity denied natural wholeness as a birthright. "Natural" indeed meant Godless. The individual must raise himself from the putrefying mire of his birth; the Christian child is born in death and must seek life, must break his imprisoning bonds.

These two images of the child come together in that "innocent yet guilty" orphan figure of the Victorian imagination, a very different pilgrim indeed from Bunyan's Christian or Wordsworth's child. The Victorian amalgamation of these disparate images suggests the precarious balance authors and readers struck between the religious and Romantic heritages. Although such Victorian children as Jane Eyre may carry the residual goodness of original innocence, they embody it as orphans, as isolated figures set adrift in desolate social landscapes, knowing their innocence and yet constantly reminded of – and often feeling – their guilt. Dickens' supreme insight into what has happened to the child on its journey into post-Romantic England yields Esther Summerson's illegitimacy and Amy Dorrit's prison birth.

The connection of innocence to prisons rather than to Nature calls our attention to another amalgamation of inherited images that the Victorians found themselves forced to make. While for Quarles and Bunyan the prison simply depicts man's fallen state, his separation from God, for the Victorians it is the chief emblem for marking man's separation from God (or any idea of "God"), from one's fellows, and from Nature. It is the chief emblem for man's aloneness. Amy Dorrit in prison is not Christian fallen, but innocence preyed upon. And when she asks if the fields are "locked up" at night, she shows how far the Victorians are from the

5

Romantics' Nature as well. Victorian Nature is remembered, heard-about, "post carded" – and always separated from the real lives of the city dwellers.[10] Carlyle remembers the "Ribble and the Aire . . ., as yet unpolluted by dyers' chemistry; tenanted by merry trouts and piscatory otters," with "no monstrous pitchy City" anywhere in sight (PP: 71). The old housekeeper in *Shirley* recalls a time, "fifty years syne," when "there was neither mill, nor cot, nor hall" on the green landscape and het mother could see "a fairish (fairy) in Fieldhead Hollow; and that was the last fairish that ever was seen on this country side" (III: 14: 740). For the Victorians the possibility of Wordsworth's "new world" with its "ennobling interchange/Of action from without and from within" (*Prelude*: XIII: 370, 375–6) has vanished with wellnigh as much certainty as the traditional "New Jerusalem" or the "fairish," leaving a "pitchy" world where no action seems really free and for which the prison seems the "natural" emblem.[11] Paradoxically, Amy Dorrit locked out of prison is "locked" *in* a city where prostitutes roam – and envy her "natural" innocence.

With prisons metaphorically – and in Dickens literally – everywhere on the landscapes, the persistent and impossible-to-answer question of the novel's pilgrims becomes "What shall I do?" – the question of Bunyan's pilgrim. Confined in such prisons, these characters are aware of nothing so much as of time's heavy burdening. Bunyan, too, found every hour a burden: he constantly specifies times, the number of days and minutes that have passed, because each marks an advance towards heaven or a fall from the narrow way. This rigorous marking of time as progress poses a stark contrast to the tomorrow-and-tomorrow weariness of so many characters in Victorian fiction. There the "restless gnawing ennui" (LDP: 337) generates the ultimate picture of a people whose idea of a *telos* has become only a vague, this-wordly hope. *Vanity Fair* provides one long tableau of a people given over to Mammon-worship and perpetual residence in Bunyan's threatening way-station; their very *material* gods are part of their stasis, their separation and hopeful insulation from the necessary "road" of the pilgrims. Clocks, with Iphigenia figures sculpted on them for ironic commentary, toll so heavily the endless cycle of their weary days that these people seem as lifeless as Thackeray's puppet metaphor renders them. Old Osborne is obsessed with the trappings of meaningful human sequence – the Peerage, the family Bible, clocks; but even that instant at Waterloo which thwarts his plans brings no sense of time's "other" reality. Only Rebecca Sharp seems to define time "traditionally." Like her biblical namesake, she looks ahead, keeps "her whole attention" turned "towards the future" (chapter 15) – and serves through her warfaring progress to parody and thus damn all the more an age whose attention to time is so determinedly secular. Becky ends precisely as so many early pilgrims: "Virtue Rewarded," the chapter title announces. But her booth, her reward, is in Vanity Fair. Only the language, with its traditional images from emblematic topography, recalls an older belief in God's intervention in history in order to save.

What makes time's impact so corrosive is the Victorian sense that the inner life is as blighted as the landscape. Meditation for human beings like Arthur Clennam or Daniel Deronda leads nowhere, except to more frustrated inaction (it is Thackeray's genius to show Vanity Fair inhabitants never meditating, except about living on £5,000 a year). Carlyle had been discussing the assaults on the "inward world" since the early 1820s, and had set himself the task – the Bunyanesque task – of recalling to his readers that "inward world" where the godborn and the demonic exist, of urging them to recognize the *fact* of an inner life that Mammon and the machine had seemed to obliterate. Bunyan showed Apollyon or Giant Despair waylaying Christian. Quarles offered his emblem (fig. 1).

> Look, look, what horrid furies do await
> Thy flatt'ring slumbers! If thy drowsy head
> But chance to nod, thou fall'st into a bed
> Of sulph'rous flames, whose torments want a date.
>
> (I: 7)

Carlyle offers Diogenes Teufelsdröckh, whose very surname *names* the "furies" of the self that waylay the soul in its journey. The Victorian novelists are determined to present, and to present as *fact*, the Giant Despair or devil's-dung of the human psyche. To illuminate this inward world Dickens not only offers the traditional fairy-tale allusions, but gives Pip an Orlick to fight, Dombey a Carker, Wrayburn a Headstone (who himself must confront a Rogue Riderhood). Charlotte Brontë offers Bertha Mason to Jane Eyre's meditations, George Eliot gives to Bulstrode a Raffles, to Dorothea a Rosamond, and to Gwendolen Harleth a Grandcourt – images of the self they would not acknowledge theirs. This suggestion of doubling or use of the *Doppelgänger* was for the novelists an essential way of insisting on an "inward world." And it is a device, Alexander Welsh has written, which "mediates between

7

the Calvinistic idea of the absolute difference between Cain and Abel and a romantic idea of personality in which evil is always threatening from within."[12] Jane Eyre is aware of her own inner turmoil, and yet like Diogenes Teufelsdröckh at the North Pole she must confront in her daylight world those insane aspects of the self whose existence within herself she refused to recognize.

This imaging of an "inward world" – whether celestial or infernal – is the preoccupying task of the Victorian novelists: they want to force acknowledgment of the vital regions of dreams and demons that a rationalist, prospering, utilitarian age would overlook ("Facts alone are wanted in life"). Bulwer Lytton, in his Preface to the 1840

Latet hostis, et otia ducis.

I PETER V. 8.

Be sober, be vigilant; because your adversary the devil, as a roaring lion, walketh about, seeking whom he may devour.

Fig. 1.   Quarles, Emblem, I: 7

edition of *Ernest Maltravers* (first published in 1837), declared that he wanted to show "life as it is": "life in its spiritual and mystic as well as its more visible and fleshly characteristics."[13] Thus Blake's "Behemoth and Leviathan" (frontispiece) seems to me the perfect emblematic illustration of what these mid-century writers were about. The drawing suggests Blake's subtle combining of both the religious tradition and the Romantic revisions of it. The God of the Judeo-Christian tradition is showing Behemoth and Leviathan to Job and his counsellors. The Romantic internalization of this "Demon Empire" is also here, minus its solipsistic tendency, since Behemoth and Leviathan *are* God's creations and not simply man's psychic projections. Blake brings together images of these demons within and of a God without, and he points to the poet's – and the Victorian novelist's – function as the prophet who insists on man acknowledging his own "Demon Empire" as well as the existence of a "power beyond the self that makes for righteousness." The artist, like Carlyle's "hero," is a *seer* speaking *unseen* "facts" to a society peopled by readers who see worldly success as a measure of godliness. Bunyan never thinks (dares) to picture God except through his Word. Blake must picture him. Carlyle must defend him – "It was not a God that did this; no!" – and assert his existence. The mid-century novelists, whether or not they believe in God, are determined to do what Bunyan and Quarles did naturally: shape the facts of their world into a religious topography and force us to see the presence of the "supernatural" in our "natural" world.[14] Bulwer's remark in his Preface to *A Strange Story* (1862) forcefully summarizes this task: asserting that "without some gleams of the supernatural, Man is not man, nor Nature, nature," he added: "[the Supernatural] is allowable to all works of imagination in which Art looks on Nature as Man's inner sense of a something beyond and above her."[15]

The Victorians, then, come to maturity with both the religious tradition – with Bunyan as its popular representative – and Romantic revisions of that tradition as substantial parts of their psychological and literary heritages. And the novel, in spite of voiced opposition from Christian and utilitarian alike, became their chief literary mode. None could have predicted, though some feared, this development at the period's beginning, in the late 1830s. "When the Lord took hold of me, I threw the novel away," one early Victorian convert stated.[16] A Benthamite, while hastening to substitute "seriousness" for "the Lord," would have said much the same thing. But if the renovated man threw the novel away, he kept on reading: "Reading Christians will be knowing Christians," Wesley had urged.[17] Thus the popularity of history, biography, essays. Macaulay's history would show England's progress – through her people's hard work and right reason (and "under Him who raises and pulls down nations at His pleasure") – and would connect that progress with the Puritan heritage. Thousands of books would tell readers how to live and how through self-help to improve their living, much as the religious emblem and example books had done and the evangelical tracts were doing. And the novel, to avoid the charge of "lying" and frivolity, had to take on the forms of history and biography which most readers associated with legitimate non-frivolous reading. It assumed, almost necessarily, the one form Carlyle judged would give it seriousness: it became an "illustrative garment of Fact" (XII: 431).

This factual biographical emphasis marks yet one more convergence of religious and Romantic traditions in a form which appealed to all of these novelists, the *Bildungsroman*. G. B. Tennyson has described this basically German Romantic creation as the form of most Victorian novels and has emphasized Carlyle's role in Calvinizing and Anglicizing it. The *Bildungsroman*, Tennyson noted, presents "the progress of the individual yet representative man as he forms his whole being," as he finds some psychological grounds for self-unity and belief.[18] Jerome Buckley adds that only when "the psychology of the child was taken seriously as an appropriate literary concern was the writing of the English Bildungsromane a possible enterprise."[19] Wordsworth's place in the development of this enterprise is of course essential: he gave the child a psychology and an environment; and, in Bulwer's apt notation, his "peculiarly German" genius brought a "singular householdness of feeling" to the depiction of the details of Nature.[20] Carlyle's role was, in *Sartor Resartus*, to amalgamate the Romantic strands of the *Bildungsroman* and the progresses of the old religious books, and to found this amalgamation in the harsh realities of contemporary social life. The result is the English *Bildungsroman*, an apprenticeship novel quite unlike the original, as Susanne Howe demonstrated. No better signal of this transformation can be had than the definition George Henry Lewes offered in 1843 for Goethe's idea of *Bildung*: "Renounce all, endure all, but develop yourself to the utmost limit."[21] This statement, which for Carlyle would constitute an endorsement of solipsism, excludes that emphasis on faith (in something beyond the self) and on the necessity of social community that Carlyle and the novelists made so important a part of their focus. Indeed, Martin Swales, in contrasting the German and English forms of the *Bildungsroman*, has written that the "consistently sustained irresolution" of the genre as the Germans developed it is not possible in English fiction, which "offers a far greater allegiance to plot, to actuality, to the linear growth of the hero to some kind of adult clarity."

Both self and world in the English novel tend to remain clear-cut – and nowhere more so than in their antagonism. Insofar as a solution is found, it usually involves a practical accommodation, a *modus vivendi* in which society and the self have at least some of their rights respected. And if no solution is found, we at least know that the struggle we have witnessed is philosophically and morally binding.[22]

Bulwer, again, offers a succinct summary of the change in the *Bildungsroman* as it established itself in England. In his 1840 Preface to *Ernest Maltravers*, he affirms that his "original idea . . . of a moral education or apprenticeship" came from Goethe's *Wilhelm Meister*. "But, in *Wilhelm Meister*, the apprenticeship is rather that of theoretical art. In the more homely plan that I set before myself, the apprenticeship is rather that of practical life" (p. vii). The emphasis on "practical life," on "common household affections" (Bulwer's phrase describing his method in *The Caxtons*) is Carlyle's precisely. And *Sartor Resartus*, with its German orphan's life and its English Editor's meditation on that life, and with its resolution in the shared concern of both "writers" over England's "two sects," constitutes the prototypical Victorian fiction.[23]

Mid-century novelists, whether influenced by Carlyle or not, worked as he had done: they represented, indeed articulated, the psychological experiences of metaphysical homelessness which they shared with their readers, and the articulation came in the language and types of the biblical tradition. Mrs Sarah Ellis, never an unbeliever, found it necessary to preface her *Pictures of Private Life* (1837) with "An Apology for Fiction." There she noted that fiction had found "authority in the writings of sincere and zealous christians"; then she cited the scriptures and Bunyan as examples of "serviceable" fictions: "The wide range of allegory affords innumerable subjects for instruction and delight, and many a weary wanderer through the valley of the shadow of death, has been cheered by the remembrance of Bunyan's pilgrim."[24] Writers, and readers, of less steadfast certainty had also this heritage of the language and visual representations from scripture and emblem books. This tradition had its roots in the habits of typologists, who read "divinely intended anticipations of Christ and His dispensation in the laws, events, and people of the Old Testament";[25] in the emblem writers, who found in all objects "an allegorical significance";[26] and in the habits of post-Reformation Protestants, for whom scriptural reading and interpretation – the locating of Providential design in the details of everyday history – were the *sine qua non* of daily religious life.[27] In the nineteenth century the English Sunday insured the continuation of this tradition of "reading"; it insured that the Bible, and Quarles, and *Pilgrim's Progress*, and *Paradise Lost* were current, a part of the nation's cultural and imaginative life.[28] Lacking Bunyan's assurance, readers and writers held all the more tenaciously to his language. They were determined to shape the facts of this world into a religious topography, making a path towards social unity in this world an analogue to Christian's progress towards the Celestial City. They used "typological symbolism" because, as Hugh Witemeyer has said of George Eliot, "it offered a way of conferring spiritual meaning upon the representation of phenomenal experience, of affirming the existence of design while yet representing the integrity of history."[29]

Thus the *scola cordis* mottoes which open this chapter suggest the shared assumptions of readers and writers about their books. Carlyle constantly addresses his readers and tries to induce them, as William Buckler has noted, to see the gritty particularity of contemporary problems "through the illuminative structures of myth/fable/history"; everything is to be seen "*sub specie aeternitatis.*"[30] Writers, readers, fictional protagonists – all are questers, bound together within the volume: authors speak to readers and emphasize the commonality of their experience. Thackeray's drawings show author and readers together, "moralist" and "congregation" (arrayed in the same "livery" of the jester); Dickens announces himself Little Dorrit's biographer while also writing marginal sermons to his readers; George Eliot is the "historian" of our progresses; and Charlotte Brontë is the editor of an autobiography whose "author" addresses the "Reader" directly.[31]

The irony here lies in the fact that this *de te fabula* aesthetic is, as Northrop Frye has noted, "the message of all romance,"[32] the message of the one literary label that most Victorian novelists, with their concern for history and "truth" and seriousness, determinedly avoided. George Eliot thought most romances "spiritual gin." Dickens, defending himself against the charges of improbability, asserted that he represented "the romantic side of familiar things." Bulwer, who did label many of his fictions "romances," carefully noted the change in emphases when he wrote "Novels." In his introductory remarks to the first edition of *Ernest Maltravers*, he notes that "the bustle, the pomp, and the stage-effect which History affords to Romance" are forbidden in the "Novel." In *The Caxtons* (1849), another "Novel," he announces that his main task has been "the completion of a simple FAMILY PICTURE."[33] Earlier, even Sir Walter Scott – whose fictions the Victorians knew so well and which Carlyle had damned so tellingly: "The sick heart will find no healing here" (XXIX: 76) – drew a careful distinction between the "marvellous" of romance and the "ordinary" of the novel (though he rather thought that both were read for amusement rather than instruction).[34] Yet of course secular romance shares the narrative linearity and the paradisal goal of the religious allegories. And the Victorian novel – paradoxically, confusedly, determinedly – became in its amalgamation of disparates anti-romance "romance," its narrative moving towards Paradise Regained, and doing it, in George Levine's wonderfully appropriate phrase, while existing on the "boundaries of fiction" and non-fiction.[35] It offers continuing witness to the truth of Carlyle's unapologetic assertion, in "The Diamond Necklace" (1837), that "Romance exists; . . . now, and formerly, and evermore it exists, strictly speaking, in Reality alone" (XXVIII: 329). (We might remember that the subtitle of Carlyle's aborted novel, *Wotton Reinfred*, was "A Romance.")

Thus, by adopting the types, analogues, and allegorical suggestions of the popular religious tradition, Carlyle and the novelists cast themselves firmly in that tradition of writing represented by Bunyan. Their plots are essentially his plot, even as the complications and variations are Victorian expressions of an age's uncertainties about the very figures it insists upon.[36] Carlyle and the mid-century novelists give us mundane life where few paradises are concretely realizable. But their quest plots and their emblematic language posit a regaining of paradise. The reader feels the pressure of these images and structures, and thus, perhaps without full recognition, feels the Bible's promises and Bunyan's progresses. He feels these sources, the author's language predicates them, the protagonists enact them. All questers: "Your homes the scene, yourselves the actors, here!"

On its primary level this need for sacred romance, this impulse away from the real, attests to a fundamental psychological need to create a golden age in order to escape those "pitchy" landscapes. Any kind of romance offers order, design, a sure identification of good and evil. As George Levine has noted, "romance implies an ordered, stable, almost static universe," while "the novel implies a growing, changing, disordered one, or one in which order can be achieved only through change."[37] Romance's structures and resolutions were so attractive to the Victorians because they seemed to provide the only certain way towards positing and insuring lasting human values in an age where the pilgrim's query "What is truth?" found a hundred answers, and none.

Northrop Frye has called romance "the structural core of all fiction," and labelled it "the secular scripture."[38] I would use the phrase "biblical romance" – that verbal pattern established by the Bible, used by Quarles and Bunyan, reformulated by the Romantics – to characterize the core of Victorian fiction, indeed of Victorian literature of the period 1837–80. The defining characteristic of this fiction is its quest to be at once secular scripture and sacred scripture. Unlike the naturalistic novel, which would adopt an almost Utilitarian definition of fact, the Victorian novel continually searched for the spiritual meaning behind the world of things, for the Romance within reality, for "natural supernaturalism." And what kept that quest from degenerating into the pale idealism of the later Pre-Raphaelites or into the Newmanized Byronism of the decadents was the continuing impact of the religious heritage through its emblematic language – the one thing writers and readers shared and found "permanent" amidst the flux.

This coming together of sacred and secular traditions – of Bunyan and Wordsworth, of Israel in Egypt and Oliver Twist in Fagin's den – receives signal illustration in the famous housetops passage from *Dombey and Son.*

Oh for a good spirit who would take the house-tops off, with a more potent and benignant hand than the lame demon in the tale, and show a Christian people what dark shapes issue from amidst their homes, to swell the retinue of the Destroying Angel as he moves forth among them! For only one night's view of the pale phantoms rising from the scenes of our too-long neglect; and, from the thick and sullen air where Vice and Fever propagate together, raining the tremendous social retributions which are ever pouring down, and ever coming thicker! (DS: 47: 620)

14

Here the Destroying Angel of the Apocalypse joins with the phantoms and "dark shapes" of fairy tales. The passage calls our attention to how much common ground religious and secular literature share (emblem drawings show demons resembling those in secular romances and in illustrated Bunyans like the one Maggie Tulliver tells Mr Riley about – MF: I: 3: 16). The novelist, that "good spirit" in Dickens' passage, would have us see how religious our secular language is. And he would show us the depths from whence comes all social unsettlement, but whose murky areas a mechanistic world view can never acknowledge. He will make us see the darkness and acknowledge it our own – and our responsibility.

In the following pages we will watch how Carlyle and the novelists explored that area, that "mere film of land," between fact and fiction, always seeing their readers as there with them, as intrinsic parts of their texts. We will watch how they use language both to create a mimetic image of the sordid realities of their world and to illuminate the process of "salvation" by which the "inward world" might survive this reality. We will examine the ways they tried to chart paths towards some form of "natural supernaturalism" in a world not much given to such unseen "realities." We will note how they used their writing – each successive book – as a continuing meditation on the way man might live *adequately* in a world whose only certainty was flux. The novels of Charlotte Brontë, Charles Dickens, and George Eliot define the tradition; those of Disraeli, Mrs Gaskell, Bulwer Lytton, and a hundred minor novelists work within it; Thackeray's especially expose its disease; Hardy's declare its death. (Indeed, the very passing of the teller from within the novel is perhaps a signal that the traditions of meditation – and the belief in the power of words – have died out of English literature and English life.)[39]

I begin this study with Carlyle because his work shows most clearly and urgently the weighing and judging and using of that heritage – religious and Romantic – which was the possession of all early Victorians. Born in a Scottish–Calvinist home in the same year as Keats, Carlyle discovered early on, in his reading of Gibbon and the Germans, that the "old theorem" by which his own father had lived had "passed away," its "immaterial, mysterious, divine though invisible character" banished by Locke and the mechanic world of the eighteenth century (XXVI: 215). Thus, to claim the Bible as factual truth and to base one's belief on *that* claim "flatly contradicted," Carlyle asserted, "all human science and experience."[40] Yet he also felt that the Romantics' response to the passing of the "old" beliefs – the effort he saw in the early Goethe to form "his world out of himself" – led to despair, to a prison of solipsism. Only coming to see, as Goethe had done, that "the Ideal has been built on . . . the firm ground of human interest and business" would free modern man from his "dungeon" – and free his art as well. Goethe's liberation from the dungeon of self, Carlyle declared, liberated his work from the "remote conventional world" represented in "*Castles of Otranto*, in *Epigoniads* and *Leonidases*," with their "clear, metallic heroes, and white, high, stainless beauties, in which the drapery and elocution were nowise the least important qualities." That art was freed to return to its "former vocation" of holding "the mirror up to Nature" and reasserting "in many-coloured expressive symbols, the actual passions, the hopes, sorrows, joys of living men" (XXVI: 213–15).

Carlyle's own "mirror" produced *Sartor Resartus* which, in its many-colored expressive ways, may be taken as the emblematic fiction for Victorian novelists. *Sartor* boldly outlines that English combination of *Bildungsroman* which is also social novel and of religious allegory which is also Romantic quest into the inner self. In presenting a nineteenth-century orphan's quest and conversion and an English Editor's meditation on that quest, Carlyle gives emphatic expression to the characteristic language and physical and psychological landscapes which his contemporaries will use, in more "novelistic" ways, to chart the journey beyond those experiences of alienation and metaphysical homelessness that so dominate the Victorian response to the Enlightenment and Industrialism, to the banishment of "fairish" and "piscatory otters," to the withdrawal of God. And in the process of his work Carlyle revitalizes the tradition of *scola cordis*: "Your homes the scene, yourselves the actors, here!"

I

Carlyle in "Doubting Castle"

In saluting Goethe's ability to move his art from the world of *Otranto* to nature, Carlyle is celebrating the banishment of romance and the return to "reality," to that world of "human interest and business" where "Romance" is possible and which Victorian novelists took as their starting point. Carlyle defined that world as "the Unseen but not unreal World" where "clear Knowledge is wedded to Religion, in the life and business of men" (XXVI: 208).[1] To mirror *this* world required a language other than the "scientific nomenclatures" of the modern Utilitarians. And the only language available was that found in the words of writers working within the "old theorem" of belief, the "extinct Hebrew" language of metaphysical reality. He saw in that language, with its ability to cobble together genres, to collapse the boundaries between fact and fiction and between "nature" and "romance," the perfect vehicle for calling readers to "Meditation" and to journeying with him towards a vision of "natural supernaturalism."

His writing, whether in fiction or in history or biography or tract, thus set out consciously to be emblematic, an "illustrative garment of Fact." The "life pilgrimage" of Teufelsdröckh or Abbot Samson, like France's journey through revolution, is "an emblem of the world's own" (as he said of Sterling's life). To lead his contemporaries "across this hideous delirious wilderness . . . to the new firm lands of Faith beyond" (XI: 60) required the romantic mirroring of human nature and society which the old supernatural language was particularly capable of rendering. He thought that by naturalizing the language of supernaturalism, he could lead his countrymen on an "Exodus from Houndsditch" (his phrase for the threadbare "old theorem") and from the Romantic dungeon, could help them create a world where mechanics and materialist philosophy did not govern all, where religion did not reduce its substance to forms of worship, where men were not simply objects impinging on each other's consciousness and freedom, where nature was something other than the grand view sought by the tourist. No wonder George Eliot celebrated him as essentially an artist and

Dickens used his "way" as a guide for his own work. *Sartor Resartus* celebrated modern man's potential to see Romance within reality, to become through his language a "Messias of Nature." And then: "All visible things are emblems" (SR: 72).

I

Sartor Resartus is the great statement of Carlyle's work of uniting religious heritage and Romantic education. No matter how revolutionary its surface – with its tote-bag collection of punctuation and allusion – its language is finally traditional, based solidly in the King James Bible and in the seventeenth-century Protestant tradition of spiritual reporting. Yet Carlyle constantly calls to his readers' attention the fact that his language is not "the product of the certainty" of God's truth, as Bunyan's allegorical language was (H: 6); it is rather a rendering of symbolic truths.

Name it as we choose: with or without visible Devil, whether in the natural Desert of rocks and sands, or in the populous moral Desert of selfishness and baseness, – to such Temptation are we all called . . . Our Wilderness is the wide World in an Atheistic Century; our Forty Days are long years of suffering and fasting.   (SR: 184)

Words from scripture may no longer "fasten" on the soul by their very literalness, they may not "dart in" upon one as they did upon Bunyan (B: 65–6). Nor may we accept Christian's encounter with Apollyon as supernatural "fact" in the way Bunyan did. For Carlyle this difference in the way we experience scriptural language underlines the vast separation between the "old" way of thinking and the new. Thus in the above passage he interprets the metaphors for the readers, reminding them of the otherness of language itself. "It is in and through *Symbols* that man, consciously or unconsciously, lives, works, and has his being," Teufelsdröckh learns; and he expresses his insight through a quotation from Acts 12: 28, though he substitutes "*Symbols*" for the "Christ" of the original (SR: 222). For Carlyle the problem was always how to make the reader recognize the unseen other which those symbols – our everyday language – suggested. In *Sartor* he at once investigates the possibility of a rebirth of this symbolic language and traces the journey of one man who must learn to use that language anew if he is to live.

In the splendid opening paragraph of *Sartor*, the Editor notes with amazement that to modern scientific man "the Creation of a

World is hardly more mysterious than the cooking of a dumpling."
Later Teufelsdröckh himself will suspect that soul for modern man
has grown synonymous with stomach (SR: 117). Both writers fear
that nineteenth-century man no longer acknowledges anything
unseen as having existence, and they fear too that our very language
has been desacralized, its symbolic content obliterated. To the
Editor, whose concerns are the killing of the "mysterious" by
science and materialism, it is only natural to choose clothes as a
subject for "philosophical" inquiry, and natural too to find a
German who has inquired. Clothes are after all visible things (in
them man's "whole Self lives, moves, and has its being," he notes
(5), in a playful shadowing of Teufelsdröckh's statement on
symbols); moreover, clothes are the first symbols, emblems of
man's first consciousness of himself as separated from his God and
his world. As for the Germans, they were from the English point of
view hopelessly lost in the abstract, their attention not enough
turned towards the "immediately practical" (7).

The Editor himself fears that such abstractions as the clothes
philosophy offers need grounding somewhere, and thus he is eager
to secure and present in the midst of snippets from the Clothes-
Volume a spiritual autobiography of the author. It is an autobiography written partly in the tradition of spiritual meditation;
Teufelsdröckh notes that "the hardest problem was ever this first:
To find by study of yourself, and of the ground you stand on, what
your combined inward and outward Capability specially is" (119).
From this "study" one "godborn" man will show us how he "found
[his] Calling" in the preaching of "the WORD" (199–200). This
self-scrutiny is what Bunyan had offered in *Grace Abounding*, where
he added at the end an account of the "Author's Call to the Work of
the Ministry."[2] But Carlyle is also suspicious of such introspection.
This suspicion is implicit in *Sartor*, and given bald statement in
Past and Present: "Methodism with its eye forever turned on its
own navel; asking itself with torturing anxiety of Hope and Fear,
'Am I right, am I wrong? Shall I be saved, shall I not be damned?' –
what is this, at bottom, but a new phasis of *Egoism* stretched out into
the Infinite" (PP: 119). Thus Teufelsdröckh emphasizes scrutiny
"of the ground you stand on," an addition neither Bunyan nor any
other seventeenth-century life-writer would sanction.

If *Sartor* is a spiritual autobiography partly in the Puritan
tradition, it is also a budding Romantic's tender tale of loss and
soulful woe. To Diogenes Teufelsdröckh we can apply Carlyle's

description of Werther (on whose woeful tale Teufelsdröckh's own "Sorrows" are modelled). The young German melts into "ecstasy at the sight of water-falls and clouds and the moral sublime," "wails over hapless love-stories, and the miseries of human life," especially his own (XXIII: 24); then he dashes off to mountains and after other will-o'-the-wisps to escape "the imprisonment of the Actual" (SR: 197).[3] Carlyle makes great fun of all of this, even as he merges the religious self-scrutinies with the Romantic's paralyzing self-consciousness until the reader sees that there is basically no difference between them, so far are both from any real, human world.

Of course the satire is more profound. Rather than being a carefully arranged, time-ordered examination, Teufelsdröckh's meditations require an Editor to sort them out, which task is especially difficult since they arrive in six paper bags marked with southern zodiacal signs. In spite of the occurrence of such touchstone words as Genesis and Exodus, these life-writings of Teufelsdröckh certainly do not have the *look* of spiritual autobiography. Indeed, were it not for their English Editor, these meditations would not look like a traditional Puritan autobiography to us either. The Englishman gives these bagged materials their *familiar* shape, even as Teufelsdröckh seems to give them a *Märchen* shape.[4] The Editor gives a Bunyanesque structure to a Romantic's quest; he sorts Diogenes' scribblings into the shape of Christian's progress. It is he who uses the Judeo-Christian terms Cain, Ishmael, Wandering Jew, to describe the self-proclaimed Wanderer. It is he who urges the correspondences with Bunyan's Christian when he points to the "burden" on Teufelsdröckh's back (182). And this earnest, foreign-suspecting Englishman's common sense never abates, even as he is always willing to see more than a "dumpling" in Teufelsdröckh's words; he always wants fact to be emblematic.

What if many a so-called Fact [in these Autobiographical Documents] were little better than a Fiction; if here we had no direct Camera-obscura Picture of the Professor's History; but only some more or less fantastic Adumbration, symbolically, perhaps significantly enough, shadowing forth the same! (SR: 202)

The Editor would answer with Keats: "A Man's life . . . is a continual allegory . . . a life like the scriptures, figurative."

The language of this perplexed Englishman calls attention to the way Carlyle is using him. The Editor is himself engaged in meditation, and is urging his reader – as Bunyan does – to compare his own life with the typical events of the text before him.[5] And yet his meditation on Teufelsdröckh's life is different from Teufelsdröckh's own meditations, and from Bunyan's, for it is cast in the present tense. In both *Pilgrim's Progress* and *Grace Abounding* Bunyan uses the past tense; the voice in each text speaks from the vantage point of the journey's end, at the attainment of the Celestial City (in the dream) or at the finding of his Calling; the voice speaks out of the certainty of heaven-sanctioned order and progress. The present tense of *Sartor*'s Editor, however, as G. B. Tennyson has pointed out in his definitive study of *Sartor Resartus*, underlines both the Editor's efforts to make "sense out of the clothes volume" and his determination "to engage the reader in the act of comprehending and pursuing the clothes philosophy."[6] Furthermore, because that tense is present, we are always at the Editor's point of awareness (or in Teufelsdröckh's philosophical present, his everlasting now), always suffering his doubts whether the ideas in the Clothes-Volume or the writings in those bags have order or lead anywhere.

Still, the Editor's comments on the writings of Teufelsdröckh differ markedly from his baffled attempts to piece together the biographical fragments left behind by his subject. The one "excited us to self-activity" (28), he announces, for it complements his own determined intuition that there is more to creation than any scientific treatise can suggest. Those bags demanded, however, "unheard-of efforts, partly of intellect, partly of imagination, on the side of Editor and of Reader" (79), if any narrative order were to be found. Editor-reader battles with the "labyrinthic tortuosities" (120) of Teufelsdröckh's life pieces and philosophical fragments much as Teufelsdröckh battles with his own more "real" demons. Parodying the "real" thing, the English Editor's language emphasizes how much every word we utter serves as a connecting filament of one vast garment. The Editor's hope is that the British reader, "with whatever metaphysical acumen and talent for meditation he is possessed of" (13), will when the work is done have "arrived with us at the new promised country" (207), perhaps even have discovered how much of a "Tailor" he himself may be. The journey towards that country is Everyman's: protagonist's, Editor's, reader's, author's.[7]

The progress of this journey exposes the reader to the main landscapes of Victorian fiction, its machines and "meadows of asphodel," its "Sloughs of Despair" and "prophetic Hebrons," its romantic mirroring of fact. The biography of Teufelsdröckh is the emblem of the whole, the "fact" that gives coherence to the fragments from the Clothes-Volume and serves as the Editor-reader's "Pillar of Fire" (161) in his own "Exodus" (81). On its surface the life story is yet one more tale of Romantic despair over an alienating and alien world. An "idyllic" Wordsworthian childhood is rapidly succeeded by a discovery of orphanage; and then the hero is "doubly orphaned, bereft not only of Possession, but even of Remembrance" (107). Drawing upon both Puritan and Romantic traditions, Carlyle pictures Teufelsdröckh as intensely aware of "being like no other," an outcast cut off from his own identity and from God. He is utterly traditionless.

As he progresses, his alienation only increases. Our "poor Hebrew" goes off to study at Nameless University, certainly an Egypt of materialist idolatry. Then he finds friendship and thereafter romance with a flower-goddess – and a broken heart. Then he makes the clichéd Romantic dash to "a world of mountains" for relief.[8] But these Alps keep no one from the Satanic School, and our poor helpless pilgrim finds his world a "dark labyrinth," one "vast, gloomy, solitary Golgotha, and Mill of Death" (164). Through this Teufelsdröckh wanders aimlessly, says the Editor, "in the temper of ancient Cain, or of the modern Wandering Jew, – save that he feels himself not guilty and but suffering the pains of guilt" (156).

We will see the force of Carlyle's use of the word "modern" and gain a better understanding of the dissociated state of Teufelsdröckh's relation to the religious and Romantic traditions by comparing his wanderings with Bunyan's own night of despair and with Oliver Twist's career. In *Grace Abounding* Bunyan reports how he discovered the hostility of the world about him:

and, after long musing, I lifted up my head, but methought I saw as if the Sun that shineth in the Heavens did grudge to give me light, and as if the very stones in the street, and tiles upon the houses, did bend themselves against me, methought that they all combined together to banish me out of the World; I was abhorred of them . . . because I had sinned against the Saviour. (B: 60–1)

Bunyan is alone in a savage external world. But he knows how to read the meaning of that savagery; the "as if" constructions tell the reader the differences between the reality of saved man and the distorted demonic vision of sinful man, and they point Bunyan's progress beyond sin. Moreover, there are words to set Bunyan free, scriptural correspondences. But Teufelsdröckh can not see the value of these words; there is no correspondence in scripture or anywhere else to his feeling of being "not guilty" (he can not even find the Devil believable). Even for the Editor the only analogy is to Cain – yet a Cain without guilt, a type that has lost its substance. Bunyan knows his guilt and its source. Teufelsdröckh can not admit a guilt he can not even conceive; to do so would be adding more idle babble to the vast vacuity his life seems to be. Lacking the assurance of the "old theorem," he remains alone, unrelieved.

Oliver Twist's innocence in the midst of evil suggests the Romantic side of the synthesis Carlyle was aiming at in his rendering of Teufelsdröckh. (Dickens' second novel began serial publication in 1837, one year before *Sartor* appeared in book form in England.)[9] In one way Dickens' child is the perfect Romantic archetype (at least as the Victorians "read" it): innocent, pure, untouched by a hostile environment, impervious to the "Demon-Empire" of self that Teufelsdröckh comes to see as his chief tormentor.[10] The "parish boy's progress" (this subtitle evokes Bunyan at the beginning) is a journey towards a happy-ever-after world utterly removed from the evil left behind; indeed, Oliver is never "wounded," in head, hand or foot, by the many Apollyons he encounters.

For Carlyle, to set this child up as an image of the innocence of childhood – of the imaginative potential of childhood – is to speak "mere *words*" in a world where so many children, violated by a mechanical society, wander as outcasts in the hellish landscapes of modern cities, and grow up warped. Thus in Teufelsdröckh he brings the Romantic child into the nineteenth-century landscape by making him as time-burdened as any Puritan sojourner (Teufelsdröckh is a "Son of Time") and as fearful ("faëry land" does not save him from "soul-debasing fear," as it does Wordsworth's child – *Prelude*, V: 451–5). The result is neither Bunyan's Christian nor Dickens' Oliver Twist, but Diogenes Teufelsdröckh – godborn devil's-dung.

Indeed, since book one the orphan's surname has been reminding us of this *fact* of his nature: his self is Puritan in make-up even if Romantic in its lack of original guilt. Edward Taylor called his own soul-searching a fall into "A varnisht pot of putrid excrements."[11] And Quarles, whose Emblems had become so much a part of Protestant religious literature, noted:

And am I sworn a dunghill-slave forever
To earth's base drudg'ry? Shall I never find
A night of rest? Shall my indentures never
Be cancell'd? . . .

(V: 13)

The same language shows up in Methodist and evangelical magazines, hymns and innumerable tracts in the nineteenth century. And in *Sartor Resartus* – except *there* Everyman is Diogenes Teufelsdröckh, not one or the other as in Bunyan, always both. In tying his Romantic "hero" so solidly to traditional religious concepts of the self, Carlyle is disavowing any Romantic equation of "soul" and "self." For him "self" is as entrapping as the Puritans announced it to be. "Man's fall," Richard Baxter wrote in his *Christian Directory*, "was his turning from God to himself; and his regeneration consisteth in the turning from himself to God. . . . The very names of Self and Own . . . are next to the names of Sin and Satan." [12] Quarles prayed: "O teach me stoutly to deny/Myself, that I may be no longer I" (Invocation). This damning of the self is Carlyle's point precisely, as it will be so often the novelists' point as well. Carlyle will not countenance any secular view of man's life. In the self is the devil who may entrap: "the Self in thee needed to be annihilated," Teufelsdröckh cries out (SR: 192). To see this is to begin to break away from "self" and to find "soul" ("descend into thy inner man, and see if there be any traces of a *soul* there," Carlyle will urge his readers in *Past and Present* – PP: 30–1). And in this discovery freedom begins.

The synthesis Carlyle ultimately works out is between harsh Christian soul-searching where self must be destroyed and Romantic self-exploration where self becomes not a thing to obliterate but to know in order to use properly ("the fearful Unbelief is unbelief in yourself" – SR: 163). Teufelsdröckh faces "a whole world of internal Madness, an authentic Demon-Empire" within himself (260). He comes to this confrontation by "falling" progressively deeper into a world where everything has lost its organic "godlike" quality and become an "object" or "thing"; all is lifeless. At the bottom of his descent is solipsistic "self-worship," which in the Clothes-Volume he will call "Demon-worship" (285), the province of Dandies and all who see, and often enjoy seeing, everything – man, nature, God – as mere hollow things without substantive meaning. Only when he is able to overcome this object-sense of himself – the sense of being "outcast," "fatherless," "like no

24

other," absolutely unique – does he begin to escape "his own Shadow" and discover himself free, "almost a God." [13]

His redemption begins, then, in the manner of Puritan life-writing, with a recognition of the demonic. He comes to see the self not as the locus of some paradise within but as the source of chaos (the imagery is of self-cannibalism, the "devouring" of his own heart). Then he "clutches round him outwardly on the NOT-ME for wholesomer food" (170), and thus begins his conquest of "the old Satanic School." In being able to look beyond himself, he enters the Centre of Indifference, that area where he has strength to say "No" to the dead mechanical world around him; he can deny the "self" and escape its imprisonment. His "pilgrimage" through the worlds of space and time, as he looks about him from the Centre, are necessary to re-establish his connection, severed since the death of Father Andreas, with the outward world which had seemed so threatening. Those "journeys" assert his historicity and his reality; they show his acceptance and understanding of himself as a "Son of Time" (155).

The Centre is then, as the Editor notes, a time of "spiritual culture." And it ends in redemption, in escape from that very static demonic world that Teufelsdröckh's surname has signified. He awakes "to a new Heaven and a new Earth," and to a new sense of nature:

Or what is Nature? Ha! why do I not name thee GOD? Art not thou the "Living Garment of God"?; O Heavens, is it, in very deed, HE, then, that ever speaks through thee; that lives and loves in thee, that lives and loves in me? . . . The Universe is not dead and demoniacal, a charnel-house with spectres; but godlike and my Father's! (186–8)

If at the Centre of Indifference Teufelsdröckh discovers the linking memory of a history, at the Everlasting Yea he loses the orphan stigma by renouncing forever his "self" (*Entsagen*) and looking outward. There is a Father and a family: "Man, with his so mad Wants and so mean Endeavours, had become the dearer to me; and even for his sufferings and his sins, I now first named him Brother" (189). Teufelsdröckh now knows his "Conversion" is real.[14]

The emphases in this "Conversion" on nature as godlike and on man as brother are founded on Teufelsdröckh's ability to *say* these facts, to speak his natural connection to the godlike which he *sees*.

Could I unfold the influence of Names, which are the most important of all Clothings, I were a second greater Trismegistus. Not only all common

Speech, but Science, Poetry itself is no other, if thou consider it, than a right *Naming*. Adam's first task was giving names to natural Appearances: what is ours still but a continuation of the same . . .?   (87)

To *speak* vision is to be an unfallen Adam. And significantly, Teufelsdröckh interprets this speaking as his "Conversion" (his word, and the Editor's), a discovery of his work or "Calling": he will preach "the Word," "speak forth what is in [him]": "man, thereby divine, can create as by a *Fiat*" (199). The questions that began his life-writing – "Who am I; what is this ME?" (53) – are answered in finding his work; it is "the mirror wherein the *spirit* first sees its natural lineaments" (162; my italics). Not the "*Know thyself*" of the "old theorem": in that quest lies the madness of solipsism. But "*Know what thou canst work at*" (163). Work connects the inward and outward worlds.

Obviously there are profound differences between this conversion and that of traditional religion. To see oneself as "divine," "almost a God"; to become an Adam before the Fall (even imaginatively); to consider (even for a moment) naming Nature God; to interpret one's Calling as a dictate to establish a new Jerusalem – a "Communion of Saints" – on *this* earth; to name man a "Messias of Nature" who will preach the "new Mythus" (194) – these ideas would not have been much more comforting than Bentham's words to a traditional Christian believer. Carlyle has given some very Romantic, human-centered readings to the language of Bunyan. Bunyan's Christian may encounter Apollyon, but he has his memory of the Word to save him. Carlyle's godborn man can only with grave difficulty keep his "Demon-Empire" from triumphing; and he carries this "Shadow" of self with him forever. No divine Word shields him vigilantly, he is always Diogenes Teufelsdröckh. Moreover, Christian is on the road, looking upward; "the world [is] cast behind him" (B: 162). To break away from "self" is for him to break with all the "world" that would not be on the way – with his wife and family, with his country: "but the Man put his fingers in his Ears, and ran on crying, Life, Life, Eternal life: so he looked not behind him . . ." (B: 148). Not so, Diogenes Teufelsdröckh. The world is always before him and man always his focus once he breaks away from "self"; and in that world and in those human beings he witnesses the godlike, and indeed finds part of his redemption. All this is Idolatry indeed, especially when we register John Sterling's complaint that there was no goal in this pilgrim's progress, that Carlyle had removed the reason for the journey since no "Living *Personal* God" awaits this Christian's arrival.[15]

But to assert a *"Personal* God" as fact, Carlyle felt, ignored the signs of the times and contradicted "all human science and experience." The actual world was man's only seedfield, the only knowable new heaven and new earth. The true "Conversion" for nineteenth-century man, he asserted, involves the defeating of solipsism by confronting the self's demons and madness and reaching outwards towards others. The Everlasting Yea, we should remember, posits nature as the Garment of God in one paragraph, the vitality of the Fatherhood of the universe in the next, and Teufelsdröckh's sense of relationship with his fellowman in the third (SR: 186–7). This *Yea* takes him literally beyond himself – next door, if no farther.[16] The failure of Romanticism, as Carlyle sees it, was its inability to escape the sense of alienation from society, the sense of Byronic uniqueness. In this it parallels those Puritans and evangelicals who failed to see how opposite "soul" and "self" were.[17] "Close thy *Byron*; open thy *Goethe*"; the names themselves have become emblems in Carlyle's text for imprisonment and for liberation into this human world.

Interestingly, the Editor who is shaping these materials, selecting what will carry some meaning to English readers, is at his most paradoxical in the most non-traditional sections. He tries constantly to clear the verbal clutter and give the reader a recognizable religious progress. Sometimes Teufelsdröckh will announce himself in the biblical "wilderness," at other times (in the same paragraph!) he will describe himself as in the "enchanted forests" of secular romances. The Editor tries to reinterpret these experiences in familiar Christian terms:

Was "that high moment in the *Rue de l'Enfer*," then, properly the turning-point of the battle; when the Fiend said, *Worship me, or be torn in shreds*; and was answered valiantly with an *Apage Satana*? – Singular Teufelsdröckh, would thou hadst told thy singular story in plain words! (185)

"*Apage Satana*" *places* Teufelsdröckh's experience in familiar spiritual geography (and "plain words" are to the Editor emblem-carrying words, we note). This same placing effort occurs after we have been through the Centre of Indifference. Here, the Editor assures us, "for the matter of spiritual culture, if for nothing else, few periods of [Teufelsdröckh's] life were richer than this," were more "favourable to Meditation." And he then concludes the chapter with an allusion that tells us how he read what we have just witnessed: "Too heavy-laden Teufelsdröckh! Yet surely his bands are loosening; one day he will hurl the burden far from him, and bound forth free and with a second youth" (182). Christian loses his burden at the Cross immediately after he has sojourned in the House of the Interpreter. If we look back through Carlyle's chapter, we notice that its emphases are on book-writing and on great men and the pilgrim's experience of each. The Editor seems to "read" the Centre events as analogous to the scenes explained to Christian in the House of the Interpreter. Like Christian, Teufelsdröckh learns "what will be profitable" for travelling further; particularly he learns, as does Christian, of the power of the Word, though his Word is human-inspired, not God-written ("thou who art able to write a Book . . . Thou too art a Conqueror and Victor; but of the true sort, namely over the Devil: thou too hast built . . . a Temple and Seminary and Prophetic Mount, whereto all kindreds of the Earth will pilgrim" – 172–3).[18] The Editor's analogy here mirrors his constant effort to find scriptural correspondences to Teufelsdröckh's life, and thus to make sense of another's life for himself and his readers by noting how it emulates the lives of traditional pilgrims. Yet the Editor himself has "naturalized" Bunyan's experience in recreating Teufelsdröckh's. Through his use of "plain words," he allows the reader to see Teufelsdröckh's world and his conversion within it as a "new Mythus," and the only one believable – because founded in "human science and experience."

Most significantly, then, the Editor's shaping allusions announce his own "Conversion" to "natural supernaturalism," to a belief that man is "incarnated Word." This conversion is clear by the time we arrive at the chapter on "Natural Supernaturalism" in book three. There the Editor declares himself: he has found, "after long painful meditation," that Teufelsdröckh's words are not "unintelligible," but "clear, nay radiant, and all-illuminating" (255). He presents the entire chapter without interruption, and labels the ideas there "the new promised country." As if to underscore the practical results of his own conversion, the Editor then immediately applies the meaning of the Clothes-Volume to English life. From many possible offerings in the book he chooses the chapters on England's rich and poor. But before inserting the description of the "two sects," he himself defines the "dandy" as a "visual object, or *thing* that will reflect rays of light" (273; my italics). A sense of wonder is obviously not part of this creature's interest. Nor is there any wonder, any sense of the Romance within reality, in this Dandy's "Sacred Books" – otherwise called "Fashionable Novels." In these everything is presented "chiefly from a Secular point of view." Words in these volumes draw pilgrims to play, not to think. Alongside these Dandies stand the Drudges, human beings whose conditions of living demand out of necessity that devotion to the self which the higher sects *choose* to practice.

Teufelsdröckh's conversion has thus had its effect on at least one reader who has meditated on his life (and his style has also "infected" the Editor's – 269). The Editor may still maintain suspicions of Teufelsdröckh's ideas – "Nature is good, but she is not the best," he warns after one particularly Adamite effusion from the Professor (59). But he endorses with energy the very non-traditional key of Teufelsdröckh's doctrine: "Man is properly the *only* object that interests man" (75): we are all our brother's keeper, indeed our brother's brother. "Yes, truly, if Nature is one, and a living indivisible whole, much more is Mankind, the Image that reflects and creates Nature, without which Nature were not" (246–7). And man is the "Messias of Nature" – if he can see the Romance within reality and preach that vision "by act and word" (220).

II

"The WORD is well said to be omnipotent in this world," Teufelsdröckh discovered; "man, thereby divine, can create as by a *Fiat*." But of course Carlyle's words could not. Setting out to bring together the Puritan God-centered world of the "old theorem" and the man-centered yet still "Romance" world of the Romantics, Carlyle had aimed to lead his readers into that "new" world where the unseen and symbolic and godlike lived in the imagination and language of man, in his ability to *name* his fellow "Brother" and to see nature as godlike. But those words which came from naturalizing the language of supernaturalism and from centering it in the world Christian had left behind him did not "create as by a *Fiat*." By 1850 and the *Latter-Day Pamphlets*, Carlyle's words lose their "natural" quality and take on all the denunciatory harshness of any "old theorem" anathema which an Ezekiel or some fiery divine might have hurled at a whoring people. The text grows as threadbare as the earlier Carlyle might have predicted.

What happens in Carlyle's progress from *Sartor* to the *Pamphlets* is significant for seeing the mid-century novelists clearly because Carlyle's struggles with the language of the "old theorem" antici- pate their own. Charlotte Brontë insisted like Carlyle on the godlike in man and nature (and believed, like him, always in some power beyond the self); but she mistrusted a language which allowed men pilgrimages that women never took alone, without a Greatheart, "because a woman." Dickens and George Eliot as much as Carlyle focused all their energies on that world behind Christian's back as the place of community and communion. Yet their own develop- ment testifies to the continuing problems and fears they and Brontë shared with Carlyle about finding a language adequate for urging their readers to see the reality and the necessity of the godlike in human life. Dickens always needed the conventional religious rhetoric (the "world that sets this right"), yet by the time of *Our Mutual Friend* the relatively simple characterizations and reso- lutions of his early novels have vanished, leaving a novel that stops rather than ends, and one where the older language seems available only to those who would "play dead." George Eliot, always fact- based, always looking to the human alone for salvation, yet chose to make a fictional end by writing a *real* biblical romance, one insisting on the necessity of asking Bunyan's question, "whether we were of the Israelites, or no?"

The many questions of Bunyan's pilgrims are central to *The French Revolution*. Though Carlyle's history does not overtly explore English life, its constant references to "Irish sans-potato" and to the Chartists, its Bunyanesque labels throughout – Eatall, Do Nothing, "Janus Bifrons, or *Mr. Facing-both-ways*, as vernac- ular Bunyan has it!" (III: 289) – and its continual direct addresses to the reader underscore the emblematic quality of the work, the spiritual nature of its words. The history, Carlyle asserts, is a "journeying together" of reader and author, each of whom, "by the nature of him, is definable as 'an incarnated Word'" (IV: 323). Carlyle wants us to experience the drama of author and Frenchmen encountering this revolution, a drama thus at once real and imaginative, at once an effort to depict France's desperate need for brotherhood and to create it among the readers. This drama takes place within our souls as Teufelsdröckh's history had (since we and the Editor together sorted out and then ordered those chaotic life- writings). And Carlyle structures the drama of France's revolution as he had that of Teufelsdröckh's life: implicit throughout are the pilgrim's questions "Who am I?" and "What shall I do?" which a nation must ask when it loses sight of its social responsibilities. And to these is added the question inconceivable to Christian in *Pilgrim's Progress* but always implicit in *Sartor*, "What shall I believe?" (II: 54) – the question a *Contrat Social* could never address.

Carlyle sees revolutionary France as a warning to England in the 1830s. There soul is synonymous with stomach and all the world is a "Thespian Stage" – with the Pit threatening to jump on to it (III: 54). And when the Pit takes over the stage, revolution comes – proclaiming brotherhood to the four winds, shouting Fraternity in a shrill voice and giving feasts in its honor. But "the *louder* it swears Brotherhood, will the sooner and the more surely lead to Cannibalism" (III: 70). And then "Dinners [will be] defined as 'the *ultimate* act of Communion'" (II: 246). It is all, finally, a "Brotherhood of Cain" (IV: 263) because it is a world utterly self-centered (quite other than the human-centred world of "natural supernaturalism" (III: 70). And then "Dinners [will be] defined as 'the *ultimate* Sense," where vice has "los[t] all its deformity" and "pleasure is pleasant" (II: 303 – Burke's famous description provides Carlyle his basic images for analyzing the horror); good and evil look quite the same. Thus Cain must be the major emblematic figure of this history because he illustrates so absolutely solipsism incarnate. He has no external reference beyond the killing of his brother. That point at which he cut himself off from Abel and from God, from man and from the unseen *real*, remains forever the defining moment of his life. For Carlyle such an act defines any deadened society which refuses to see that "God's Universe" is something more than "the work of the Tailor and Upholsterer mainly" and which labels as human "mere buckram masks that went about becking and grimacing" (II: 212). With a world declared to be all surface, the "Demonic that is in man" must burst out:

French Revolution means here the open violent Rebellion, and Victory, of disimprisoned Anarchy against corrupt worn-out Authority: how Anarchy breaks prison; bursts-up from the infinite Deep, and rages uncontrollable, immeasurable, enveloping a world; . . . till . . . the Uncontrollable be got, if not reimprisoned, yet harnessed, and its mad forces made to work towards their object as sane regulated ones. (II: 211–12)

This emphasis on madness and sanity Carlyle and the novelists will use repeatedly to suggest both psychological and social injustice.[19]

At the root of such madness lies the failure of those whose instruments are words to have any understanding of man as "incarnated Word" or, indeed, any sense of what a word properly is. Literature – which "must either found on Belief and provable Fact, or have no foundation at all (nor, except as floating cobweb, any existence at all)" – is in France signified by Beaumarchais' *Figaro*, with its "thin wiredrawn sentiments and sarcasms"; and by *Philosophes* who believe that "in spiritual supersensual matters no Belief is possible" (IV: 31; II: 59,14). The Church is dead, moving only in some "skilfully galvanised" state (III: 155). And "the King can give no order, form no opinion; but sits there, as he has ever done, like clay on potter's wheel" (III: 182).

The only living voice here is, finally, the voice of historian Carlyle. He knows and sees the "spiritual supersensual" that is obscured for all France; he knows where "Madness and Horror and Murder" lie, and where Sanity may be found. And through his own voice he can show that man is indeed an "incarnated Word" who can be a nation's "Fire Pillar" and lead it out of captivity. Man *will* do God's work (or else Satan's). Carlyle's strategy for insuring that his words will tell as reality on the reader is to create a narrative voice which is carried by the present tense, a verbal strategy adopted to force the "British reader" into the book's drama as an active participant. He writes in the present tense and, near the end, tells the reader why:

For indeed it is a most lying thing that same Past Tense always: so beautiful, sad, almost Elysian-sacred, "in the moonlight of Memory," it seems; and *seems* only. For observe, always one most important element is surreptitiously (we not noticing it) withdrawn from the Past Time: the haggard element of Fear! Not *there* does Fear dwell, nor Uncertainty, nor Anxiety; but it dwells *here*; haunting us, tracking us; running like an accursed ground-discord through all the music tones of our Existence; – making the Tense a mere Present one! (IV: 81)

The drama is thrown around us, into our minds, *here* – not distanced as "history." And the tense choice emphasizes the themes of the history: *seeming* versus *reality* are indeed the issues the French Revolution poses for British readers.

And they are the issues Carlyle will always pose as he calls on his readers to "meditate earnestly these things," to focus on the way *seeming* – defined as surface, imaged through words suggesting theatrics, animals, digestion, and madness – has got interlaced with *reality* – defined as the "unseen world" and imaged through emblematic language. But Carlyle fears that British readers will less and less recognize any difference between the two, or else prefer seeming above reality. Then the human-centered world becomes a *self*-centered one, attention to the godlike in nature becomes a worship of materialism, and "external varnish is the chief duty of man" (LDP: 289), rather than, as in Ecclesiastes, the worship of God or the godlike.

The present tense appeals to Carlyle because of his fears, increasing to certainty during the 1840s, that this "varnish" was suffocating England's inner life: it deadened the imaginative response to language, deadened fellow-feeling, and finally deadened anything human. Carlyle needed a style that would force the reader's attention. He found the present tense a particularly disconcerting one for readers. Implicitly carrying "fear" and "uncertainty," it prevented readers from relaxing in the romance of the past. Carlyle thus employed the present tense for both rhetorical and thematic effect in *The French Revolution*, and used it tellingly in juxtaposition to the past tense in the *Heroes* lectures and in *Past and Present*. Juxtaposing past and present tenses added urgency to his theme of the contrast between past and present: the one offers order (and heroes who could enforce it); the other disorder, madness, absolute uncertainty of going anywhere. And in each work (as well as in *Sartor*) the constant intrusion of the present tense and of a voice from the reader's present reinforces Carlyle's view that it is extremely difficult to sustain an ordered world – or a linear narrative. Chaos constantly threatens. Yet Carlyle finally abandoned the tension these two tenses offered, and the hope their juxtaposition implied. In the *Pamphlets* his tense is only the present one – leaving us and him in a world directionless, Godless, humanless, and utterly material: as "natural" as Bunyan's.[20]

If this seems a long way from the interests of the novelists, Dickens' own experiment with the past and present tenses in *Bleak House* and in *Our Mutual Friend* should suggest the rightness of that present tense for depicting madness and fear, and for describing Dedlocks and Veneerings and Podsnaps. Charlotte Brontë's increasing narrative sophistication shows in her juxtaposition of the tenses – of narrator's present and narrative's past – in *Shirley* and in *Villette*; and in both novels the present tense is very consciously associated with fear and uncertainty, the past tense with the "sunny imaginations" of "romantic readers." George Eliot too, though she never left her historian's past tense perspective, yet constantly forces her readers into the present through her direct addresses ("provincial families, still discussing Mr Peel's late conduct on the Catholic question, innocent of future gold-fields, and of that gorgeous plutocracy which has so nobly exalted the necessities of genteel life" – Mid: 1:6). More interestingly, she manages through constant allusion and through the mottoes which preface chapters in her later novels to create a tension between a timeless, changeless past invoked by those references and the fluctuating uncertain past that she is creating; those allusions provide the same analogy to known order that the past tense does for Carlyle and for Brontë. (The alternations in *Daniel Deronda* between the "Jewish" half of the novel and the English half have the sharp antithesis of Carlyle's own past and present juxtapositions: godlike order versus demonic chaos.) Carlyle and these novelists had to have the biblical romance structure, in allusion and in verbal strategies, to provide a "mirror" of order against the mirror of present reality. The present tense, like the fictions which the novels unfold or the intrusions of contemporary "phenomena" into Carlyle's texts, underlines their "realism" and focuses for us how far their own emblematic language is from the "mere *words*" of their characters, whether Edward Rochester, Paul Dombey, or Bobus of Houndsditch.

The phrase "mere *words*" (H: 8) is Carlyle's; he used it to express his own fear of what was happening to language and to the reader's sense of it in an Age of Machinery. His work after *The French Revolution* shows a man increasingly doubtful of the ability of language to suggest the godlike. There is a passage in *Chartism* (1839) that particularly illuminates the way he wanted to use, and wanted readers to hear, words. In it Carlyle is considering the basic question that animates the English *Bildungsroman* which is also social novel: "What is injustice?"

What is injustice? Another name for *dis*order . . . The real smart is the soul's pain and stigma, the hurt inflicted on the moral self . . . As *dis*order, insane by the nature of it, is the hatefulest of things to man, who lives by sanity and order, so injustice is the worst evil, some call it the only evil, in this world. All men submit to toil, to disappointment, to unhappiness; it is their lot here; but in all hearts, inextinguishable by sceptic logic, by sorrow, perversion or despair itself, there is a small still voice, intimating that it is not the final lot; that wild, waste, incoherent as it looks, a God presides over it. (XXIX: 145)

The present tenses here assert the reality of present chaos. The biblical allusion implicitly relocates past order in this present, in the power of each individual. The phrase "small still voice" is from 1 Kings 19: 11–12, where Elijah waits in the wilderness for God to appear, as always, through a natural occurrence. But after wind, earthquake, and fire come and no God, there is heard unexpectedly "a still small voice" – which is God. Carlyle, placing that voice within man, makes Everyman the "incarnated Word." Romance can exist in our reality.

Yet fearing that this voice was becoming only "ancient dialect" to modern man, Carlyle sought other correspondences outside the Bible and the religious tradition for enforcing "natural supernaturalism" on the consciousness of his audience, and he sought them in England's own history, "in our veins." In the *Heroes* lectures, especially in the first, and in *Past and Present* he offers a romantic mirroring of England's past: in the Pagan Norsemen (whom he names as England's "true progenitors" and the source of its language – H: 16, 32), and in Abbot Samson and his monastery, he locates the emblems of English life where there was at once sincere communion between human beings and between them and the invisible world about them. Those old Norsemen and Samson are alike both in their manly "solemnity and depth" and in their "childlike" simplicity (H: 7; PP: 118); they participate in the godlike instinctively, without self-consciousness. They differ only in the nature of their awareness. "Paganism emblemed chiefly the Operations of Nature," Carlyle avows; "Christianism emblemed the Law of Human Duty, the Moral Law of Man. One was for the sensuous nature," one "for the moral" (H: 98). But the sensuous *first*, for "Man is a born idol-worshipper, *sight*-worshipper, so sensuous-imaginative is he" (FR: IV: 227).

In the first of the *Heroes* lectures Carlyle considers the nature of this original idolatry by investigating the passing of the godlike into scientific "object" status in English thought and the desacralization of the English language into "mere *words*."[21] In the remaining lectures he presents brief spiritual biographies of men who said "No" to this smashing of the Word's power. He begins by trying to clear away the notion that the pagans were irreligious heathens. Those old Norsemen, he declares, are sincere and honest like their descendents. If their way of worship looks like "quackery," like a "jungle of delusions, confusions, falsehoods, and absurdities," that is due to the evolution of the Englishman's consciousness (H: 3–5). Paganism *was* the sincere expression of early Englishmen's hearts. It is "the . . . creed of our fathers; the men whose blood still runs in our veins . . . Unconsciously, and combined with higher things, it is in *us* yet, that old Faith, withal" (16, 41). That old faith is, of course, not the Judeo-Christian belief but a faith which is, in everything but name, "natural supernaturalism." Those Norsemen lived in a period when to give something a name was not to distance oneself from it, but to acknowledge kinship with it, *awe*-ful relation to it.

To the wild deep-hearted man all was yet new, not veiled under names or formulas; it stood naked, flashing in on him there, beautiful, awful, unspeakable . . . Mark at present so much: what the essence of Scandinavian and indeed of all Paganism is: a recognition of the forces of Nature as godlike, stupendous, personal Agencies, – as Gods and Demons.   (7, 19)

What Carlyle is trying to effect here, and in the language of the Romantics ("ennobling interchange/Of action from without and from within"), is a re-experiencing of that feeling of God in nature which the pagan and medieval mind had experienced as fact and the Romantics as symbolic truth.[22] He wants his audience to see that a consciousness of nature and man as emblems of the divine is not some foreign (i.e., German) or heathen notion, but a "possession of the Present," a formative part of the English consciousness.

Furthermore, for Carlyle such a recognition is an essential part of man's mental and psychological growth. To ignore or obliterate the first and natural part of one's formation is to leave a vacuum – and thus to deform the moral self as well. There is no contradiction between the natural and the moral because when rightly seen they are inextricably connected. And *seeing* Scandinavian Paganism as an original part of England's religious heritage is crucial to modern England because it offers a vital religious sense quite separate from the ideas and "ancient dialect" of the Judeo-Christian tradition. It asserts the magical powers of every man's language.

Carlyle is very aware that his evangelically influenced audience will be suspicious of such pagan nature worship. Thus he addresses himself both to the definition of idolatry as defined in the Bible and to the failures of the English Puritans to appreciate man's need for it. Idolatry as the Prophets defined it, he asserts, is self-conscious worship, not instinctive; "no man's mind *is* any longer honestly filled with his Idol or Symbol . . . 'You do not believe,' said Coleridge; 'you only believe that you believe!' " (122). The Puritans were right to protest this kind of idolatry; their world was full of sensual idolatries, of false idols. But their one blind-spot was their hatred of forms: "the naked formlessness of Puritanism is not the thing I praise in the Puritans; it is the thing I pity" (205). In smashing the materialist idols, these men also smashed England's "natural" inherited sense of what "natural" means, of what "natural supernaturalism" is (Carlyle throughout uses the word

"Nature" as a synonym for God). Ironically, that smashing began the desacralizing of words as well, until now they are more and more "encasing wholly every notion we form," are casting "a wrappage of traditions" between us and the godlike about us; they have become "mere *words*," nothing else (8).

Carlyle's heroes have fought this emptying of the "reality" from words. All can speak and act, can say *"Fiat lux"* to some degree ("Napoleon has words in him which are like Austerlitz Battles"). To suggest in each of his biographical sketches the nature of the lives of his heroes, Carlyle imposes on their histories, as David L. DeLaura has shown, the same "pattern of experience" as he had used for Teufelsdröckh's battles.[23] All "wander like unrecognized unregulated Ishmaelites," feeling outcast and unheard (165); all are determined to live "in the inward sphere of things" (155); all ask the questions of nineteenth-century meditation: "What am I? What *is* this unfathomable Thing I live in, which men name Universe? What is Life; what is Death? What am I to believe? What am I to do?" (54). All become, finally, what Carlyle names the "true" hero, an "incarnated Word." Of the man of letters he says, simply: "he is the light of the world; the world's Priest; – guiding it, like a sacred Pillar of Fire, in its dark pilgrimage through the waste of Time" (157). The statement, with its images from the Bible, evokes a Romantic conception of the artist and the power of language, and it defines precisely the basic "creed" of all mid-Victorian novelists, of Brontë and George Eliot and Dickens and Thackeray: in their fictions, as in Carlyle's "non-fictions," only man leads his fellows beyond the City of Destruction, past the Valley of Humiliation.

And yet *Past and Present* shows Carlyle's increasing fear that language was becoming more and more theatrical, no Pillar of Fire creating union but rather a "'Schnüpsel [Pickwick] the distinguished Novelist'" arousing "universal hep-hep-hurrah" (PP: 60). Carlyle's book is thus at once a second *Chartism* and a spiritual biography, a history of England now, enclosed in St Ives workhouses, and of England then, centered on Samson and his monastery. As he had done in *Sartor*, Carlyle presents himself as the Editor, aiming to "instruct men how to know Wisdom, Heroism, when they see it," and asking them to meditate on his "Meditation" (PP: 42). The book begins in prison and ends with a vision of a "green flowery world," begins in a "Dantean Hell" and ends in Heaven. The landscape between these points is equally polarized: the "formed" world of Abbot Samson and the "enchanted," demonic, "inorganic" world of the industrial present. This latter-day England is populated by a group of demons escaped out of Bunyan (or Samson's prisons) for a more profitable and applauding nineteenth-century world: Pandarus Dogdraught, Bobus of Houndsditch, Plugson of Undership, Sir Jabesh Windbag, Alcides Dolittle, Aristides Rigmarole, Blank, and – for chorus – the Dead Sea Apes, all thrashing about in "Stygian mud-vortexes" and similar swamps. Only Madame Bubble is needed to complete the picture.

It is a Devil's brood, placed in England for the contrast of Semblance and Reality, or Past and Present. Carlyle would force his readers to "meditate" on this juxtaposition, on the topsy-turvy world they inhabit so willingly.

Thou shalt descend into thy inner man, and see if there be any traces of a *soul* there; till then there can be nothing done! O Brother, we must if possible resuscitate some soul and conscience in us, exchange our dilettantisms for sincerities, our dead hearts of stone for living hearts of flesh. (30–1)

He urges his countrymen to do what Teufelsdröckh and a thousand Puritan life-writers had done; and he shows them that to descend into the depths of history is to discover in one's own heritage a time of real organic unified life.

Abbot Samson himself, by sheer force of will and work, governed England successfully because he lived in a world where "men then had a soul" (53) and could thus see beyond their own selves. A religious man, he yet operated by few of the outward signs of religion. In his England religion was "not a diseased self-introspection, an agonising inquiry" (66). In him was no worry about preparing for the after-life, no concern with the kind of "spiritual rubbish" (96) that characterizes the religious exercises of the present. Samson looks absolutely secular in comparison with the modern divines. "But this too, if we examine it, was right," Carlyle declares. "For it is *in* the world that a man, devout or other, has his life to lead, his work waiting to be done" (118). *Work* is the key: "in Idleness alone is there perpetual despair" (196). "*Laborare est Orare* . . . true Work is Worship . . . a making of madness sane" (205–6).

Carlyle's meditation here, focusing on the redemptive power of work for man and society, announces what became a Victorian gospel. The male protagonists of Dickens and all of the protagonists of George Eliot and Brontë see the question "What shall I do?" as the essential question demanding answer if they are to *live* here in this actual world. Carlyle in considering work, as Albert LaValley has noted, uses Pauline language to state ideas which are quite the opposite of St Paul's: "in Carlyle's religious structure, man the laborer replaces Christ as redeemer and the new heavenly Jerusalem is no longer the completed Body of Christ but an apotheosis of the very process of labor itself."[24] And this is not solipsism. As in *Sartor* and *The French Revolution,* Carlyle sees man's ability to work and his actual working as a way towards sanity, an affirmation of the God within and of a Divine Power beyond the self. Only by working does man establish ties between his inner self and his external life, between himself and his fellows – and thus live sanely and wholly. He breaks out of "enchantment," out of bondage.

But the idleness, enforced or chosen, and the earnest Mammon-working of England in 1843 tell a very different story, one of self-idolatry and thus of "perpetual life-in-death" (PP: 245). The Present is Madness, Insanity, because it lives so completely on the periphery, so determinedly away from that "inner man." It acknowledges no possibility of, or need for, Romance in reality. The only modern person capable of doing Samson's work is the Irish Widow, and she does it by disease rather than by exacting firm leadership. It is Cain's demonic world indeed when one proves one's sisterhood in the Widow's manner. It is a nightmare world too when Idleness alone is the chief labor: dilettantes doing nothing, and workers not allowed to do anything, all sitting "enchanted." The only actual laborers are the industrialists, and they are "earnest" chiefly about the "making of money" (148). Everywhere the main religious activity is "Idolatry of Sense" (149), and the worshippers' basic prayer, "during hours of mastication and rumination, which they call hours of meditation," is a demonic echo of Christ's parable of the rich man: "Soul, take thy ease, it is all *well* that thou art a vulture soul" (189). "Gospel of Enlightened Selfishness" indeed. Or else Cannibalism. And utter isolation:

Isolation is the sum-total of wretchedness to man. To be cut off, to be left solitary: to have a world alien, not your world; all a hostile camp for you; not a home at all, of hearts and faces who are yours, whose you are! It is the frightfulest enchantment; too truly a work of the Evil One . . . Encased each as in his transparent 'ice-palace'; our brother visible in his, making signals and gesticulations to us; – visible, but forever unattainable: on his bosom we shall never rest, nor he on ours. It was not a God that did this; no! (271)

Words, the mind: they are reduced to uninterpretable gestures. There is no better image for the world of Victorian fiction than Carlyle's picture here of a human being in his "ice-palace," his words reduced to meaningless physical movements effecting nothing. The picture tells us about Esther Summerson and Lady Dedlock and Arthur Clennam, about Rosamond Vincy and Tertius Lydgate, about Lucy Snowe and her world – all making signals, and no one hearing or knowing how to interpret. But Carlyle's last sentence is usually omitted. Such certainties few who follow him can share.

By 1850, with another revolution in France that was anything but liberating and more Chartist petitions and industrial insurrections at home, Carlyle had come to see England as a nation of bipeds lodged permanently in a "dusky potent insatiable animalism" which was once called "Doubting Castle" but is now found to be the "promised land." Because "the chief end of man" is even more than before "to make money and spend it" (LDP: 18) or to pile up Scrip, "British Industrial existence seems fast becoming one huge poison-swamp of reeking pestilence physical and moral; a hideous *living* Golgotha of souls and bodies buried alive" (27). Thus "enchanted" man is happy to find himself amongst fellow "doleful creatures," for he is "no longer a man, but a greedy, blind two-footed animal, 'without soul, except what saves him the expense of salt and keeps his body with its appetites from putrefying'"; "nothing now but a human money-bag and meat-trough" (258). The world is one "enormous Life-in-Death" (320).

The static and lifeless quality of Carlyle's images and ideas in these *Latter-Day Pamphlets* shows us how his vision has failed. Although he continues to speak of a man-centered moral world, his invocation of the wrath of God and his constant references to biblical destruction show him trapped in the very old clothes he had been so long trying to help England shed. And he knows it. In language which acknowledges its own hollowness, he proclaims: "My friend, I have to speak in crude language, the wretched times being dumb and deaf: and if thou find no truth under this but the phantom of an extinct Hebrew one, I at present cannot help it" (325).

Thus the controlling tone and imagery of the *Pamphlets* have their origin in the Puritan language of bestiality and excrement used to damn the "natural" idolatrous self, for Carlyle now sees England as the Puritans had: as idolatrous and "natural." The polarized world of the romantic mirror that he had always invoked in his Condition-of-England pictures has lost any image of the idyllic "green world." Romance does not exist in reality. There is no suggestion of tension between past order and present anarchy. Instead, we get the incessant declamations of the present tense and the jagged rhythms of sentence fragments. The "knights-errant" of old, fighting "against dragons and wizards in enchanted wilder-nesses and waste howling solitudes" (87), would defeat no enemy in modern England, Carlyle declares, for they would be trapped in some "red-tape" establishment of government. Furthermore, they would find the "human" beings about them sitting, like the Dead Sea Apes in *Past and Present*, in "Suspended animation" (157) or else "wandering in an extinct world of wearisome, oppressive and expensive shadows" (285), a world "without lungs, fast wheezing itself to death, in horrid convulsions; and deserving to die" (133). These people live spiritually – or is it respectably? – by amalgamat-ing good and evil, right and wrong (80, 162); to worship, they kiss the outsides of their Bibles (314) and raise statues to Hudson the Railway King (which statues rust "in the sooty rain" – 264). Their God is property, their "highest Priests" lawyers (284), and their one creed "external varnish" (284, 289). And yet with all these "spiritual" aids, they never "escape from that inexorable all-encircling ocean-moan of ennui" (337). Having completely denied all inward life, they are finally no different from the animals who share their "nightmare wilderness": pythons, megatherions, flabby monsters, predatory wolves, hyenas, owls, mud-gods, creatures that walk upon their bellies, drowned dogs, donkeys, and – of course – pigs: "Hrumph!" All living together happily in Doubting Castle.

No wonder Clough felt Carlyle had led his contemporaries into the wilderness and left them there. Yet the people who populate the English sections of *Daniel Deronda* and every part of the London of *Our Mutual Friend* are these same figures who sit ape-like kissing their Bibles in the *Pamphlets*, and they attest to the adequacy of Carlyle's signs of the present times. But George Eliot and Dickens escape Carlyle's despair. Seeing his readers applaud his words but never act on their message destroyed his belief in the efficacy of words – and effaced his generosity of spirit. Words had become simply "mere *words*," objects of appreciation if well said. Indeed, "if you talk well, you will go to Heaven, the modern Heaven of the English" (LDP: 187). If men are "such stuff as dreams are made of," as he had so often insisted, the madness latent within them – the injustice, blindness, disunity, animality – had for Carlyle welled up, only to be accepted by his countrymen as quite ordinary and normal in a world where good and evil had the same look and thus the same meaning. No still small voice was heard, or needed. The hope of the earlier Carlyle, his belief in a "green flowery world," his vision of the Romance within reality, and his certitude that some hero, some "incarnated Word," would yoke the polarities together and lift England from enchantment: all these have vanished in the face of that brave new world and the people in it. England lives happily ever after in Doubting Castle.

III

There is a passage ending *The French Revolution* which seems to me to place very adequately the Victorian novelists' sense of language, of their audience, of themselves as writers:

And so here, O Reader, has the time come for us two to part. Toilsome was our journeying together; not without offence; but it is done. To me thou wert as a beloved shade, the disembodied or not yet embodied spirit of a Brother. To thee I was but as a Voice. Yet was our relation a kind of sacred one; doubt not that! For whatsoever once sacred things become hollow jargons, yet while the Voice of Man speaks with Man, hast thou not there the living fountain out of which all sacrednesses sprang, and will yet spring? Man, by the nature of him, is definable as "an incarnated Word." Ill stands it with me if I have spoken falsely: thine also it was to hear truly. Farewell.   (IV: 323)

Sacred words versus jargon: the polarity is the polarity of Carlyle's works and of the novelists' – a past, whether imagined or re-membered or real, of natural and social wholeness, and a present in Doubting Castle; a past of true Words and a present of "mere *words*." Charlotte Brontë, Dickens, and George Eliot in their very different ways place their readers under the same injunction: "Ill stands it with me if I have spoken falsely: thine also it was to hear truly." So too would Bunyan have said.

2

The terrible beauty of Charlotte Brontë's "Natural Supernaturalism"

No novelist in this study is so closely aligned with Carlyle in explicitly confronting the religious and Romantic heritages as is Charlotte Brontë. Her background – born in an Anglican (but strongly Methodist-influenced) parsonage, reading with her brother and sisters the works of the Romantics – parallels Carlyle's early years. And her novels, in their ideas and language, show striking affinities both to the questions Carlyle had been asking since 1827 and to his ways of exploring them. True, her works are all set back in the opening decades of the century, and the "social" concerns, even in *Shirley*, seem peripheral to the personal dilemma, the reason–passion conflicts that she took as her subject. That, however, is the point: Brontë begins where Carlyle did, with the individual and the necessity for individual transformation if the godlike is ever to manifest itself in the world around us. Carlyle's question "What is Justice?" is hers (PP: 18). And his concern about the "hurt inflicted on the moral self" by injustice is her central theme. To chart it she places an orphan at the center of each of her novels, and structures each work on the pattern of the Calvinized *Bildungsroman* Carlyle created in *Sartor Resartus*; she presents the environment that surrounds and often entraps this central figure in a manner very similar to the social world Carlyle depicted in *Sartor* and in *Past and Present*; and she insists that religious feeling centers on living in this world. A reviewer of *Jane Eyre* noted Brontë's "faculty of discerning the wonderful in and through the commonplace."[1] Few more succinct definitions could be made of Carlyle's "natural supernaturalism."

Charlotte Brontë significantly parallels Carlyle, then, in the forms of her fiction, in its ideas, and in its characters. She emphasizes the common response of the early Victorian artist to the post-Romantic world – and emphasizes it in a unique way as well.

43

Because the protagonists in her novels published during her life are women, Brontë widens Carlyle's emphases – woman has a *Bildung* of her own, a radical assertion in the 1840s – and explores the dangers of an oversimplified assertion of the spiritual, self-defining nature of work when that work does not mean the same thing for women as it does for men.[2]

I

When *Jane Eyre* appeared, Charlotte Brontë worried that its lack of any "subject of public interest" would forestall critical approval. Her book was, she said, a "mere domestic novel," hardly the work Dickens and Thackeray were presently offering each month, and certainly not one concerned with hungry-forties Condition-of-England questions.[3] French reviewer Eugene Forçade, however, found a very solidly represented social world in the three volumes. He noted in them "a drama in which society . . . plays more or less the cruel and tyrannical role assigned to fate in the tragedies of antiquity," and praised Brontë for her refusal to "call down a fiery judgment" on that society. These words, from a critic whose ideas about her work Brontë endorsed, suggest how urgently contemporary – even "social" – her novels seemed to her readers.[4] Like her adored Thackeray, she is concerned to analyze the "warped system of things" (Preface, *Jane Eyre*), but her approach to social matters is in no way so immediate and direct as his. Her place of analysis is always from within, her one viewpoint always the inner self's effort to chart the boundaries between the private and social worlds.

Yet the outer world is important in her novels, and especially her choice of that period she called the "giant adolescence" of the nineteenth century (S: III: 14: 726), the first two decades when the effects, or disasters, of the French and Industrial Revolutions had begun to tell heavily on English life.[5] Schiller had noted that in this new mechanized, class-conscious society, man had become a "fragment": with "the more rigorous separation of ranks and occupations . . . the inner unity of human nature was severed too, and a disastrous conflict set its harmonious powers at variance."[6] Carlyle described this period which Brontë uses as one of "rag-gathering and rag-burning days" when the question "what next?" was the ultimate one because poets and philosophers *had* to seek some "new Mythus" to replace the threadbare ideas about church

44

and state and society inherited from the previous century (SR: 253, 194). In book three of *Sartor* he suggests Teufelsdröckh's own Centre of Indifference as an emblem for this new age of transition which followed the rationalist-industrial revolutions. And the machine, whether it be a mechanistic-materialist philosophy or the steam-belching loom which affronts its operative, stands as the central symbol of the transition: in its dehumanizing, in its severance of man from other men, from nature, from God, and from himself, it is the uninspirited dead image of the new age. Charlotte Brontë's backgrounds reflect this analysis and her characters suffer the psychic fragmentation and human isolation caused by the social upheaval. Hers is a world in progressive flux, its only certainty that the machine will not vanish – neither from the landscape nor from the internal world.

Like Carlyle, Brontë refuses to endorse any preoccupation with "life" after death as an answer to the fears aroused by so much change. Such an attitude, her novels suggest, constitutes an escape from the duties here. All her novels assert a this-worldly ethic. Self-knowledge is nowhere possible unless the individual can find some work, some activity that will define the self in relation to other human beings. Yet this work amounts to nothing if it enslaves the self, if it so deadens the inner imaginative life that true fellow-feeling becomes impossible. "Our Works are the mirror wherein the spirit first sees its natural lineaments," Teufelsdröckh noted (162). This is precisely Brontë's assertion: work in her novels is a spiritual issue, a way of *sane living*.[7] Thus she places each of her novels in the period when the immense rigor of that quest to "know what thou canst do" first became apparent.

The scene of Brontë's books, whether the setting is Yorkshire or an allegorical Labassecour, is essentially like that world Teufelsdröckh found so threatening. And the two key elements which define this scene are religion and work. *Jane Eyre*, set during the period of the Luddite riots and the early Romantic poets, presents a Carlylean celebration of poetry and genius as forces which, in spite of Mammon, "reign, and redeem" readers from "the hell of [their] own meanness" (III: 6: 473). Not only does this statement suggest the function Brontë assigns Romantic poetry, but in the aside to her 1847 readers about Mammon's threat to their imaginative lives, she at once adds a topical note and underlines the dehumanizing influence the alliance of money and religion plays in the novel. Q. D. Leavis has pointed out that the presentation of

Brocklehurst, that representative of formal Evangelicalism, does more than assail the evangelical offense against life; in him and his biblical phrases Brontë illustrates how "Religion has thus become a means for imposing class distinctions *based on money*."[8] It is an unholy alliance indeed, elevating all that separates man from natural feeling and from nature.

For Brontë nature and the truly religious are inextricably connected; they constitute an alliance which does not oppose, as do all of the novel's "religious" figures, a genuinely human and creative life lived in this world. The fact that even the decent, non-hypocritical religious figures in *Jane Eyre* are cut off from nature signifies how little use the old Mythus has become in a post-eighteenth-century world. Helen Burns's way of life finally affirms Brocklehurst's notion of (charity-)man's "vile bodies" and "immortal souls" (I: 7: 72). Helen is never seen in any relation to nature; her life is completely centered on the world to come and her duty in it. This evangelical heritage has an even more destructive effect on St John Rivers. Nature for him is a threat, something to crush much as he crushes the flowers under his foot (III: 5: 464). Indeed, this is how he uses religion: to repress all natural feeling. His love of God and his use of the time-worn phrases of worship and devotion serve to cut him off from love and feeling, and from his own self; they are, finally, ways of self-aggrandizement as deadly as any Benthamite calculus since they are used to insure a place in the New Jerusalem. St John Rivers is a Diogenes Teufelsdröckh determined not to acknowledge the "Demon-Empire" of feeling that is part of the dual-natured self. To do so, he seems to think, would be to lose his mansion in heaven; it would constitute a denial of degenerate man's salvation. For Jane, who sees his fire within, he thus becomes an "automaton" (III: 5: 466). His religion is as deadening as Brocklehurst's or Eliza Reed's, as death oriented as Helen's. His notion of "duty," like Helen's "doctrine of endurance," Jane Eyre's autobiography at once scrutinizes and redefines.

Shirley's actual social background is defined by much more than religion, though Brontë's insistence to her publishers that the curates were necessary to the novel suggests how much of a piece is the church's place in her sense of the social picture;[9] and the opening page's allusion to the Puseyites urges the reader to see the novel's analogies to the present and the barrenness of contemporary religious institutions. *Shirley*'s panoramic picture is one of a nation and its individuals in the "throes of a sort of moral earthquake" (I:

2: 37). There is no patriotism, little real fellow-feeling, a "great gulf" between classes (III: 2: 502), and nothing – certainly not the church – that seems in a position to redeem. In giving life to these abstractions, Brontë so draws her characters and their contexts that any 1840s reader would almost certainly have seen Carlyle's analysis behind her ideas and *dramatis personae*, no matter what the author's sources.[10] Indeed, Carlyle's ideas about work provide the best way of placing the characters against the social background, since work is the constant topic of the men and women in the novel, and the issue of creative self-defining work its dominating idea.

"The latest Gospel in this world is, know thy Work and do it," Carlyle wrote in *Past and Present*, echoing the idea he had used since "Characteristics." "'Know thyself:' long enough has that poor 'self' of thine tormented thee" (PP: 196). For Carlyle man's work offered him the opportunity for defining himself, and thus for redemption. It broke the entrapment of self, in both Puritan and Romantic senses. The discussions of work between Shirley and Caroline are virtually a gloss on this idea – with the signal difference that it is woman's work they are discussing. For Caroline labor might not "make a human being happy," but "successful labour has its recompense; a vacant, weary, lonely, hopeless life has none" (S: II: 1: 257).

Shirley alone knows her work and thus her duty; they are inseparable, in Brontë as in Carlyle. As Robert Bernard Martin has noted, Shirley "represents the older aristocratic position, one slowly being overtaken by the Moores and Yorkes," by the new manufacturing classes and their new ethic.[11] No better illustration of Carlyle's "Aristocracy" – "A corporation of the Best, of the Bravest" (C: XXIX: 160) – exists in English fiction than this fiery spirit. Her comments on heroes, on the need to reverence and admire what is great and good (S: II: 1: 245–6, 25), would fit easily into any Carlyle passage on man's "faculty of Reverence." Carlyle traced the breakdown of social order and the "sullen revengeful humour of revolt" that pervaded the lower classes to the "decay of loyalty in all senses, disobedience, decay of religious faith" (C: XXIX: 149). There could be no "loving companionship" with one's fellows, Teufelsdröckh noted, until all classes experienced "the Higher" as something quite unconnected with rank and money (SR: 251). Brontë makes the same analysis in *Shirley*. With few exceptions the gods of the men in power are "the world," money, machinery – nothing "Higher" in any spiritual sense.

Though Shirley herself is "aristocratic" in the most noble sense of the term, oppressive forces surround her. She sees in the manufacturers Moore and Yorke, and in Mr Helstone, the rector, a fundamental selfishness. Robert Moore cares for nothing beyond his "gods" – trade, mill, machinery – and shows no understanding of his workers' claims on him. His conversion at the novel's close is in terms of *its* work ethic ("let the worst come, I can work" – III: 12: 678) and of its demand that man must render "justice to his fellowmen" (III: 7: 616). Yet the language he uses to describe this change of heart suggests how warped he has been by his work: "The machinery of all my nature; the whole enginery of this human mill: the boiler, which I take to be the heart, is fit to burst" (III: 7: 604). The other manufacturer, Yorke, does not speak in such metaphors, and is indeed an ideal "Captain of Industry," responsive to and responsible for his employees. Yet he is "dead at heart," the narrator announces (I: 4: 55). Brontë's judgment on him is made in Carlylean language: "he is a man without awe, imagination and tenderness"; "his religion could not be that of one who knows how to venerate" (I: 4: 55).[12]

Except for the good but ineffectual Mr Hall, *Shirley*'s priests offer as sorry a spectacle as spiritual guides as the manufacturers do as earthly helpers. The curates and Helstone provide reason enough for "the wide-spread spirit of disaffection against constituted authorities" (I: 4: 63) that marks the social realm of the novel. The curates are least interested in religion, most in status and rank (and Brontë's satire on them provides some of the real fun of the novel). As for Mr Helstone, his name suggests the nature of his religious feeling. His "duty" he perceives to be more martial than religious ("he should have been a soldier," the narrator tells the reader – I: 3: 44). "To hunt down vermin [i.e., anyone who dares question established authority] is a noble occupation, – fit for an Archbishop," he pronounces (I: 3: 51). Justice has no place in his system. His sense of the vocation his clothes indicate is nil. And, in the context of the novel's emphasis on work, he is damned all the more by his declaration that "the great knowledge of man is to know himself, and the bourne whither his own steps tend" (I: 4: 65). Helstone has no idea of the existence of any inner self, nor any notion of the sources of his militaristic energies. His words about something "Higher" are based on class-feeling rather than religious belief.

In the West Riding of Yorkshire, Shirley is the truth-teller, the voice of justice towards "our fellow creatures." Only one other character occupies such an animating position: William Farren, the worker. It would seem impossible for a reader of 1849 to hear him and not remember the commands shouted to Captains of Industry in *Past and Present*:

Invention may be all right, but I know it isn't right for poor folks to starve. Them that governs mun find a way to help us: they mun mak' fresh orderations . . . (S: I: 8: 154)

I thought it shameful that, willing and able as I was to work, I suld be i' sich a condition that a young cratur about the age o' my own eldest lass suld think it needful to come and offer me her bit o' brass. (II: 7: 365)

Brontë's presentation of this man, "disposed to be honourably content if he could but get work to do" (I: 8: 155), disposed to believe that the hierarchical position of his superiors requires them to answer such questions as his, parallels Carlyle's depiction of the workers' condition. Her Farren, like Carlyle's workers, exposes the hollowness of the 1840s' Plugsons.

The closing pages of *Shirley* offer a lament for all that the world of the millowner has replaced. Though Shirley marries a millowner's brother, and they seem ideal employers, the narrator's last-page, present-tense emphasis on the banishment of the green world underlines how man's new "setting" is finally anti-life, and emphasizes too, in the passing of time, where we stand in 1849. A manufacturer's "daydreams" have created, in the place of a green Hollow where "fairish" once ran, *our* landscape of "stone and brick and ashes." Machine-centered English life offers the individual almost no way to assert his/her inner life in creative sustaining work, and offers few landscapes for the imagination to work upon.

Surely it was Brontë's despair about the effects of such "daydreams" and about a woman's oppression by such an environment that caused her to move her last novel away from England. *Villette*'s main landscape is the allegorically-named Labassecour, where the reader encounters very little suggestion of machines and factories and almost no hint of the political (except in Paul's speech attacking tyranny and injustice). Because Labassecour is "infinitely less worried about appearances" than "dear old England" (III: 31: 450), it is the only place where a family significantly named Bretton can make an adequate life for itself, and where a single woman can find work and independence.

Nevertheless, even here the inevitability of Carlyle's diagnosis cannot be escaped. If the machine, *per se*, plays no role in *Villette*, the novel's world is governed by the deadened forms of religions that go hand-in-hand with mechanic life. And these forms are totally inimical to psychological and intellectual freedom. No matter how we may squirm over the novel's anti-Catholicism, *Villette* remains utterly radical in its insistence on the worn-out nature of religion's clothes. Sects and churches here would find a ready home amongst the "doleful creatures" running in and out of Carlyle's churches. Catholic tracts and Methodist ones Lucy pronounces alike in their "excitation to fanaticism" (III: 36: 508). And she sees "incumbrances and trivialities" in Presbyterian, Lutheran, and Anglican churches. Her "last appeal" is to the Bible alone, she asserts (III: 36: 513–14). That religion as represented by its churches has any place in man's struggle for unified existence is finally denied by the "marriage" – of minds and hearts alone – which joins Protestant and Catholic before the novel's end. Church and sect are not important.

The purpose of setting in all of Brontë's novels is, then, to counterpoint the quests towards "Freedom and Renovation" (V: III: 41: 578) of her protagonists with that deadening landscape which shadows those quests. The social world and those who constitute it are increasingly blocked from real feeling, unable to acknowledge any life beyond the seen and quantifiable. The quest to sustain imagination, fellow-feeling, and freedom in such an atmosphere is the subject of the autobiographies of Jane Eyre, Lucy Snowe, and William Crimsworth, and of the biography of Caroline Helstone and Shirley Keeldar. Brontë's novels are thus English *Bildungsromane*, novels of the self's development – radically different from other spiritual biographies of the period only because three of them focus on the development of a woman's inner life. But their psychological terrain is the same as that of the period's most famous autobiography of an orphaned soul: "Our Wilderness is the wide World in an Atheistic Century . . . To me also, entangled in the enchanted forests, demon-peopled, doleful of sight and of sound, it was given, after weariest wanderings, to work out my way into the higher sunlight slopes" (SR: 184). That Brontë's heroines also achieve a certain happiness attests to her romance impulse; that her final heroine, Lucy Snowe, can achieve that happiness – "Freedom and Renovation" – only in exile and alone attests to Brontë's continually darkening sense of the alienating nature of English life. *Villette* is bleak, but in significant ways more affirmative than Carlyle's *Latter-Day Pamphlets*.

II

Although Charlotte Brontë may not have conceived of herself as a sage in the Carlyle mold, the subtitle of *Jane Eyre* and the form of all her novels indicate that she saw her task as something more than a writer of mere domestic fictions: "An Autobiography. Edited by Currer Bell" would have asked any serious reader to acknowledge the book's place in the long line of spiritual autobiographies and biographies that aspired to teach by illustrating one man's self-conquest amidst Vanity Fair's allurements. Brontë intended her novels to "delineate the likeness of the earthly pilgrimage of man," as her words in an 1849 Preface to *The Professor* suggest:

I said to myself that my hero should work his way through life as I had seen real living men work theirs . . .; that, before he could find so much as an arbour to sit down in, he should master at least half the ascent of "the Hill of Difficulty." . . . As Adam's son he should share Adam's doom, and drain throughout life a mixed and moderate cup of enjoyment.   (xi)

It was the arbor of the Hill of Difficulty which tempted Christian to "sleep in the day-time" and thus leave off attention to his soul's progress. The allusions to Bunyan and to the Bible which figure so prominently in this Preface pervade all of Brontë's novels, which are structured around the journeys of their protagonists through the "dreary wilderness" (JE: II: 10: 354) of this world. Thus, with these allusions, and with the idea that the task of fallen man is to work unceasingly towards some goal, Brontë places herself within the religious tradition of life-writing, a tradition whose central characteristic was the report of how the individual responded to God's calling.[13]

Yet Jane Eyre, reporting the details of her life, presents her young self not as a sinful child but as a suffering innocent living amongst people who think she is innately unregenerate. This emphasis focuses that aspect of Brontë's fiction which runs quite counter to the Puritan-evangelical heritage and which caused contemporary critics to question whether Currer Bell has "any defined notions of religion at all."[14] Brontë's emphasis on the innocence of the child (an emphasis she will give up in *Villette*) aligns her fiction with Wordsworth's child ("and I grew up/Fostered alike by beauty and by fear" – *Prelude*, I: 301–2) and with Carlyle's Teufelsdröckh. And with them, as we have seen, the quest is not towards the New Jerusalem but into the self as a mode of escape from the experience of despair and alienation. The goal of this quest is not for Brontë that substituting of "self" for "soul" which marks a crucial difference between Romantic and Puritan self-scrutinies; no more than Carlyle does Brontë intend a merely secular way of thinking about oneself, even if her contemporaries saw that in the novels.[15] Rather, she attempts to discover new modes by which the soul may be realized through the self, indeed a new synthesis of the old religion and Romanticism. Her protagonists *will* gain the right to sit down in Bunyan's arbor without fear of losing the parchment scroll.

This synthesis is, in all but name, the "natural supernaturalism" which Teufelsdröckh discovers at the end of his pilgrimage. His experience did not serve as the source of the quests of Brontë's protagonists, but it provides the clearest context and model for understanding the nature and importance of her blending of the religious and Romantic traditions, and it focuses her essential concern: the effort to define the relation of Romanticism to the moral self's struggle. It is the preoccupying question of the Victorian Romantics because it deals with man in relation not simply to himself and nature, but to a social world and to God (however "God" is defined). Thus Brontë's novels are studies of the Victorian orphan rather than the Romantic child. Her protagonists, like Teufelsdröckh, begin their conscious life feeling "like no other" (SR: 107), at once innocent and "fallen." William Crimsworth, in *The Professor*, is born at his mother's death and cared for out of political expediency by an uncle who, after sending his nephew to Eton, cuts him adrift and denounces all familial ties as "humbug." Jane Eyre's "very first recollections of existence" involve her dependent status; at Gateshead she is a "discord," a "thing," "like nobody there" (I: 2: 10, 13). Caroline Helstone's "dark recollection" of her father is of a drunken, cruel man who loathes her; of her mother she has no memory at all. As for Lucy Snowe, she *tells* nothing about her childhood except that her godmother had rescued her from kinfolk – but only for six months, after which there was "a long time, of cold, of danger, of contention" (V: I: 4: 94). As a result of such isolation, all of these protagonists ask Teufelsdröckh's question: "Who am I; what is this ME?" (SR: 53). Caroline Helstone wonders, again and again, "What was I created for . . .? Where is my place in the world?" (S: I: 10: 194).

Jane Eyre is a book of such questions, of "the ceaseless inward question," "Why was I always suffering, always brow-beaten, always accused, for ever condemned?" (I: 2: 12). Because it poses these questions so overtly, it is the Brontë novel where the search after answers involves most centrally and overtly the clash of Romanticism and the old religious heritage. In his extraordinary discussion of the language of fire in the novel, David Lodge makes this point:

Jane Eyre is remarkable for the way it asserts a moral code as rigorous and demanding as anything in the Old Testament in a universe that is not theocentric but centred on the individual consciousness . . . The sanctions of Old Testament morality – punishment by fire and water, destitution, exile, solitariness – are still very much in evidence on both the literal and metaphorical levels, but the symbolic art of the novel presents them as extensions of the individual consciousness.[16]

The autobiographical form Brontë chooses emphasizes this combining of Romantic and religious heritages. Jane Eyre, in telling her story, is doing precisely what Bunyan and Baxter and eighteenth-century Methodist autobiographers did: "reviewing [her] past experience" in order to discern "the shape of the divinely ordered whole which [her] life was becoming."[17] Hers is indeed a history of finding her Calling.

Jane's experience in the red-room stands at the novel's beginning as an emblem of this Romantic-religious dilemma. That room, with its throne-like bed and "great looking-glass," Jane associates with images of isolation (cold, damp, "decaying fire," jail) and ideas of being an outcast which will recur throughout the novel. But the episode serves as a warning of the exile possible if one chooses to indulge the self and forget others. That mirror – a constant in Romantic poetry and in religious emblem books – alerts us to the scene's significance: the mirror suggests entrapment, but it also suggests the way to liberation. A scene from Quarles, involving the image in a glass (and carrying a motto about vanity from Job 15: 31), tells us how to read the young Jane's experience (fig. 2):

Look off, let not thy optics be
  Abus'd: thou see'st not what thou should'st:
Thyself's the object thou should'st see,
  But 'tis thy shadow thou behold'st:
    And shadows thrive the more in stature,
The nearer we approach the light of nature.
                                        (*Emblems*, II: 6)

The older Jane, narrating her life, uses the mirror to show her young self in the midst of formation, with Vanity Fair or freedom as the alternatives. The child sees her image – "half fairy, half imp" – as some phantom out of a story (I: 2: 12). But she will come to see these "shadows" as part of her inner life which she must *know* if she is ever to see herself whole. One of the quotations Quarles affixes to his emblem of the vanity-mirror announces Jane's quest: "if thou canst not apprehend the things within thee, thou canst not comprehend the things above thee: the best looking-glass, wherein to see thy God, is perfectly to see thyself." [18]

Jane's situation in the novel both initially as an unwanted orphan and later as a governess (an adult orphan, really, so placeless and unconnected is that Victorian archetype), is one that tempts her to a Romantic assertion of self. Although Bessie's song of "the poor orphan child," with its traditional pilgrim's progress iconography and yet its ironic reminiscences of Wordsworth's "Lucy Gray," promises that God is a friend of the outcast child, the God that Jane

Sic decipit orbis.

JOB. XV. 31.

*Let not him that is deceived trust in vanity; for vanity
shall be his recompence.*

Fig. 2.   Quarles, Emblem, II: 6

actually hears about is one associated with the hypocrisy of Mrs Reed and Brocklehurst. Or, at best, it is the God of "inexpressible sadness" which Helen Burns worships (I: 8: 81). Jane's response to scripture indicates what she wants from a God. Her readings of Revelations, Daniel, Genesis, and some Old Testament narratives excite her because they are "interesting" to her case; they offer correspondences to her feelings of injustice; they stimulate her imagination because they are *narratives* with ends where promises are fulfilled and sufferings rewarded (I: 4: 35). As apocalyptic works these biblical stories allow her to discern a pattern to experience as well as an end of injustice and a reward for bearing it. (And it is an apocalyptic pattern that the older Jane gives to the narrative of her life.) The young Jane's experiences of denial have mandated for her a God whose love and justice she can feel. Thus her questions to the dying Helen Burns – "Where is God? What is God?" – bring no answer that is comprehensible to her (I: 9: 96). Jane's *feeling* of injustice is not touched by that God who comforts Helen or abates Brocklehurst.

Even while the young Jane listens to Helen Burns on the New Testament and strives to imitate Maria Temple, she is at the same time discovering the joys, few as they are, of this world: she discovers the wonders of Miss Temple's hearth fire and her fellowship; and she comes upon the "great pleasure" (I: 9: 88) available in the natural world lying beyond Lowood's walls. This Romantic sense of nature as a resource for the soul, indeed as the one force outside the self in essential harmony with it, has been with Jane from her beginning consciousness of her orphan state. And Brontë parallels Jane's maturing consciousness of nature with her "religious" questioning. Thus Jane's conclusion that "This world is pleasant – it would be dreary to be called from it, and to have to go – who knows where?" (I: 9: 93) is counterpointed with Helen's death – and not to the advantage of the God of sadness Helen worships.[19]

The figure of Maria Temple perfectly embodies the ambiguity Brontë intends to project. Her first name alludes to the traditional Christian Mythus; yet her surname suggests that human affection and love of God can coexist in one individual living in this world. Ostensibly, Jane receives religious instruction at Miss Temple's hearth; in reality this teacher provides Jane with the comforts of nature: a home, fellow-feeling, even a surrogate mother. Her marriage and her removal from Lowood cut Jane loose; "allegiance to duty and order" (I: 10: 99) are again mere abstractions to her and thus meaningless without their living palpable embodiment. Maria Temple's departure throws Jane back into her "natural element" (I: 10: 100) – "natural" here carries some of the resonances it carries in Bunyan – and sends her out again, as she phrases it, "to seek real knowledge of life amidst its perils" (I:10: 100). She is once more "quite alone in the world; cut adrift from every connection" (I: 11: 112). The first phase of Jane Eyre's journey is thus complete; she now enters upon the stage of larger temptations at Thornfield.

Jane's journey from Lowood, like Teufelsdröckh's after the Blumine affair, is a journey after the undefinable: "I longed for a power of vision which might overpass that limit [of the hill]; . . . I believed in the existence of other and more vivid kinds of goodness, and what I believed in I wished to behold" (I: 12: 132). But it is more. I do not think it over-allegorizing to see that night-journey to Thornfield and the Gothic nature of that aptly-named house as the beginning of her discovery of the world of Romantic passion as it involves the adult; it is the beginning of her experience in what Carlyle called the "Satanic School" or "dungeon" of man's life. On his own journey Teufelsdröckh finds "what a Gehenna was within" and experiences the "laughter of Demons" that form the self's creative power. Jane's journey to Thornfield and then away presents her with the chance for maturity and self-fulfillment because it exposes her to the demons of passion that lie within and that she must acknowledge hers.

Superficially, Thornfield will seem the scene of Jane's liberation. She will see it as a "home" (II: 7: 303) and Mr Rochester as a "relation" whose attentions allow her, for the first time, to cease "to pine after kindred" (I: 15: 180). At Thornfield her restlessness finds it first real outlet. Early-on, walking along the house's third floor, her "imagination [had] created and narrated continuously" a life full of all lacking in her "actual existence" (I: 12: 132). Then Rochester comes and "the green flowery Eden in [her] brain" (his description of her visionary thought – II: 1: 399) seems to become fact. But this reaching towards self-fulfillment is mocked by the mad laughter of Bertha Mason, who also occupies the third floor. Hers is a laughter which, in the eyes of the autobiographer, provided a warning that no real fulfillment comes in self-indulgence and in isolation from one's fellows.[20] The Romantic quest into self must be accommodated to experience in the outer world.

The tension in Brontë's language in this section of the novel

56

underlines Jane's dilemma. On the one hand, she shows the Christian pilgrim's concern with time – "your claim to superiority depends on the use you have made of your time and experience" (I: 14: 164) – and his fear of exalting man above God. But she also shows Jane more and more unable to resist the blandishments and exaltations of the world as Rochester presents them (he promises a world like that in the vanity-mirror emblem, one "fairer, godlier, greater"). Looking back, the narrator notes: "He stood between me and every thought of religion . . . I could not *in those days* see God for his creature of whom I had made an idol" (II: 9: 346; my italics). As her Lowood experience had tempted Jane to turn from traditional religion to nature by showing its comforting power, so Thornfield tempts her to fashion a god for herself from nature. Her adoration of Rochester and her sense of his love suggest to the young woman that *this* life can be divine, that no promise of salvation is needed when nature so reflects her wishes.

Thus the older Jane, meditating on these earlier feelings, has only one model for describing her dilemma: Bunyan's description of Christian's pilgrimage towards his home in heaven, a journey beset on every side by ideas that depict this earthly life as paradise. For the older narrator, her past history, precisely because it does correspond to the traditional model, shows her readers "God's voice speaking instruction and doctrine,"[21] as Bunyan's life had. Her narrative warns of the dangers of vanity and idolatry, even in a world where, as we shall see, the supernatural has been naturalized in a very Carlylean way.

This possibility of idolatry is the central challenge to the post-Romantics. As I suggested in discussing Carlyle, the heirs of the Romantics, struggling to reconcile the inherited Puritan tradition with that sense of nature's consoling power which Wordsworth especially had made available, faced this very Hebraic problem of idolatry, and with it the terrors of self-indulgence and, finally, of solipsism, when man is tempted to name himself another god. Owen Barfield has suggested that idolatry for the Hebrews involved essentially a "subjective emptiness," a phrase which aptly defines Jane's fear of her idolatry: she knows that she faces the loss of her own identity in Rochester's consuming passion.[22] As the older Jane notices, her worship of Rochester was, in fact, an admission that the "old" God had never been a felt belief for her, had never been the reality nature had been because it had never offered her the warmth that the natural world had. The reason the autobiographer begins her history with the red-room experience is to alert us at the outset to the temptations Jane will face throughout her quest. In the "half fairy"–"half imp" image from the red-room, we get defined the essential antithesis of her experiences at Thornfield, and we also get the either-or images of nineteenth-century woman that Jane refuses to tolerate. Rochester would make Jane a "fairy" (II: 9: 337) in *his* world. Yet his first wife – to whom he doubtless promised the same rewards – lives an imp, her shrieking laughter mocking the unknowing governess. And Jane will see that to become the "fairy" is to align herself with the self-indulgence of the imp (in the vanity-mirror emblem, the self's "shadows thrive" the more the "world" takes over). Either position isolates her from the world of "human action and experience."

But the subtlety of Brontë's art is fully revealed in the way she makes Rochester symbolic for Jane not only of the "natural" warmth but also of the dangers of the Romantic quest. Harold Bloom has pointed out that this quest

is from nature to the imagination's freedom (sometimes a reluctant freedom), and the imagination's freedom is frequently purgatorial, re-demptive in direction but destructive of the social self. The high cost of Romantic internalization, that is, of finding paradises within a renovated man, shows itself in the arena of self-consciousness. The quest is to widen consciousness as well as to intensify it, but the quest is shadowed by a spirit that tends to narrow consciousness to an acute preoccupation with self. This shadow of imagination is solipsism.[23]

Rochester represents this solipsism in full force. He appropriates the judgment of God as his own ("I know my Maker sanctions what I do" – II: 8: 322) and conjures "mak[ing] our own heaven" (II: 9: 337). It is a heaven where he would completely deny the real and necessarily social world in which man must live and exercise responsibility. Rochester would much prefer to take Jane to the moon if need be. Indeed, his whole history is one of a wanderer through Gehennas of the self, even as he tries to escape the "hell" (III: 1: 393) of his own life. Philosopher Eric Vogelin has said, in speaking of the Romantic cult of Satan, that the "man [who] contracts heaven and hell into his Self" dooms himself to a "satanic existence" as the only reality.[24] This self-imprisonment is precisely what Rochester accomplishes.

His consciousness of his solipsistic acts at once alienates him and, in the end, redeems him. To his pastor and his lawyer he asserts, "I am little better than a devil at this moment; and . . . deserve no doubt the sternest judgments of God, – even to the quenchless fire and deathless worm" (II: 11: 368). The last phrase alludes to Isaiah's description – which Christ also uses – of the outcast, he who transgresses God's law (Isaiah 66: 24; Mark 9: 44, 46, 48). It is this self-preoccupation and Rochester's inability to conceive of his situation as other than doomed necessity which finally separate him and Jane.

And the depth of Brontë's intelligence and art forces such a separation. In her Romantic thrust towards self-fulfillment, Jane has become trapped in self-consciousness, a self-consciousness bred by her almost innate sense of herself as a discord and an outcast. Such peace and connection as she enjoys with Rochester are reason enough to forget all else in contemplation of her own joy; her quest seems realized in its palpable happiness. Indeed, she finds herself wondering "why moralists call this world a dreary wilderness" (II: 10: 354); nature itself seems to sanction her feelings: "Nature must be gladsome when I was so happy" (II: 9: 324). And her mirror underlines her "rejoicing heart":

While arranging my hair, I looked at my face in the glass, and felt it was no longer plain: there was hope in its aspect, and life in its colour . . . I had often been unwilling to look at my master, because I feared he could not be pleased at my look; but I was sure I might lift my face to his now, and not cool his affection by its expression. (II: 9: 324)

Yet her next look into this glass is strikingly different in the image of the imp it presents: Bertha's "discoloured," "savage face" stands before that mirror with Jane's wedding veil on her head (II: 10: 358). The opening lines of Quarles's text for the vanity-glass emblem describe what Jane will learn from these two reflections:

> Believe her not, her glass diffuses
> False portraitures: thou canst espy
> No true reflection; she abuses
> Her misinformed beholder's eye . . .   (II: 6)

Neither image is a "true reflection" of Jane. The "Eden" she has made of Thornfield and its orchard (II: 8: 311) has for a time obscured the metaphysical wilderness she does actually live in and has caused her to "shut [her] eyes against the future" in the face of such present joy. Yet the reality – and Jane's strong if intermittent sense of it – is suggested in a statement she makes during her one absence from Thornfield, for the death of Mrs Reed: "I still felt as a wanderer on the face of the earth" (II: 6: 285). Jane's real place is that of a post-Romantic: it is in the wilderness full of temptations to turn from God and worship elsewhere that the Israelites and Christ wandered, that Bunyan "dreamed," and that Carlyle placed Teufelsdröckh's Everlasting No.

The shattering of Jane's false Eden takes place when she discovers the reality of Rochester's previous marriage and the truth about Bertha Mason. Significantly, one of Jane's first responses to this confrontation scene is her acknowledgment that nature has never been at one with her, except in her imagination: "A Christmas frost had come at midsummer," she says, yoking metaphor to reality; and then she turns to the Bible for her language, giving up metaphor for simile and underlining her sense of the *real*: "My hopes were all dead – struck with a subtle doom, such as, in one night, fell on all the first-born in the land of Egypt" (II: 11: 374). The equation of her hopes with the Egyptians underlines their pagan (or worldly) nature, and emphasizes Jane's still outcast state; her hopes have been in reality an attempt to escape the responsibilities of time-centered modern man.

That she chooses language from Psalms rather than from the biblical histories she enjoyed as a child indicates her confusion and her want of a certain road to journey along; there now seems no pattern, no scriptural correspondences for her; she fits into no narrative, only the poetic present. She finds comfort in the words of the Psalmist who feels cut off from God: "'Be not far from me, for trouble is near: there is none to help'" (II: 11: 374; Psalm 22). Yet in her despair Jane's only aid, her one "life-like idea," is her "remembrance of God." It is not the traditional God of Helen Burns (that "life-*like*" tells us how unsure Jane is of tradition). Nor is it the pantheistic God Wordsworth sometimes suggested. Teufelsdröckh, in the midst of the Everlasting No, found "the Infinite nature of Duty still dimly present to me; . . . if my as yet sealed eyes, with their unspeakable longing, could nowhere see [God], nevertheless in my heart He was present, and His heaven-written Law still stood legible and sacred there" (SR: 162). So it is with Jane.

Ironically, Rochester had seen this, and yet had been helpless to *see*. Disguised as a gypsy-seer, he had looked at Jane's brow and heard the forehead saying: "Reason sits firm and holds the reins, and she will not let the feelings burst away and hurry her to wild chasms . . . Strong winds, earthquake-shock, and fire may pass by: but I shall follow the guiding of that still small voice which interprets the dictates of conscience" (II: 4: 252). The allusion, as I noted in discussing Carlyle's use of it, asserts that God is no longer part of nature as he had often been for Moses, but is a quiet voice speaking to man's soul. The New Testament overtly transfers that voice to the inner self ("The Kingdom of God is within you" – Luke 17: 21). And the traditions of Puritan meditation mandated the "apprehension of the Word as an insistent inner voice."[25] This tradition is the basis for Carlyle's assertion of the God within and of "natural supernaturalism." For him it was this "small still voice" alone which promised man that "injustice will not be his final lot," that "*sanity* and order" will come – that he can defeat madness (my italics).

Thus Jane's "voice within me" (III: 1: 379) demands that she leave Thornfield. It gives her "whole ME" (SR: 167) the strength to confront Rochester's demand that she "must become a part of [him]" (III: 1: 387); she is able, as he has never been, to assert a true superiority over the deadened world they both perceive. She phrases her self-assertion in the conventional language of "Preconceived opinions": "Do as I do: trust in God and yourself. Believe in heaven. Hope to meet again there . . . I will keep the law given by God; sanctioned by man." But with a significant addition:

> I will hold to the principles received by me when I was *sane*, and not *mad* – as I am now. Laws and principles are not for the times when there is no temptation . . . They have a worth – so I have always believed; and if I cannot believe it now, it is because I am *insane – quite insane*: with my veins running fire, and my heart beating faster than I can count its throbs. (III: 1: 403–5: my italics)

Jane's preoccupation here is with insanity and with words. She at once recognizes the unlimited powers of the self-centered imagination, and asserts her way of controlling its excesses: the Word is still her "stay" and guide; it has power against the demons. With this insight Jane conquers the inner "Demon-Empire" whose image is Bertha Mason. "We were born to strive and endure," she says. It is this Carlylean insight that shows what Jane has learned from Helen Burns and that affirms Brontë's place alongside Carlyle in the synthesis of Romanticism and the inherited religious traditions. The reality of the insight and the signal of what Brontë is doing are validated in one phrase: "trust in God *and yourself*." This "and yourself" is the superbly Victorian addition, the phrase that takes us two centuries from Bunyan: there, in that self, is the real knowable center of the godborn.[26]

Jane's last wilderness struggle – after her dream of the moon's command to "flee temptation" (III: 1: 407) – brings the final denial of the conventional Romantic escape to nature. More importantly, it brings a definition of what endurance means. Teufelsdröckh had tried to see nature as "his Mother and divine" (SR: 151). Jane too turns "to the universal mother, Nature" (III: 2: 412) for repose and nourishment. Failing this, she asks for death that will make her part of the natural world ("Hopeless of the future, I wished but this – that my Maker had that night thought good to require my soul of me while I slept; and that this weary frame, absolved by death from further conflict with fate, had now but to decay quietly, and mingle in peace with the soil of this wilderness" – III: 2: 415). Her death wish, like that one she uttered before Rochester's pleadings (III: 1: 381), recalls the wish of the Israelites to die in Egypt or in the wilderness in order to escape the God-imposed command to go onward (Numbers 14: 2). Significantly, "The wish to have some strength and some vigour returned to me as soon as I was amongst my fellow-beings"; "Human life and human labour were near. I must struggle on: strive to live and bend to toil like the rest" (III: 2: 416). Jane's final wilderness journey urges the necessity of living and working and moving onwards with others, and denies Rochester's solipsistic belief in self. The description by *Sartor's* Editor of the Wanderer's clutching "round him outwardly on the NOT-ME for wholesomer food" (SR: 170) describes Jane as well. She has begun her escape from that abyss that haunts so many Romantic questers.

Teufelsdröckh is able, through that imaginative apocalypse in the Rue de l'Enfer, to affirm himself by annihilating the devil's-dung part of the self: "and my mind's eyes were now unsealed, and its hands ungyved" (SR: 186). To unsealed eyes the universe becomes "godlike, and my Father's," and man becomes "my Brother" (SR: 188). Feminine Nature, with its suggestion of Paganism and cyclical time, is not enough. It is man's very suffering and his discovery of his ability to endure it that affirms the godborn within, and enables him to act. Jane Eyre's lesson is the same – except that she does not come to the realization alone. While Carlyle seems to remain within the Puritan tradition (where salvation involves only man and his God) by showing Teufelsdröckh's "conversion" occurring in isolation, Brontë insists that human aid and communion are vital to Jane's salvation. This *human* insistence makes her triumph all the more convincing.

The Moor House section of the novel reveals the subtlety and profundity of Brontë's handling of Jane's quest. Following the "guiding light" to Moor House, Jane begins her own imaginative apocalypse, for she finds at last a real family and home. To complete her development, Brontë exposes her to the falsity of the old religious language as she had at Thornfield exposed her to the falsity of Romantic (and romantic) speech. Jane must fully understand the irrelevance of the "old theorem" to living in this world amongst one's fellows. Brontë concentrates her attack on the deadness of the old religion in the figure of St John Rivers, whose other-worldliness affronts that present world of fellow-feeling which, Jane has learned, is essential to life.

Rivers has no sense of nature as the garment of God, no sense that it can offer any consolation. For him religion's function is the "pruning and training" of nature (III: 6: 479), the nature of fallen man. He sees himself as the Christian pilgrim, "an alien from his native country – not only for life, but in death" (III: 4: 451). Heaven alone is his home; like Bunyan's Christian, he has turned his back on this "world." Yet, though he describes himself as a "Christian philosopher," Jane suggests that "pagan" would be the better label (III: 6: 479). In aligning him with the heathen gods, she at once points the very worldly nature of his own concerns with "great ends" and "lofty eminence" and calls the reader's attention to this last temptation of her own wilderness journey. St John's kind of self-denial is so killing because it so completely denigrates the worth of this world and the necessity for fellow-feeling between human beings. It would destroy precisely what invigorates Jane and validates all endurance and struggle. His way is the counterpart of Rochester's threat: each would take away her liberty of mind, one by giving utter rein to passion and thus destroying sane ordered life; the other by killing passion, suppressing feeling, and desiccating all not directed towards heaven. And each man has the same goal: to find – "make" – his own New Jerusalem, utterly unconnected with this world.

While St John's temptation never moves Jane's passions as Rochester's had, it touches her more than Helen's piety because of St John's intense spiritual power. His appeal to her to "work" is sufficiently strong to cause her to agree to go with him to India as a missionary though, savingly, she refuses to marry him. "Remember," he says, "we are bid to work while it is day – warned that 'the night cometh when no man shall work.' Remember the fate of

Dives, who had his good things in this life. God gave you the strength to choose that better part which shall not be taken from you!" (III: 9: 533–4). It is this (superficially Carlylean) appeal to the "better part," that which Christ defined as lasting, which nearly causes Jane to follow the path of Christian denial that St John marks out for her.

Brontë concretely dramatizes Jane's rejection of this path for a *via media* between Romantic reaching and Christian denial in the scene where she hears a voice calling her. "I contended with my inward dimness of vision, before which clouds yet rolled . . . 'Shew me, shew me the path!' I entreated of Heaven . . . I saw nothing: but I heard a voice somewhere cry – 'Jane! Jane! Jane!'" (III: 9: 535–6). The "still small voice" speaks again. Since it is Rochester who calls, however, our temptation is to suggest that the world of passion displaces the traditional religious creed.[27] Such a view oversimplifies the complexity of Brontë's idea. Again Carlyle's use of the language of the "old theorem" clarifies the reading. St John, in his exhortation to Jane to see her duty as working towards a heavenly home, is glossing a passage from the twenty-first chapter of Revelation which he has chosen for the evening reading: "he sat there, bending over the great old Bible, and described from its page the vision of the new heaven and the new earth – told how God would come to dwell with men" (III: 9: 532). This vision is the source of Carlyle's "natural supernaturalism": God comes to dwell within and all about man as soon as he breaks free of the prison of self ("and I awoke to a new Heaven and a new Earth. The first preliminary moral Act, Annihilation of Self . . ., had been happily accomplished" – SR: 186). But St John Rivers refuses to acknowledge the literal meaning of the words "dwell with men," insisting instead that they validate his belief that all believers (i.e., those who agree with him) will find a mansion in heaven. Thus, where he aligns duty with working towards heaven, Jane aligns it with love of one's fellowman (and notes how Rivers has "put love out of the question" – III: 9: 535). This recognition that redeeming work involves first of all a generous concern for one's "brother" is precisely Carlyle's emphasis. And Brontë's "work" is his, too: "Yes here, in this poor, miserable, hampered, despicable Actual, . . . here or nowhere is thy Ideal: work it out therefrom . . . Up, up! Whatsoever thy hand findeth to do, do it with thy whole might. Work while it is called Today; for the Night cometh, wherein no man can work" (SR: 196–7). Whatever meaning work has, in this yoking of the words of the world-weary Ecclesiastes with those of Christ, is centered in this actual world.

Jane's journey throughout is towards that actual daylight world, towards her duty and work there. As David Lodge has noted, the "sequence of night and day, day bringing relief from the trials and terrors of the night, is one of the basic rhythms of the book."[28] It is also the basic rhythm of the Bible. Brontë uses this rhythm for Jane's narrative in order to emphasize how Jane is to get beyond the solipsism implicit in the Romantic assertion of the self; what the "moon" and the voices of the night and Bertha Mason represent, in Romantic poetry and in *Jane Eyre*, has to be incorporated into the daylight world of reality. Thus Jane's first evaluation of the voice which calls "Jane!" is to label it "the work of nature": "*She* was roused, and did – no miracle – but *her* best." But immediately Jane utters a prayer which takes her, she feels, "very near a Mighty Spirit; and my soul rushed out in gratitude at *His* feet" (III: 9: 536–7; my italics). The movement from feminine to masculine pronoun is decisive. Like Teufelsdröckh, Jane finds no escape in feminine nature; like him she acknowledges "that the universe is godlike and my Father's." And the older Jane implicitly agrees with the comment of Teufelsdröckh's Editor: "Nature is good, but she is not the best" (SR: 59).

Thus Jane is eager "to search – to inquire – to grope an outlet from the cloud of doubt, and find the open day of certainty" (III: 10: 538); like the figure in Quarles' vanity-glass emblem, she knows that the soul "seeks the noon of grace," else all is shadow. Her journey to Ferndean is a quest of exploration, to see if it offers the possibility of work and relationship. Significantly, her daylight revaluation of that voice removes it from nature: "it seemed in *me* – not in the external world." And then she compares the shock of feelings aroused by this inner voice to "the earthquake which shook the foundations of Paul and Silas's prison." Jane is free once for all, "the doors of the soul's cell" opened, the prison of self conquered (III: 10: 539).[29]

This discovery is expressed as an apocalyptic affirmation of time lived in this world. First, there is Rochester's giving of his watch to Jane (III: 11: 570), a gesture at once repudiating his earlier fancy of imprisoning her on his watch guard (i.e., in his own heaven – II: 9: 341) and marking his acknowledgment of her liberation from the time-deadened world where he was her idol and they were to live on the "moon." Jane's relocation of the voice from nature to within and her sense of a Father-God are an assertion of her place in the on-going time-bound world of Judeo-Christian history. Accepting its burden rather than fleeing it makes time a Carlylean "seedfield" where man is able to free himself from time's limitations by using it creatively.[30]

The only slackness in Brontë's handling of the novel's resolution is her presentation of Rochester's change of heart. His withdrawal to the wilderness of Ferndean following his separation from Jane and the death of Bertha Mason is finely done. The wilderness, traditionally an emblem of both temptation and repentance, of acknowledgment of the need for some aid beyond the self if one is to avoid utter despair, suggests his liberation from the idolatry of self and from his sense that there is no freedom. Kierkegaard has said of despair: "Only that man's life is wasted who lived on, so deceived by the joys of life or by its sorrows that he never became eternally and decisively conscious of himself as spirit, as self, or (what is the same thing) never became aware and in the deepest sense received an impression of the fact that there is a God, and that he, he himself, his self, exists before this God, which gain of infinity is never attained except through despair."[31] Certainly we feel Rochester's developing awareness of something beyond himself when he describes to Jane his growing consciousness of "sin." But this impression is weakened by the sense we get that he has made of Jane what she had once made of him: an idol. She has gone beyond this in her spiritual education. But his description of his prayer concludes: "and the alpha and omega of my heart's wishes broke involuntarily from my lips, in the words 'Jane! Jane! Jane!'" (III: 11: 572). Yes. But God or Christ is the Alpha and Omega of Revelation (Rev. 22: 13, 21: 6). Brontë, with so much quotation from the Apocalypse, begins to make it seem that for Rochester Jane is the New Jerusalem. This echo of idolatry jars, and diminishes the complexity of the presentation of Jane's quest, one beyond this very idolatry.

Tellingly, the novel's final paragraphs are given over to St John Rivers and the traditional image of time's end. The older Jane quotes from two letters Rivers had written. In the first he hopes "I am happy, and trusts I am not of those who live without God in the world, and only mind earthly things" (III: 12: 575). The second ends the novel; in it Rivers uses the penultimate verses of the Bible to prophesy the nearness of his much-longed-for death and resurrection. His scripture-based words focus subtly the "natural supernaturalism" that is Brontë's aim; he alludes to Philippians 3: 19–20 (where Paul discusses those "whose God is their belly"), verses used by Quarles in an emblem featuring a conversation between "Divine Cupid" and "Venus," "queen of false delights" (fig. 3). Again, St John gives us the heaven–Vanity Fair contrast, as in the emblem. But Jane asks us to consider his marriage to heaven in the context of the three marriages – those of herself, and Diana and Mary Rivers – which also close her autobiographical account.

Hæc animant pueros cymbala ; et illa viros.

PHILIPPIANS III. 19, 20.

They mind earthly things, but our conversation is in heaven.

𝔙enus. 𝔇ibine 𝔠upid.

Fig. 3.   Quarles, Emblem, II: 8

This contrast constitutes Brontë's "retailoring" of the scripture, her redrawing of the emblem: she asserts that the New Jerusalem can mean at once what St John "sees" – the Celestial City – or it can be part of a "new Mythus," can mean the "natural supernaturalism" of *this* world. Divine Cupid in the emblem declares, "Let swine love husks, and children whine for toys." Jane does not love this "world," she loves the godlike she finds there – the godlike in husband and family and fellow-feeling. Her apocalypse has been the discovery of the "open day" and what it bids her do; it has been a clear vision of the godlike dwelling in this world amongst one's fellows. St John may write warning her against godlessness, but for Jane those "earthly things" – being "vision" and "right hand" to Rochester – are what validate the godborn in her life, what signify her "spiritual majority" (SR: 199). And Brontë emphasizes this in the richly allusive language Jane uses to describe her marriage, words placed between St John's two letters:

I have now been married ten years. I know what it is to live entirely for and with what I love best on earth. I hold myself supremely blest – blest beyond what language can express; because I am my husband's life as fully as he is mine. No woman was ever nearer to her mate than I am; ever more absolutely bone of his bone, and flesh of his flesh . . . To be together is for us to be at once as free as in solitude, as gay as in company. We talk, I believe, all day long: to talk to each other is but a more animated and an audible thinking.   (III: 12: 576)

These words are not "mere *words*," they are God-validated ones. The conversation of Jane and Rochester *is* in heaven, the one that men and women establish here. We *know* nothing else.[32]

Jane Eyre ends, then, like the Bible and *Pilgrim's Progress*, with a vision of apocalyptic marriage because the *modern* Christian's very struggle in a world which seems godless has been validated; eyes have been unsealed. The "human tears" yoked with "Divine joy" (III: 12: 578) which Jane feels about Rivers' anticipation of his heavenly end signify her sense of his loss and of the *awe*-fulness of her gain. St John has had to smother feeling completely in order to testify to his vision of the New Jerusalem and his place there. For Brontë such action is a denial of the godborn in man, of that which requires him to live amongst his fellows with responsibility for them. Jane's last-page comparison of St John to Bunyan's Great-heart is thus meant in part ironically (Greatheart takes women and children to heaven, they do not progress alone; Brontë's Jane *is* Christian, is Everyman – she is not Christiana). For Brontë the

Greatheart in a post-eighteenth-century world is that "still small voice" – the "voice within" which is *not* man-made and which does respond with genuine fellow-feeling to the genuinely human, to the godborn, in others, which does lend a "right hand" to them, here. Jane says of St John: "His is the exaction of the apostle, who speaks but for Christ, when he says – 'Whosoever will come after me, let him deny himself, and take up his cross and follow me'" (III: 12: 578). But Jane's own autobiography has shown us that "self-denial" has not just a supernatural focus, that to deny the isolating "natural" self is to discover the soul's power and to gain the self-reliance necessary to confront the deadened, spirit-crushing world around one. But this self's assertion requires absolutely the acknowledgment of some world, some "NOT-ME," beyond the self that will make *sane* life possible. Then is living possible, for the soul is freed.[33]

Jane Eyre is Brontë's synthesis of both the religious tradition's loathing of this world as the prison-house of the soul and the Romantic's impulse towards some "paradise within." The Miltonic echo of "We entered the wood, and wended homeward" (III: 11: 573) suggests the growth beyond the Thornfield Eden of unlimited, and finally insane, indulgence of the passionate self. And the image of Ferndean, "deep buried in a wood" (III: 11: 550), validates Bunyan's sense of this life as a wilderness of struggle – with Carlyle's qualification: beyond this wilderness, for the modern Christian, lies the unknown:

May we not say, however, that the hour of Spiritual Enfranchisement is even this: When your Ideal World, wherein the whole man has been dimly struggling and inexpressibly languishing to work, becomes revealed, and thrown open; and you discover . . . that your "America is here or nowhere"? (SR: 196)

Not that visionary country – "the busy world, towns, regions full of life" (I: 12: 132) – glimpsed from the third floor of Thornfield, but at Ferndean, "deep buried in a wood."

III

The novels that follow *Jane Eyre* suggest that Brontë was not satisfied with her working out of the quest after a "new Mythus." *Jane Eyre* still contained too much of "romance," not enough of the *real* which alone would validate that "still small voice" within; the Actual was still too idealized. And the issue of what a woman's *work* could in *reality* be in mid-century England had not been boldly confronted. To make her fictional worlds more severely real, Brontë turned first to social realism in *Shirley*, then to allegorical realism in *Villette*. And there, at last, in the somber drama of Lucy Snowe, the romance world is reduced to the subterranean level of the novel; it becomes a part of the narrator's inner self. In the process of this reworking of her themes, the Jane Eyre voice which assumed the reader's applause hardens into Lucy's utter skepticism that a reader will tolerate anything beyond the "romantic" and pleasant.

The issues discussed in *Shirley* and their connection to the other novels are best indicated by the devoir which Shirley had written while a student as a gloss on the sons of God/daughters of men passage in Genesis. This gloss tells of the "dawn of time" and an orphan girl for whom the green wilderness alone is a "mother." The girl, Eva, finds her situation as the "centre" of all things an intolerable prison: "She asked, was she thus to burn out and perish, her living light doing no good, never seen, never needed . . . when something within her . . . restlessly asserted a God-given strength, for which it insisted she should find exercise?" Then, in a dialogue whose imagery is drawn from the Apocalypse, she summons a "Comforter" ("Lord, come quickly") and her prayer is answered. The result: "the bridal hour of Genius and Humanity," of the sons of God and the daughters of men (III: 4: 548–53). The whole thing, which reads somewhat better than this synopsis (even as Shirley's juvenilia), gives an emblem of the novel's situations and suggests why it is so static and, finally, unsatisfying.

In the first place, Brontë's two protagonists are more examples of certain stances than complex human beings. The devoir's Eva is split into Shirley, the orphaned aristocrat given to paeans to "my mother Eve, in these days called Nature," as well as to noble works to help the poor; and into Caroline Helstone, the orphan seeking to define herself through work and also longing for a mother and a home of love. Though any reader would be hard-put to identify the devoir's Genius with the brothers Moore, they are the counterparts of the heroines: the one a self-centered manufacturer whom Caroline pines after, the other a tutor worried that his class is a barrier to his love for Shirley. The issues of *Jane Eyre* – Romantic self-assertion versus self-abnegation – are discussed by these characters, particularly by Robert and Caroline, but they are not explored in any significant manner. Robert Moore comes to awareness of his own selfishness after experiencing a "Cain-like desolation" (III: 7: 610); yet this is not shown, only reported by him. And in a novel with a sharply observant omniscient narrator, this telling is not convincing in the way it is in Brontë's "autobiographies."

Caroline Helstone's presentation is more complex. There are splendid interior monologues where she asks, like the Eva, the questions of spiritual autobiography about her place and her work. She views life as a struggle, not after heaven – "The soul's real hereafter, who shall guess?" – but after self-definition which is achieved first by work, then by love. She feels that virtue does not "lie in abnegation of self," in a self-denial which leaves no room for creativity but only for "undue humility" and "weak concession" (I: 10: 194). And she asserts that a life spent waiting for the "bliss" of the next world and a life without real work have the same end: one of wretched waste.

God surely did not create us, and cause us to live, with the sole end of wishing always to die. I believe, in my heart, we were intended to prize life and enjoy it, so long as we retain it . . . I believe single women should have more to do – better chances of interesting and profitable occupation than they possess now. And when I speak thus, I have no impression that I displease God by my words; that I am either impious or impatient, irreligious or sacrilegious. (II: 11: 440–1)

The situation is convincingly presented, and suggestively counter-pointed by the hymns the Wesleyans sing in the novel, hymns whose texts assert that the fire of apocalypse alone will vindicate "This struggle for life" (I: 9: 162). There is a sense here that the rigidity of the social world – its religion, its class system, its conventions that demand that a "good woman" be "half doll, half angel" (II: 9: 395; the "bad" is a "fiend") – forces this psychological deadening and entrapment in the self. The world around one throws the sensitive human being – and particularly a woman who lacks the assigned work-role a man has – back into herself, and offers no way for realizing her godborn potential.

But this subtle presentation of the imprisoned self in society – so much an advance over *Jane Eyre* in social, unromantic terms – is not developed. Indeed, it nowhere coheres with the other side of Caroline Helstone that involves her "yearning to discover and know her mother" (I: 11: 208) and her pinings after Robert Moore and "the little parlour of [his] house [which] was her earthly paradise" (II: 13: 281). After a long and near-fatal illness (the result of the understandably wearing effect of such longings), she finds her mother and then her lover. She is happy, but the reader cannot see how the more assertive, and assertively questioning, side of her nature has been satisfied. It is as romantic an ending as *Jane Eyre*'s, without any of the superb dramatic resolution of that novel (and none of its sense that a woman might feel the necessity to define at least her domestic role).[34]

Thus the marriages at the end of the novel represent no imaginative apocalypses. The insights are recounted, not felt; they are not the result of struggle and experience. *Shirley* is so static because Brontë is unable to dramatize the novel's central questions which Caroline has posed: the way a woman can break out of forced role-imprisonment and become a creative part of daily social life. The decision to split the Jane Eyre protagonist in two – one woman assertive and whole, one passive and outcast – and to make one the symbol of self-integration for the other, is probably responsible for the novel's failure. Brontë makes Shirley's unity with feminine maternal Nature an end in itself, not a stage in the passage towards "spiritual majority" as it had been for Jane Eyre (or for the Eva of the devoir). And with her money, Shirley has few problems of doing what she chooses. There is thus nothing to be done with this title character (except to allow her some often very satiric thrusts hurled at various worshippers at Vanity Fair who cross her path). The decision to make Caroline a "domestic" Shirley might have been more significant had her woman–angel contradiction been explored and had Brontë not made her search for a real mother a counterpart to Shirley's relation to Nature; this undermines the complexity of the issues of what Nature and human relationship represent for the post-Romantic woman.

Although the narrative side of *Shirley* thus marks no advance over Brontë's earlier romance (indeed, it is even a palpable concession to her sense of the reader's debased tastes, their "elegant love of the pretty and pleasing" – III: 14: 724), the narrator herself faces with a severe scrutiny the social issues her characters gloss over. This voice, which begins by announcing to the reader that "romance" is not on the menu, but "Something real, cool, and solid, . . . something unromantic as Monday morning" (I: 1: 7) and ends by satirizing the reader's "quest" for a "moral," is a voice of 1849 damning on page after page any notion that time means progress. She supplies the modern framework for a novel set forty years back, in an age where there was something heroic evident in men. She damns the present-day Manchester school for its heroless nature in attacking Wellington; like Shirley, she withers those with no faculty for reverence. She notes the slavish submission of all human creatures to mercantile interests. And she muses often about the reader's desires for anything but reality in novels he looks into (he always finds "the actual, simple truth" a "lie" – III: 14: 722). She alone dispels the "lived happily ever after" nature of the story itself. At the end her voice undercuts the "romance" she has just told by displacing its green world and throwing the reader into the ashy landscape of the present. Her closing presentation of the result of the "daydreams" of Robert Moore removes any appreciation the reader might have had for the industrialist's Carlylean conversion within the story. The reader can take no comfort: the Robert Moores make bleak the world we live in; the poetic Louis Moores, no matter what the extent of that "world . . . in [their] own head and heart" (III: 6: 589), do not preserve the fairies nor anything natural around one. It is this narrator's voice alone which makes *Shirley* a true social novel of the 1840s; it reminds the reader that Chartist disturbances *now* constantly disprove the idea that some lasting good has come out of past actions. The narrator refuses to traffic with any modern celebration of progress. And she challenges the reader, with that last tableau of the vanishing fairies, to feel any satisfaction as well. Imagination itself has been debased. Indeed, the closing paragraph satirizes the very readers who want a "moral" tale full of instruction:

The story is told. I think I now see the judicious reader putting on his spectacles to look for the moral. It would be an insult to his sagacity to offer directions. I only say, God speed him in the quest! (III: 14: 740–1)

This narrator, having given her "romance," and then added the report of the vanishing "fairish" and oak trees, suspects few "Christian" readers any longer care a whit for the "moral" they are offered, no matter what they say; the "unvarnished truth" they do not want. Harsh reality does not suit their need for poetic justice; they want only "the sheer fiction" of their "own imagination."

In *Villette* this suspicion of the readers has become fact: readers are superficial, they want entertainment in the guise of pretty instruction, they require "romance" for their leisure hours rather than guidance for their souls. In this final novel Brontë unites *Shirley*'s narrative voice with that of an equally severe protagonist. And the result is a book whose first-person voice constantly challenges the reader's "sunny imaginations" (III: 42: 596). Unlike

Jane Eyre, who assumes the "Reader's" avid assent to whatever she does, Lucy Snowe does not trust her readers to accept anything unromantic or painful. Again and again she draws some "wild dreamland" calculated to please them – only to destroy it with a

Cancel the whole of that, if you please, reader – or rather let it stand, and draw thence a moral – an alternative, text-hand copy –
Day-dreams are the delusions of the demon.   (I: 6: 117–18)

The voice's bitterness rules all, even to the last page, where it interrupts the narrative of the storm to allow the "quiet kind heart" and "sunny imaginations" of some reader to envision a "union and a happy succeeding life" for the doomed protagonists. Brontë's life-writer feels quite certain that her readers find "demons" wonderfully appealing, as long as they are sunny. Real truth frightens them. To Lucy Snowe it bears a terrible beauty.

Villette is a rewriting of Brontë's previous fictions, a meditation on the ideas and language that have preoccupied her writing life. It differs from the earlier books in jettisoning, or at least chastening, all of the elements that had before defined her fiction. The protagonist's exile from England, an exile necessary if she is to find any liberating creative work, does away with the social world suggested in *Jane Eyre* and depicted in *Shirley*; and the title's emphasis on place underlines the reader's sense that the environment of England in the 1850s is so alienating for an unmarried woman that she cannot live adequately there (it gives added point as well to Lucy's outcast status, for in Labassecour she is indeed "like no other"). Oddly enough, Brontë also dispenses with the natural world which she had presented even more luxuriantly in *Shirley* than in *Jane Eyre*. While *Villette* contains storms and other natural metaphors, they have more the symbolic force they have in Shakespeare and the Bible rather than in Wordsworth. Brontë carries over only one element from her past work: the Puritan autobiographical form with its depiction of life as a stern pilgrimage and its allegorical treatment of experience.[35] Even this form is chastened: the incidents that formed so much of the action and the Gothic elements of *Jane Eyre* are gone (except for some stage business with a "nun"). That world of romance, as Andrew Hook has noted, "is almost wholly internalized within the mind of the novel's protagonist, Lucy Snowe."[36] The novel thus becomes in essence a "drama of consciousness," or what Robert Colby has called "an allegory of the imagination coping with the world outside itself."[37]

74

Villette is indeed an allegory very much in the tradition of *Pilgrim's Progress* and of *Sartor Resartus*. The use of names, both of places and of characters, recalls Bunyan and Carlyle: Villette, small town; Labassecour, the farmyard; Rue Fossette, Ditch Street. This rather patent allegorical device provides Brontë, curiously, a means of exploring with more subtlety and suggestiveness than she had ever displayed the issues of the place of a woman and her Romantic imagination in a harsh daylight world from which God seems totally absent.

What allows this subtlety is Brontë's grounding of the language of the novel more solidly in the Bible and Bunyan than even Carlyle had done (if that is possible!). If the goal in *Villette* were heaven, it would be very difficult for the reader to distinguish it from many Puritan and Methodist biographies and allegories (even to the anti-Papist passages). There are constant references to Bunyan, constant askings of "Whence did I come? Whither shall I go? What should I do?" (I: 5: 107); damnings of Rousseau's natural man (III: 34: 484; III: 38: 538); the sense of this life as a "hopeless desert" (I: 15: 228); invocations of one of the fiercest Gods outside of Hannah More's tracts or Mr Spurgeon's tabernacle; the belief that every experience has its biblical analogue (even Lucy's cry "Peace, be still!" – from Mark 4: 39 – is not heeded: man's words do not order nature as Christ's words did). Sacvan Bercovitch, discussing Puritanism and the self, helps us to see precisely what Brontë is doing with this language. He notes that the "christic correspondence" the Puritans invoked to describe their own progressings indicates their "*need* for an infallible correlative to the self."

To this end, they turned to scripture as the safest way also to regulate conscience . . . And to this end, every Puritan biographer wrote, in one degree or another, as though he were bringing the scriptures up to date through his subject's life. The result is a conventionalized rhetoric that blurs the difference between metaphor and experience.

And this blurring allows a "synchronizing of author, reader, and scripture."[38]

Brontë's language in *Villette* is calculated to effect precisely this synchronizing. She shows Lucy Snowe, with her desire for freedom to work here, in the Actual, constantly using biblical language, and for two reasons: to provide a correlative to that self of intense, and intensely suppressed, feeling which Lucy fears; and to show that her independent self-asserting actions are justified by their scriptural correspondences to Christ's life. Like Bunyan, Lucy distrusts fictions ("romance"), she loathes play-acting (even as she feels a "keen relish for dramatic expression" – I: 14: 211), she distrusts the ornamental nature of language, and she thus needs to "blur the difference between metaphor and experience" – else she will find herself practicing self-idolatry. Brontë thus, in presenting this modern woman's progress, uses language as Carlyle did in *Sartor*. Lucy's goal is independence; a heaven beyond is not her focus. And the language, as it synchronizes author, readers, characters, scripture, retailors the old Mythus. Brontë makes, and asks her readers to make, new interpretations; she asks that they see the "natural supernaturalism" of language itself – and thus the "natural supernaturalism" possible in their lives if they can witness the power of language.

Yet Lucy's world is a much more severe one than Carlyle would have accepted (at least before the late 1840s). She begins her autobiography as his heroes begin their careers, declaring that man's life is not "a May game" but a "stern pilgrimage through burning sandy solitudes" (PP: 287) which constantly threaten isolation. But Carlyle's conclusion – "It was not a God that did this; no!" – severs his world from *Villette*'s. Like Arnold, Lucy Snowe finds that "A God, a God their severance ruled." And her God is the terrifying wrathful God of the Old Testament, Job's "King of Terrors" (III: 37: 533): "When I tried to pray I could only utter these words: 'From my youth up Thy terrors have I suffered with a troubled mind'" (I: 15: 232). Her quotation is from the Prayer Book rendering of Psalm 88, which concludes: "Lover and Friend hast thou put far from me, and mine acquaintance into darkness." The Psalm summarizes the novel.[39]

For Lucy Snowe, as for so many Puritans and evangelicals *before* conversion, life begins in the Everlasting No – there is nothing else, no moral order, no good discernible in the world; all is suffering. Lucy lacks completely Jane Eyre's *feeling* of the injustice in her life, nor has she any of Jane's conviction of original innocence. Self-abnegation is forced on Lucy as on Caroline Helstone by a life-denying world where she has no place. Carlyle described Teufelsdröckh's analogous state:

Disbelieving in all things, the poor youth had never learned to believe in himself. Withdrawn, in proud timidity, within his own fastnesses; solitary from men, yet baited by night-spectres enough . . . all a grim Desert . . . and no Pillar of Cloud by day, and no Pillar of Fire by night, any longer guides the Pilgrim.   (SR: 142, 161)[40]

76

The opening four chapters of *Villette* demonstrate how completely Lucy Snowe's world is Teufelsdröckh's. Indeed, like the red-room episode in *Jane Eyre*, these chapters (the only ones set in England) provide an emblem for the novel. Ending with her work for Miss Marchmont, they present Lucy's apprenticeship to sorrow. As Miss Marchmont's life and name suggest, Lucy's experience will be a journey towards the acceptance of renunciation which is the lot of Everyman. This apprenticeship prepares Lucy to see existence as "desolate" (I: 6: 110), the future as "dead" (I: 12: 175), and her "Inscrutable God" (I: 4: 99) as one who has made it "a part of his great plan that some must deeply suffer while they live." "I thrilled in the certainty that of this number, I was one," she comments (I: 15: 229); the "thrilled" focuses her obsessive need of Bunyan's paradigm.

Yet Lucy has sufficient inner strength so that a sighting of the Aurora Borealis inspires her to hear a voice urging her to become a Christian pilgrim, to "Leave this wilderness, and go out hence" (I: 5: 104). (Brontë's use of the passive in "A bold thought was sent" helps to underline the sense that neither Lucy nor the reader knows if God is behind this voice; it is not the "still small voice" that dwells within Jane Eyre.) So Lucy goes to London and on to Villette where, for a time, her work quite literally saves her. But the school's long vacation comes, and "now that the prop of employment was withdrawn" (I: 15: 228), the night-spectres that have haunted her psychic life assert themselves. Perhaps only Dickens' Headstone is a better illustration than Lucy Snowe of Carlyle's dualistic psychology: "I seemed to hold two lives – the life of thought, and that of reality; and, provided the former was nourished with a sufficiency of the strange necromantic joys of fancy, the privileges of the latter might remain limited to daily bread, hourly work, and a roof of shelter" (I: 8: 140). These joys lead, in the vacation, to Lucy's "wandering in solitude" and to her wish for suicide in the absence of "some fellow-creature to help." And they lead at last to that long night journey that takes Lucy to the Catholic confessional. Lucy shares Teufelsdröckh's state: like him she finds "Hope a false idol" (I: 15: 232; SR: 158–9). And each, "doubting God's existence" (SR: 161), seeks "any opening for appeal to God" (I: 15: 232) in a world which is "void of Life, Purpose, Volition" (SR: 164). Teufelsdröckh discovers that his wish to defy is evidence of the godborn. But for Lucy Snowe – and this is part of Brontë's stern psychological realism, her sense that such defiance does not come unaided by others – the German's resolution is not at hand. It comes only with the help of some "fellow creature" (though only at the end of her autobiography will Lucy allow any assertion of her need of another human being to be part of her daylight world of "reality").

When she awakens from her night journey, Lucy at first sees all around her as "spectral"; but in reality she is in "a very safe asylum; well protected for the *present*" (II: 16: 244; my italics). She emerges from the Everlasting No that had seemed her lot only with the aid of the aptly named Brettons, those representatives of home who had once before taken her in (a stay she had identified with that of "Christian and Hopeful beside a pleasant stream" – (I: 1: 62). At their home in Villette Lucy begins to gain strength, to turn towards the outside world (the "NOT-ME") for "wholesomer food." This Centre of Indifference Robert Langbaum has described, in words carrying special force in Lucy's case, as "the stage when the individual, after an iconoclastic period in which tradition has been rejected and conviction lost, first changes direction. The change of direction begins when he discovers his own feelings and his own will as a source of value in an otherwise meaningless universe." [41] Brontë places Lucy once again with the Brettons because they provide a link with the one "pleasant" memory of her past; like Teufelsdröckh in his Centre, Lucy is reintegrated in time, her reality is confirmed in the re-establishing of connection with others. The Brettons help her to begin that learning process which will culminate in her seeing that goodness and even happiness do exist in the present, real world, that they are not foolish delusions of demons. The Brettons are in Labassecour in order that Lucy may *see* that home, in England or anywhere, offers freedom and love when one can achieve the imaginative vision of it. This family brings into her imagination a real sense that human happiness is not necessarily "real" only in romances, that something other than an expectation of terrors can be a part of her life. No wonder the often harshly judging autobiographer announces at this point that she had "a new creed . . . a belief in happiness" (II: 23: 334). Her education in feeling is beginning.

Lucy's education is a long process, one expressed and explored as a debate between reason, a part of reality, and imagination, a part of Lucy's "world of thought" and feeling. She, like Teufelsdröckh, becomes a "Spectre-fighting Man, nay one who will one day be a spectre-queller." And in order to live a healthy creative life she has to recognize that these spectres arise from her own nature – the

Romantic world of feeling – and that they form a *natural* part of the self. What Lucy must learn is that her freedom lies not simply in the power to feel, but in the further ability to evaluate those feelings. She must not simply release her hitherto suppressed emotions but she must also understand and evaluate their worth, and their danger, in the real daylight world. She must come to see that "the natural character" is not a thing to be obliterated as it is in those books from which she quotes so often (she uses "natural" here precisely as Bunyan does) but to be acknowledged and built upon (II: 17: 252).

Brontë dramatizes Lucy's growth by focusing on her relationship to the workings of the imagination as represented by the art of others and by her own "fictions." She goes to a concert, to a gallery, and to the theatre. At each of these we watch Lucy's determined detachment, her refusal to credit what does not seem "real" – which always means the human rather than the artful. At the gallery she gazes at a Cleopatra and at a series of four paintings called "La Vie d'une femme," none "a whit like nature" (II: 19: 274; here the word is not used as Bunyan would use it; Lucy uses it as a synonym for "reality"). At the concert (prefaced by one of the many emblem-mirrors Brontë uses throughout the novel; Lucy does not recognize herself here), all her attention is focused on the men and women present (especially the King and Queen, in whose faces Lucy reads a very personal story). Only at the performance of the actress Vashti does Lucy's habitual reserve in *writing* of her experiences break down – as it does also in the two great night journeys:

It was a marvellous sight: a mighty revelation.
It was a spectacle low, horrible, immoral.   (II: 23: 339)

In the latter sentence Lucy tries to censure the intense spontaneous involvement suggested by the first one, precisely as she also uses references to the King of Terrors and traditional religious phrases of renunciation to check her desires for, or her approaches to, happiness. In the Vashti scene we get to that inward world which Lucy is determined to control, indeed to hide, and we witness its dangers. We witness as well the acknowledgment forced on Lucy that *imagined* "reality" can be *real*; it has in it "nature" that can not be dismissed with the label "romance."

Lucy's writing of her own "love stories" makes even more clear to her the "naturalism" – the reality – of the imagination. The older narrator *sees* that in narrating her relationship with Dr John, she at once creates "reality" and yet witnesses the reality of his "romance" life. For her he is an "idol" whose history she sees and presents as a romance narrative for sunny imaginations, an uninterrupted movement towards a happy-ever-after. In her closing of his story, she validates his life with biblical language:

> In short, I do but speak the truth when I say that these two lives of Graham and Paulina were blessed, like that of Jacob's favoured son, with 'blessings of Heaven above, blessings of the deep that lies under.' It was so, for God saw that it was good. (III: 37: 533)

For Lucy these figures *seem* never to have left Eden.

The "hero" of her real love-story will be no such romantic figure as Dr John, but the plain, acerb Paul Carl David Emmanuel. And this story – her *history* – Lucy presents in the most severe language of anti-romance. Yet that history becomes biblical romance, a movement at least to the "House Beautiful," for this "hero" of her real story becomes finally her "Greatheart." The allegorical suggestions of his first and last names tell all: Paul, the hero of St Pierre's romance *Paul et Virginie* and also the reborn apostle whose words suggest the "natural supernaturalism" possible for man who sees (man can throw off the "old man" and "be renewed in the spirit of [his] mind" – Ephesians 2: 23; he can learn to believe: "if any man be in Christ, he is a new creature: old things are passed away; behold, all things become new" – 2 Corinthians 5: 17); and Emmanuel, "God with us," Isaiah's prophesied Messiah, the deliverer of the Hebrews out of their captivity. And of Lucy Snowe out of her psychic wilderness of despair which comes from her inability to believe in herself. Paul is really Carlyle's "Messias of Nature" (SR: 220), one who aids others to free themselves through thought and action; he gives Lucy a new conception of "the natural character."

Paul Emmanuel is for Lucy the "Greatheart" (III: 38: 542) who will lead her safely onward past her inner Apollyon, the imagination which unreined provides "delusions of the demon." He is a man of "inward sight" whose mind becomes Lucy's "library," "collyrium to the spirit's eyes" (III: 33: 472). He is the "incarnated Word" who shows her the joys rather than the terrors of an imaginative life. (Interestingly, Lucy will not report their conversations or Paul's letters which she so treasures; the mature woman will not risk the fictionalizing that language seems necessarily to involve.) Thus Paul is very much a Greatheart of *this* world.

Bunyan's says: "It is my duty . . . to distrust my own ability, that I may have reliance on him that is stronger than all" (B: 342). Brontë's Paul teaches Lucy to rely on herself – a self understood, its "reality" and its "fancy" brought together in her own work. It is no idle term that Brontë employs when she has Ginevra Fanshawe, again and again, idly call Lucy "Diogenes." M. Paul helps Lucy to discover the godborn within herself by showing her the redeeming power of love. And there is nothing of idol-worship here, nothing of the earlier pining after Dr John. During Lucy's second night journey (at the Fête), when imagination ungoverned by reason takes control, she perceives "the symbols of Egypt," the idol gods, all about her. But the next day brings knowledge of how deluded she has been (and also knowledge of the true nature of the "nun"). She is indeed winning "Freedom and Renovation" (III: 41: 578). And "conversion" – as Teufelsdröckh used the term.

The moment of this conversion occurs when Lucy *feels* Paul's acceptance and can use the word "home":

I was full of faults; he took them and me all home. For the moment of utmost mutiny, he reserved the one deep spell of peace. These words caressed my ear: –
"Lucy, take my love. One day share my life. Be my dearest, first on earth."
We walked back to the Rue Fossette by moonlight – such moonlight as fell on Eden – shining through the shades of the Great Garden, and haply gilding a path glorious, for a step divine – a Presence nameless. Once in their lives some men and women go back to these first fresh days of our great Sire and Mother – taste that morning's dew – bathe in its sunrise. (III: 41: 591–2)

This passage marks Lucy's imaginative apocalypse, her "new heaven and new earth." The King of Terrors has no place here.

Yet, though Paul Emmanuel shows her the meaning of "natural supernaturalism," his teaching does not replace this King of Terrors. That figure is always, and paradoxically, very real to Lucy Snowe the narrator. This inscrutable God who does not hear her voice praying for the still waters exists as a felt representation, a verbal sign, of much of Lucy's reality, and to him Lucy gives her resigned allegiance throughout her meditation:

His will be done, as done it surely will be, whether we humble ourselves to resignation or not . . . Tired wayfarer, gird up thy loins, look upward, march onward. Pilgrims and brother mourners, join in friendly company. Dark through the wilderness of this world stretches the way for most of us: equal and steady be our tread; be our cross our banner. (III: 38: 534)

The passage offers its tribute to the traditional vision of apocalypse (these pilgrims, like Bunyan's Christian, are "reliant in the issue to come off more than conquerors"). Yet its emphasis on man's joining together "in friendly company" with his fellows shows the influence of M. Paul. Lucy does not, like Christian, any longer "put her fingers in her ears," nor does she become a second Miss Marchmont lost in thirty years of hatred because of the "burden" placed on her back by this terrible God. Lucy's sense of the importance of life *here* is underscored by the abrupt reversion to quotidian reality in the paragraph following this stern passage: "On a Thursday morning . . ." Like Teufelsdröckh, Lucy struggles to redeem the wilderness of the here and now. She does not seek escape in the future or in the past. That "promised land" that she continually witnessed only in "dying dreams" (II: 21: 309–10) is here, at the Faubourg Clotilde.

And she achieves "if not Victory, yet the consciousness of Battle, and the resolve to persevere therein while life or faculty is left" (SR: 184). After having decided, in her Centre of Indifference where romantic fantasies promised splendors, on a "belief in happiness," Lucy Snowe comes like Teufelsdröckh to renounce that, and finds "Blessedness" in that renunciation (SR: 190–1). (The nun machinery serves Brontë well in showing the fatuousness and waste that comes of self-indulgent fantasies.) As Teufelsdröckh concludes, "Till the eye have vision, the whole members are in bonds" (SR: 197). Paul Emmanuel, Lucy Snowe's spiritual bridegroom, brings her the vision – the spiritual apocalypse – and helps her find her way through the wilderness to a "home." Thus she promises him to be a "faithful steward" in his absence, an allusion to Christ's parable and a *placing* of her sense of Paul (III: 4: 587). The very writing of the autobiography, like her work at the school, is proof of the permanence and worth of Paul's teaching – and of her stewardship. Like the Puritan's autobiography, Lucy's meditation is an assertion of the exemplary nature of her experience, of its "christic correspondence" and thus the religious worth of its words. Paul's death may seem unbearable to the reader, but it is not killing to Lucy Snowe because she has been delivered from the wilderness of the self, she is "not friendless, not hopeless, not sick of life, and seeking death" (III: 41: 582) even if she is alone. She can assert by working and then by writing this record her spiritual victory before the world.

Charlotte Brontë, then, derives from the religious tradition the structures and many of the images that she uses to represent the struggles of her protagonists. And in using these images to explore the "Demon-Empire" within, she gives them a Romantic reading as well, as Carlyle did. Yet the resolutions of her novels are determinedly post-Romantic; they parallel the paths Carlyle had chartered for saving man from the Romantic traps of self-consciousness and from Centres of Indifference. Brontë's insistence on life as a pilgrimage has Carlyle's emphases, as does her selection of the orphan as the symbol of man's metaphysical homelessness. Her novels use and thus illustrate the Calvinized *Bildungsroman* that *Sartor* had made available to Victorian England. Yet the patterns and the language were Brontë's own, originated out of the same needs and concerns that drove Carlyle to his Teufelsdröckh. The necessity of incorporating the Romantic discovery of ways of escaping the deadness of a rationalist-mechanistic world into the older religious Mythus confronted both writers, and their solutions are the solutions of those Victorian artists trying to deal with past and present, and with language presenting all things *sub specie aeternitatis* or else becoming "mere *words*."

Brontë's meditation on the traditions she inherited yields, finally, *Villette*, the most austere and terrifying and, as George Eliot noted, "preternatural" (GEL: II: 87) English *Bildungsroman* of the mid century. Though Carlyle does not stand directly behind it, the ethic of *Sartor* – the self-annihilation and renunciation, the exaltation of work as alone giving the human being purpose and identity – is its ethic, and one asserted with unrelieved seriousness. Neither Dickens nor George Eliot could ever allow themselves to imagine so severe a world. For them as for Carlyle, "Hope" is a sustaining "possession" (SR: 158). Though Brontë uses the word, those who sow in tears are allowed little joy in this last recasting of her ideas. (Paulina tells Lucy that biographies present "Hope" constantly eluding the "wayfarer" – III: 32: 465.) And the human justice which her heroines cry out for is nothing finally but "a red, random beldame with arms akimbo" (III: 35: 495). Brontë's is a terrifying vision of this life.[42] And though it has so much affinity with Carlyle's, his insistence that man will have justice or will revolt separates them. His God is not Brontë's, for his will not tolerate injustice; the "small still voice" will drive a man to assert a "no." Brontë's final "voice" is, or becomes, a memory of a man who suggests that God can be immanent: Emmanuel, God-with-us. But always outside and beyond as well: "A God, a God their severance ruled"; always a King of Terrors. Only "romantic readers," with "sunny imaginations," can believe in any happy union at the end of *Villette*. For Carlyle, the Romantic impulse was an impulse of affirmation. For Brontë, it was a way towards dangerous daydreamings of a freedom that was not possible. For both, though, the impulse, amalgamated with the traditional religious heritage and chastened by it, made *this* world bearable because together they gave the human being a way to believe in himself/herself and to work in that belief:

We walked back to the Rue Fossette by moonlight – such moonlight as fell on Eden – shining through the shades of the Great Garden, and haply gilding a path glorious . . .

The "life of thought, and that of reality" come together here, in the "new heaven and new earth" – the one "promised land" that is not the romance of "dying dreams."

3

Transmutations of Dickens' emblematic art

Charles Dickens is the Carlylean novelist of the nineteenth century. He declared his allegiance publicly in speeches, in allusions in his essays, in the dedication of *Hard Times*, and in the Preface of *A Tale of Two Cities*; he told Carlyle so privately: "I am always reading you faithfully and trying to go your way," he wrote in 1863, repeating what he had been saying for over two decades.[1] Carlyle provided Dickens with the "spiritual and intellectual atmosphere," the current of ideas, that Arnold saw to be so necessary to creative work of the highest seriousness. Carlyle's language and the conversion pattern that *Sartor Resartus* made available to the Victorians give us the best critical medium for looking at Dickens' novels, even as they focus very clearly the great divergences between the "prophet" and the novelist.

Dickens is always close to Carlyle in his analysis of the "Condition of England" questions, even if he shows a palpable *joy* in life never to be found in Carlyle. The "iron barrier" (BH: 8: 99) between classes Dickens traces to human selfishness in all of its manifestations; the death-in-life realities of modern life he locates in the machine-centered nature of industrial England and in the money that it has made so plentiful. And his plea, like Carlyle's at the end of "Signs of the Times," is always for a change of heart: "To reform a world, to reform a nation, no wise man will undertake; and all but foolish men know, that the only solid, though a far slower reformation, is what each begins and perfects on *himself*" (C: XXVII: 82). To show this reformation Dickens turns, as did his contemporaries, to Carlyle's combination of Puritan self-scrutiny and Romantic internal quest. The journeys of Arthur Clennam, Pip, and Wrayburn bear palpably Teufelsdröckh's signature.[2]

But these quests are not Carlylean without qualification because Dickens is increasingly unable to believe in the transcendental reality that Carlyle always asserts. In *The Old Curiosity Shop*, to be sure, we can find quite straightforwardly in the story of Nell's journey the conventions of popular religious literature. By the time of *Dombey and Son*, the supernatural has been reduced to the natural operation of the human heart, however many angels may surround Florence and Paul on the frontispiece. And after *Dombey*, the realm of natural supernaturalism becomes more and more a small human society and, finally, something alive – if at all – only in the imagination. Agnes may point upward, Little Dorrit's voice may suggest "all that great Nature was doing" (II: 34: 790). But in *Our Mutual Friend*, "playing dead" is, according to Jenny Wren, the only way to participate in any of the "supernaturalism" impossible in real life. Everything is memory of fictions – not Bunyan's "recall" of God's promises, not Wordsworth's recall of the child's natural goodness, not Teufelsdröckh's sighting of God's presence in his fellow man – but simply playing dead to avoid facing the demonic life around one.

The imagery of this last completed novel, like that of *Latter-Day Pamphlets*, is the imagery of the dunghill. But Dickens' reaction to such a world is the very opposite of Carlyle's. The latter looks down, sees a whoring people, and announces that if they cannot believe in a God of love and mercy, then a God of vengeance will visit damnation on their "dismal swamp." Dickens sees that swamp swallowing up the few really *human* people about, but he finds "no rent in the leaden canopy of its sky" (OMF: I: 12: 191), no exit except in a death that promises none of the repose it had promised Nell, none of the justice missing in this world that Esther Summerson knows will be part of the next. Romantic nature has given way utterly to Bunyan's unaccommodated nature – but there is no God above to redeem anything. Against this reality of modern life Dickens found the effort to suffuse the merely human with supernatural meaning finally impossible, for the merely human was, "In these times of ours," quite generally the "Brute Beast," whether respectably dressed or not, and quite happy to be that. Such a world tempts Dickens to name nature Satan rather than God.

His last novels show this bestial world coming to prevail just as the earlier ones show a (pseudo-)Romantic world of childlike goodness triumphing. Those Victorian critics who complained of the loss of Pickwick's cheerful England simply ignored their own and the age's requirements for fiction, which requirements Dickens subscribed to without question. "The exact truth must be there," he said to Forster, and he reasserted this idea in most of his prefaces.

86

He certainly sanctioned Carlyle's assertion that fiction was "an illustrative garment of Fact"; otherwise it was worthless. Against charges of exaggeration and untruthfulness, he merely noted that "the very holding of popular literature through a kind of popular dark age, may depend on such fanciful treatment."[3] With truth increasingly hard or impossible to get at, the novelist's responsibility was to find ways to force his readers to *see*.

This chapter examines Dickens' "popular literature": his use of the religious and Romantic traditions he inherited and found redefined in Carlyle, and his increasing inability to make his fiction a *scola cordis* in the face of the "hollow empty hearts" of modern life.

I

Dickens' description of his work as "popular literature" directs us to the sources of his art. No novelist in this study cares more that his art be a "popular art," none relies more on the inherited popular literary traditions, secular and religious. Beside the allusions to fairy tales, ballads and Romantic poetry that recur throughout his novels, there are quotations from the hymns of Isaac Watts, borrowings from the old emblem writers, and constant allusions to Bunyan (who, according to Macaulay, was better known in the nursery than Jack the Giant-killer). The quest motif is central to his writing. And *Oliver Twist*'s subtitle, "The Parish Boy's Progress," told readers what Dickens had in mind, as did Nell's allusion to Christian within the text of *The Old Curiosity Shop* (15: 175). The pilgrim's questions "Who am I?" and "What shall I do to be saved?" have amazing potency in his novels, which also show a persistent probing of Christian's declaration of his goal: "I seek an Inheritance incorruptible, undefiled, and that fadeth not away" (B: 148).[4]

The old inheritance plot (which George Eliot was to use with such meagre results in *Felix Holt*) Dickens adopts again and again. And no matter what melodramatic echoes from the stage this plot carries, he also means us to hear its emblematic or allegorical echo even as he gives the most literal reading of the convention. Oliver Twist looks for his lost family, young Martin Chuzzlewit would be a legatee, Arthur Clennam fears his inheritance (and the Dorrits get theirs, at the end of volume I!). *Our Mutual Friend, Great Expectations, Bleak House* – all turn about wills and bequests. Even *Dombey and Son*, where the plot is turned on its head and the legator is anxious to pass on the patrimony, gives us language that insists on a moral reading. The title of chapter 5, "Paul's Progress and Christening," alerts readers at the outset to the double-edged meaning of the scenes that follow. Mr Dombey is speaking:

So that Paul's infancy and childhood pass away well, and I see him becoming qualified without waste of time for the career on which he is destined to enter, I am satisfied. He will make what powerful friends he pleases in after-life, when he is actively maintaining – and extending, if that is possible – the dignity and credit of the Firm. (5: 48–9)

For readers acquainted with the Bible and Bunyan as Dickens' readers were, the chapter title, the emphasis on "after-life," the concern with time, ring with damning irony against Dombey.

Indeed, "I have used similitudes" might rightly have been imprinted on the covers of the novels since the cover illustrations were suggestive both of the plot and of Dickens' allegorical intentions. He took as much care about the composition of these illustrations as he did with his text because his emphasis was so visual – again, so much a part of popular art. Q. D. Leavis has noted his "habit," learned from Hogarth, Gilray, and a tradition of moral illustrations, "of visualizing character and situation as types," and his "instinctive practice of moralizing a spectacle, with an expectation of wildly exaggerated characteristics and of a satiric intention."[5] Michael Steig, in his invaluable *Dickens and Phiz*, notes how Dickens and Hablot Browne share ways of condensing allusion "in a form reminiscent of the poem-plus-picture of the emblem book"; and he reminds us that Victorians, at least through the mid-1850s, certainly "read" art emblematically.[6] Dickens' visualizing, embleming habit came, then, out of the inherited tradition. As Samuel Pickering, Jr, has noted, "in Dickens' early novels, strict Protestants found a familiar world. Not only were the characters often clearly recognizable moral types, but the form of parts publication itself was almost second nature to 'bible Christians' raised on religious narratives." Furthermore, to put a child at the center of a novel was not a Dickens innovation; it was already "a hackneyed convention of religious publications" by the time of *Oliver Twist*. And dying youngsters like Little Nell simply repeated a pattern which evangelical magazines had been using for decades. (Indeed, there were anthologies of children's deathbed scenes, all proving the values of obedience and goodness.)[7]

Dickens' art is thus essentially an emblematic art, growing out of Bunyan, the emblem writers, fairy tales, the Hogarthian satirists, and out of the Bible (no language is less abstract than the Bible's, particularly in the Old Testament). And the signal thing about this art is that as Dickens matures, the allegorical echoes become more urgent, the emblems of man's separation from God more *real*, more literal in their use. The eccentric early names – Quilp, Bumble, Jingle – give way to the typical naming of Murdstone, Dedlock, Vholes, Merdle, Mrs General, Veneering; even Bar and Bishop and company walk unadorned, and otherwise uncharacterized, into the morality play before us. For Dickens as for Carlyle, the language of the "old theorem" is finally all that is available to express "reality." No matter how complex his art becomes, Dickens' increasingly bald use of the types and images of the religious tradition testifies to his Carlylean desperation that the language and the fundamental belief which gave it power have become for most readers what they are for Dombey and Podsnap, "mere *words*" useful for describing how one lives prosperously in "Anno Dombei 18 –."

The traditional emblems that Dickens used throughout his career are of course transformed and secularized – as they were by Carlyle as well. The "personal and psychological" ideas which, as Rosemary Freeman has shown us, Quarles and those who followed him present in their emblems, Dickens retains, but he incorporates a Romantic understanding of man and nature into his reading of the tradition.[8] As he uses the emblems, they carry the personal and psychological content of both traditions, Bunyan's pilgrimage and the Romantics' internal quest. But Dickens' progressive disenchantment with the idea of "supernatural" – or even the Romantics' "natural" – reality finally turns those traditional emblems into anything but the images of man's separation from God or of man's own divided nature (though they remain that as well). By the time of *Our Mutual Friend* the traditional emblems have been reduced to almost photographic pictures, literal images of a reality having nothing to do with anything beyond what the eye can easily see.

Although the emblems which Dickens uses most often – the shipwreck, labyrinth, birdcage or prison, and dunghill – are now critical clichés in Dickens studies, their traditional religious context has never been adequately discussed. As used by Quarles and the eighteenth- and nineteenth-century evangelicals who appropriated them for their own doctrinal ideas, emblems illuminated man's separation from God and promised that the Divine Love of Christ could save: Christ would rescue man's soul from the waters, show the way out of the imprisoning labyrinth, if man could only learn to see beyond his self. To begin the process required a fleeing of the self-centered life, one often imaged (as in *Pilgrim's Progress*) by a picture of a figure fleeing the city: "Come, my beloved," Christ says to the soul, "let us go forth into the field" (IV: 7); and the soul – or Bunyan's Christian – follows. In an England where the urban landscape loomed as an overwhelming fact of man's existence, these emblems from the tradition, reinforced and even redefined by Wordsworth, had an extraordinary appeal for Dickens and for his readers. Indeed, in many of his novels, a traditional emblem generates the metaphorical structure.

The Old Curiosity Shop presents the traditional emblems almost unchanged. Little Nell begins her fictional journey lost in the city: "I have lost my road," she says when we meet her for the first time (1: 45); and before long she is urging her grandfather, "Let us be beggars, and be happy" in the open fields away from the demonic, Quilp-haunted London (9: 122). Like Christian, she constantly

PSALM CXLII. 7.

Bring my soul out of prison that I may praise thy name.

Fig. 4.   Quarles, Emblem, V: 10

associates the Bible's promises with the events of her trip (her grandfather has "no memory for the words" of her prayers – 15: 175); and she constantly seeks the road that offers the promised "end." Associated with her throughout – even when she is offstage – is the birdcage which she must leave behind before she goes on her journey, and which Kit guards zealously until he is able to take it to her in the village of her death. Dickens uses this traditional emblem (fig. 4) to underline the earthly imprisonment of Nell's soul (she constantly thinks about death). In the death-bed drawing (fig. 5), Cattermole places a bird – uncaged – on the windowsill beside an hourglass (with the pilgrim's book in the dead child's hand). The text and the illustration ask readers simply to recall the emblem they all knew, and its meaning:

> My soul is like a bird, my flesh the cage,
> Wherein she wears her weary pilgrimage
> Of hours . . . (V: 10)

Fig. 5. Cattermole, "At Rest"

The emblem and the idea will become a constant of Dickens' work.[9]

Martin Chuzzlewit marks his first significant use of the dunghill emblem, and it too is presented quite traditionally as a sign for selfishness. Carlyle, as we have seen, chose his wanderer's surname to suggest the Puritan definition of the natural self. Young Martin Chuzzlewit, going to the American Eden ("the grim domains of Giant Despair" – 23: 442) to make his fortune, finds a place of "offal" and ooze. The reader at once sees the man's chief characteristic emblematized (and the Preface, published with the last number, called attention to selfishness as the book's theme). Young Chuzzlewit's journey into that wilderness is a journey into the Victorian Everyman's heart of darkness, as it is in all of Dickens' novels. Meditating on the corruption around him, Chuzzlewit learns to "read" its typical significance.

PSALM LXIX. 15.

Let not the water-flood overflow me, neither let the deep swallow me up.

Fig. 6.   Quarles, Emblem, III: 11

It was natural for him to reflect – he had months to do it in – upon his own escape and Mark's extremity. This led him to consider which of them could be the better spared, and why? Then the curtain slowly rose a very little way; and Self, Self, Self, was shown below . . . Short as their companionship had been, he felt in many, many instances, that there was blame against himself; and still inquiring why, the curtain slowly rose a little more, and Self, Self, Self, dilated on the scene. It was long before he fixed the knowledge of himself so firmly in his mind that he could thoroughly discern the truth; but in the hideous solitude of that most hideous place, with Hope so far removed, Ambition quenched, and Death beside him rattling at the very door, reflection came, as in a plague-beleaguered town; and so he felt and knew the failing of his life, and saw distinctly what an ugly spot it was.   (33: 597)

Dickens' handling of Pip's progress to the sluice-house and Orlick is foreshadowed here, in the allegorical rendering of Chuzzlewit's "conversion."

Dombey and Son, focusing on pride, is built around the emblem of the shipwrecked soul on the River of Death and Life. But in this novel Dickens begins to refocus the traditional emblematic meaning. Quarles took his text for the emblem (fig. 6) from Psalm 69: 4: "Let not the water-flood overflow me, neither let the deep swallow me up." He added for epigram:

> My soul, the seas are rough, and thou a stranger
> In these false coasts; O keep aloof; there's danger:
> Cast forth thy plummet; see, a rock appears;
> Thy ship wants sea-room; make it with thy tears.   (III: 11)

With *Dombey* as evidence, it could be argued that Dickens took this idea of tears (a constant in devotional literature) more literally than was salutary for his fiction. He needed this very traditional emblem for his work, however, because it was the image his readers associated with spiritual isolation (Brontë also uses it – JE: II: 11: 374).

But Dickens' use of this emblem shows us graphically the changes he has to make in his reading of it, and of all the emblems he will use. Of course, he draws upon the traditional meaning: the shipwrecked soul and the "River of Death" are represented very clearly on the monthly covers of the novel (fig. 7: the life-to-death voyage of man is shown at the bottom, with a telescope pointing towards heaven and maimed clocks lying on the sands). A passage that Dickens cancelled from the proof of the novel's last page underscores this traditional meaning. The "voices in the waves" which we have heard since Paul's birth and which old Dombey

93

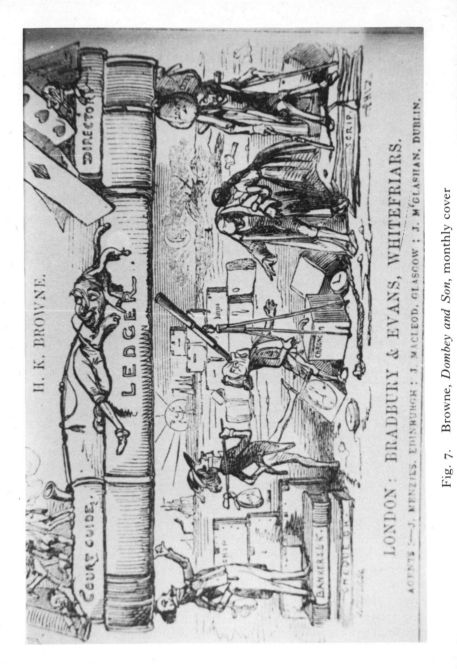

Fig. 7.   Browne, *Dombey and Son*, monthly cover

comes to hear at the end, speak to him "of Florence and their ceaseless murmuring to her of the love, eternal and illimitable, extending still, beyond the sea, beyond the sky, to the invisible country far away."

Never from the mighty sea may voices rise too late, to come between us and the unseen region on the other shore! Better, far better, that they whispered of that region in our childish ears, and the swift river hurried us away!   (DS: 62: 833, n. 6)

Bunyan's bridgeless River of Death is here, and the soul's tears to help man cross it.

But this conventional reading is by no means Dickens' focus. (I suspect the cancellation of the passage was not simply due to lack of space in the closing number, but to Dickens' sense that such rhetoric was "mere *words*," unresponsive to the novel's emphases as he wanted readers to take them.) Although *Dombey*'s frontispiece – published with the closing number, and containing angels and other

Fig. 8.   Browne, *Dombey and Son*, frontispiece (detail)

95

signs of the supernatural – shows Browne's knowledge of the emblem's traditional nature, it also underlines the new emphasis Dickens has given it (fig. 8). Rather than Christ standing on the shore reaching forth his hand, Browne presents Florence and her child rescuing a drowning Dombey. The daughter returns him to life, her child sustains him – human love regenerates. Now this point is hardly startling in discussions of Dickens. But what strikes us increasingly about Dickens' use of the emblematic tradition is his determination to have it both ways: to invoke God and yet celebrate man as man's only knowable aid, to appeal to the God of tradition and to the human love of felt experience.[10]

It is precisely here that the difference between Dickens and Carlyle begins to make itself felt. Both were determined "to save traditional concepts, schemes, and values which had been based on the relation of the Creator to his creature and creation," even as they had to reformulate them in a world where that Creator seemed so far away as to be hardly knowable at all.[11] As we have seen, Carlyle was always able to reconcile the godlike and the human perspective. His use of the shipwreck topos, George Landow has noticed, particularly demonstrates this double perspective.

In the traditional Christian uses of the situation of shipwreck, the author and reader alike view the disaster from the vantage point of divine law; in romantic and post-romantic uses, they view – or experience – the destroying waters from within the sinking vessel, for the existence of divine law is itself in doubt. Carlyle's complex and ironical use of this imagery . . . arises in the fact that although he concentrates on the situation of shipwreck from within, he is ultimately able to believe in a transcendental order of the kind that enables or requires us to judge the mariner from without.[12]

Carlyle never doubts the existence of the unknowable God.

Dickens does. The luxuriant prose which surrounds the death of little Paul and calls attention to divine love and the "older fashion" of immortality undoubtedly comforted his readers in a religious way. But the excesses of the prose and the very conventionality of the rhetoric indicate, I think, Dickens' fear that he does not know what he can believe. Much more credible to him is the "natural supernaturalism" he finds in human beings, the kind emblematized in the frontispiece where Florence, not the angels, saves her father. Dickens can effectively dramatize the idea of a spiritual meaning in a daughter like Florence and in the "childlike" people around Sol Gills; he can give literal representation to Christ's celebration of children and to his commandment to "Love thy neighbour as thyself.'' In this he is like Carlyle, who located the ''region of the Supernatural'' in the recognition of the interdependence of self and others. ''Society is the genial element wherein [man's] nature first lives and grows,'' he wrote in ''Characteristics'' (XXVIII: 10). But if Carlyle finds community the passageway to the divine, Dickens places his emphasis on genial society as an end in itself. Only there can man experience the godlike; only there can he find a basis for belief.

This emphasis on community becomes all the more important because *Dombey* marks a radical change in Dickens' attitude towards nature. In the famous passage, ''Oh for a good spirit who would take the house-tops off,'' there is an extended meditation – one of the longest in his novels – on what nature means to Victorian England. It is a statement that deserves our attention because its ambivalences are central to the development of Dickens' art.

It might be worth while, sometimes, to inquire what Nature is, and how men work to change her, and whether, in the enforced distortions so produced, it is not natural to be unnatural . . . Alas! are there so few things in the world about us, most unnatural, and yet most natural in being so! . . . Look round upon the world of odious sights . . . Vainly attempt to think of any simple plant, or flower, or wholesome weed, that, set in this foetid bed, could have its natural growth, or put its little leaves forth to the sun as GOD designed it. And then calling up some ghastly child, with stunted form and wicked face, hold forth on its unnatural sinfulness, and lament its being, so early, far away from Heaven – but think a little of its having been conceived, and born, and bred, in Hell! Those who study the physical sciences, and bring them to bear upon the health of Man, tell us that if the noxious particles that rise from vitiated air, were palpable to the sight, we should see them lowering in a dense black cloud above such haunts, and rolling slowly to corrupt the better portion of a town. But if the moral pestilence that rises with them, and, in the eternal laws of outraged Nature, is inseparable from them, could be made discernible too, how terrible the revelation! . . . Then should we stand appalled to know, that where we generate disease to strike our children down and entail itself on unborn generations, there also we breed, by the same certain process, infancy that knows no innocence, youth without modesty or shame, maturity that is mature in nothing but in suffering and guilt, blasted old age that is a scandal on the form we bear. Unnatural humanity! When we shall gather grapes from thorns, and figs from thistles; when fields of grain shall spring up from the offal in the by-ways of our wicked cities, and roses bloom in the fat churchyards that they cherish; then we may look for natural humanity, and find it growing from such seed. (47: 619–20)

The traditional view of a divinely ordered nature lurks behind this passage in the sentimentalized images of the simple plant putting out its leaves to the sun. But the image of nature that prevails is that of the unnatural. Man's effect has been felt everywhere, and the result is the corruption and perversion of nature. Carlyle always manages to view the world from a godlike perspective: *his* God will take the house-tops off and make us see if we fail to gain vision. Carlyle is determined to believe that there are natural laws which will assert themselves. Dickens, however, interprets those "natural" laws differently. That dense black cloud is clearly differentiated from the "moral pestilence"; it is nature itself converted into a form of bestiality.

And where can man turn for protection? The remembered emblems that imply a heavenly perspective persist even to *Little Dorrit* and *Our Mutual Friend*. "Far aslant across the city, over its jumbled roofs, and through the open tracery of its church towers, struck the long bright rays, bars of the prison of this lower world" (LD: II: 30: 741) – but the wan belief of the Dickens of *Little Dorrit* is signaled by the dragging phrases of this sentence. That weariness is signaled again when he recapitulates Florence Dombey's emblematic "Saving" of her father in Lizzie Hexam's rescue of Wrayburn from the waters. Dickens can no longer maintain the Carlylean perspective, the conviction that there is a God who will change all. Even in Little Nell's world of clearly contrasted good and evil, he reveals his uncertainty: Nell wonders whether *Pilgrim's Progress* "was true in every word, and where those distant countries with the curious names might be" (15: 175). By the time of *Dombey*, Dickens seems a doubly terrified Bunyan, seeing man's bestiality but lacking belief in a transforming God. In *Our Mutual Friend* Lizzie's act of redeeming rescue is counterpointed at the novel's beginning by the "modern" reading of the emblem: her father is a fisher of men.

If Dickens comes to see little hope from a transcendent force, he also loses faith in the salvation the Romantics had suggested could be found in nature itself. His changing attitude towards the great Romantic archetype of the child shows his tenuous hold on any certainties about original innocence. Little Nell seems close to the Romantic child. The dunghills that mark Christian's beginning touch her only as she must come into contact with Quilp or suffer nightmares about him. Like Oliver Twist (though in no way so passive), she survives trial after trial untouched by the wretched world, constantly dreaming of nature's splendors, always looking forward and upward (she stares out of windows as much as Dinah Morris in *Adam Bede*). She is the Romantic child who will never need ask with Christian, "What shall I do to be saved?" She is saved, and has indeed instinctively revised the Pilgrim's question: "What shall I do to save him!" she says of her grandfather (42: 403).

Yet, Peter Coveney has noted, neither Nell nor any other of Dickens' children is essentially like those of Blake and Wordsworth because each is constantly associated with death.[13] One of Nell's meditations underlines this point. She is staring into the river:

She bent over the calm river, and saw [the stars] shining in the same majestic order as when the dove beheld them gleaming through the swollen waters, upon the mountain tops down far below, and dead mankind, a million fathoms deep. (42: 396–7)

As in Quarles' emblem of Flesh and Spirit (the Spirit stares away from this earth, the Flesh gazes delightedly at a prism, and the motto urges men to "consider their latter end"), Nell sees the spiritual world beyond (fig. 9). But she focuses on the skeleton of the

DEUT. XXXII. 29.

O that men were wise, that they understood this, that they would consider their latter end!

Fig. 9.   Quarles, Emblem, III: 14

99

emblem: death is release and repose, not rebirth. There is none of Christian's nor Christiana's joy here.[14]

After *Dombey*, Dickens' treatment of the child changes. Little Dorrit, for example, is a Nell seen through unsentimental eyes. Born in a prison (Clennam sees her as a caged "small bird" – I: 9: 100), her road is towards no freedom but always back to the prison of her birth. As for nature, she knows nothing of the happy landscapes Nell remembers. "Thinking of the fields, ain't you?" the turnkey asks her. Her questioning reply, "Where are they? . . . Does anybody open them, and shut them? Are they locked?", indicates her alienation from the Romantic view of nature as the beneficent mother; the world beyond the city has at best been imagined reality for her (I: 7: 68). And when, free, she gets to the great Romantic sublime, the Alps, she is quite unable to separate her sense of them from the figure of Blandois, the novel's bona fide devil, who stands before them and colors all with his sneers (II: 3: 443).[15] From *Bleak House* onward, Dickens' children are born in isolation and grow up as outcasts; they are stunted in will, purposeless, almost without identity. His good adults, like those in Carlyle, may always retain something of the childlike (too much perhaps for our credulity) as if only this quality will serve as touchstone for the really human in man or woman. But even this childlike quality is ruthlessly satirized in the figure of Harold Skimpole, that "child" utterly free of time, responsibility, and human feeling. He is indeed, as Q. D. Leavis has said, the "serpent" in Jarndyce's garden.[16] And he shows us how harsh Dickens is on his own – and on his readers' – sentimental attachment to the Romantic child.

A fuller look at the two major emblems he uses, one dealing with a combination of prison and labyrinth emblems and the other with the dunghill, will help us to see further into the transmutations of Dickens' art. Quarles' verses combine the images of the prison and the labyrinth as a reflection of man's spiritual condition in this world (fig. 10):

> Fond earth! . . .
> . . .
> Thou art my prison, and my home's above;
>   My life's a preparation but to leave thee:
> . . .
> The world's a lab'rinth, whose anfractuous ways
>   Are all compos'd of rugs and crook'd meanders:
> No resting here . . .

This gyring lab'rinth is betrench'd about
On either hand with streams of sulph'rous fire . . .

(IV: 2)

Losing one's way in a labyrinthine world is also the condition of living in Dickens' urban England. As with Quarles, the emblem at once marks the City of Destruction in which men live (in *Bleak House* a red glow hangs over the city, and an "infernal gulf" at its center – Tom-all-Alone's – draws everyone towards it) and the horrors of the alienated self (Pip writes that he is taking the reader "into my poor labyrinth" – GE: 29: 253). Like Quarles, Dickens looks in sorrow on "the multiplicity of paths in the labyrinth trodden by the sons of Adam" (LD: II: 12: 539). And like Quarles, he even sees that it is man's concentration on self that isolates him –

PSALM CXIX. 5.

O that my ways were directed to keep thy statutes !

Fig. 10.   Quarles, Emblem, IV: 2

though for Quarles man is separated from God, for Dickens he is separated from his fellows. Where Dickens alters the traditional signification of the emblem is in his assertion that the good and selfless are as lost in the labyrinth as the selfish. Pip may be isolated from Joe and Biddy by his own self-interest. But Esther Summerson, Amy Dorrit, and Arthur Clennam also find life, as Teufelsdröckh did, "wholly a dark labyrinth" (SR: 152), with "no pillar, cloud, nor star" (Quarles: IV: 2; SR: 161) to guide them to union with God or with their fellows.[17]

The case history of Arthur Clennam perfectly illustrates this alteration Dickens has made in the traditional implications of the prison–labyrinth emblems. Bunyan's Man in the Iron Cage knows that he is responsible for his entrapment: "I have provoked God to anger, and he has left me; I have so hardened my heart, that I cannot repent." He knows that his self-centered nature has led him to prison, that "the Lusts, Pleasures, and Profits of this World" have beguiled him; "but now every one of those things also bite me, and gnaw me like a burning worm" (B: 167). In contrast, Arthur Clennam's listlessness arises from his not having the vaguest notion why he is imprisoned. He only knows that he feels trapped in a "labyrinth" which was his inheritance from the sternly Calvinistic home of his youth (LD: I: 2: 18). His life is one "weary pilgrimage of hours" through a world that has turned on him as it has on Bunyan's caged figure. In his youth he felt the clock "growling" at him. In his adulthood he walks in a London where houses "frown" on him and mud "splashes" him and furniture threatens him; and like Teufelsdröckh he has no notion of why he is so outcast. He has only "the shadow of a supposed act of injustice" and three initials on a watch (D.N.F.) to fill the blank that stands for the cause of his dis-ease. Even the remnants of his Calvinistic upbringing form part of his painful ambivalence; the questions meditation has taught the wayfarer to ask simply haunt him because there are no answers. Calvinist – or Romantic – self-questioning provides a form that does not lead to redemption or self-enlightenment, just to more questions.

That the burden of this pilgrim, like those afflicting all of Dickens' later travellers, is called a "shadow" tells us how far we are from Quarles and Bunyan and their certainties. Clennam has been brought up in a sternly Calvinistic home where an obsessive emphasis has been placed on man's innate depravity and on money as a sign of God's blessings on the good. Dickens uses Clennam's case to illustrate the killing of the Word's power that has accompanied evangelical religion's commercial success; together religion and commerce have "weighed, measured, and priced everything." And "what could not be weighed, measured, and priced," Clennam notes, "had no existence" (I: 2: 20). It is Atheist's world, where only what is seen has reality (B: 248–9). Only Vanity Fair is paradise, for earth has become the *axis mundi*.

The earth was made for Dombey and Son to trade in, and the sun and moon were made to give them light. Rivers and seas were formed to float their ships; rainbows gave them promise of fair weather; winds blew for or against their enterprises; stars and planets circled in their orbits, to preserve inviolate a system of which they were the centre. Common abbreviations took new meanings in his eyes, and had sole reference to them. A.D. had no concern with anno Domini, but stood for anno Dombei – and Son. (DS: 1: 2)

The world of Merdle and Mrs Clennam is the same, and it offers Clennam no more knowledge of the New Testament God of love "than if he had been bred among idolaters" (LD: I: 3: 69). Which, in effect, he has, for the Dorrit code of business is little different from that of Dombey or Merdle, except in its religious lexicon.

Each time Bunyan's pilgrim falls into a net, remembrance of the Bible's promises rescues him. At the bridgeless River of Death, Christian despairs of a way to pass on to the Celestial City: "here he in great measure lost his senses, so that he could neither remember nor orderly talk of any of those sweet refreshments that he had met with in the way of his Pilgrimage" (B: 266). But finally he does "call to mind" God's goodness – and is saved once more. No such language resonates for Clennam, neither that of evangelical religion nor that of commercialism. Paradoxically, Dickens shows that nineteenth-century evangelical life, clothed in anything but filthy rags, has made Bunyan's way impossible for the sensitive human being. The "fierce dark teaching of his childhood" (LD: I: 27: 310) forms for Clennam a "broad road" leading towards a psychological hell: "Strait was the gate and narrow was the way; far straiter and narrower than the broad high road paved with vain professions and vain repetitions" (I: 27: 310). In the modern world the only sacred way lies around one, and it is a Carlylean way: "Duty on earth, restitution on earth, action on earth; these first, as the first steep steps upward" (I: 27: 310). Earth *must* be the place of godlike action – if there is a God.

Dickens has thus stripped the emblem of its traditional meaning –

because men have, no matter how pious their "vain professions." Unlike Bunyan's pilgrim, Clennam can "never mount on wings of words to Heaven," nor stay on the strait road because he knows them.[18] Instead, he must turn to the Carlylean prescription of work. "Labour is Life," Carlyle had urged, whereby man first awakens "to all knowledge, 'self-knowledge' and much else, so soon as Work fitly begins" (PP: 197). Clennam's progress in self-discovery indicates Dickens' rereading of the vanity-mirror emblem: to "perfectly see thyself" is for Clennam to see "what he was to do henceforth in life" (Quarles, II: 6; LD: I: 16: 183). The cancelling of the Puritan's "Who am I?" and the stress on "What shall I do?" –

PSALM LV. 6.

O that I had wings like a dove, for then would I fly away, and be at rest!

Fig. 11.   Quarles, Emblem, V: 13

do, not to be saved, but to live adequately in this world without fear
– is inevitable in a period when the traditional God seems so
unknowable and the sources of one's self often so uncertain.
"Properly thou hast no other knowledge but what thou hast got by
working," as Carlyle said (PP: 197).

The Merdle world in which Clennam tries to work suggests the
other emblem essential to our getting at the sources of Dickens' art,
the image of the dunghill (fig. 11). Quarles wrote:

> And am I sworn a dunghill-slave for ever
>   To earth's base drudg'ry? Shall I never find
> A night of rest? shall my indentures never
>   Be cancell'd? Did injurious nature bind
> My soul earth's 'prentice, with no clause to leave her?
>   No day of freedom? Must I ever grind?
>
> (V: 13)

The lines summarize Arthur Clennam's meditations throughout
Little Dorrit, and also Pip's in *Great Expectations*: they apply to the
selfless and (in the traditional usage) to the selfish, to Everyman. As
Pancks tells us, "we are always grinding, drudging, toiling, every
minute we're awake": "There you are with the Whole Duty of Man
in a commercial country," he adds, inverting Ecclesiastes and
showing the literal reading an Age of Mammon and Machinery has
given its traditional religious ideas (LD: II: 13: 154).

The dunghill emblem receives more and more emphasis in
Dickens' later novels until the thing it signifies becomes the chief
component of the physical landscape. This is due to Dickens'
increasing sense that selfishness in the guise of respectability is the
chief barrier to genuine community in England. He adopts
Carlyle's often-stated diagnosis that selfishness masquerading as
respectability is society's most insidious disease, undermining
utterly man's ability to discriminate good and evil, and causing him
to prefer "cobbling together two Inconsistencies" to choosing the
good (XXVIII: 254). "Of all blinds that shut-up men's vision,"
Carlyle wrote in "The Diamond Necklace," "the worst is Self."

How doubly true, if Self, assuming her cunningest, yet miserablest
disguise, come on us . . . not as Pride, not even as real Hunger, but only as
Vanity, and the shadow of an imaginary Hunger for Applause; under the
name of what we call 'Respectability'! (XXVIII: 326)

A belief in respectability, he declared, "gradually winnows away
[men's] souls" by causing them to cease to see – or to care to see –
any difference between good and evil.

The number of times selfish respectability and the dunghill emblem appear together in later Dickens attests to his acceptance of Carlyle's diagnosis. In *Bleak House* only those who live within Jarndyce's home fail to use the word with approbation; everyone else is preoccupied with "this necessity for self-concentration," as Mrs Jellyby happily phrases it (23: 296). The lawyer Vholes particularly makes the case, for "Mr Vholes is a very respectable man." Dickens even puts him in a gig, the image Carlyle made notoriously synonymous with respectability (and that gig, Esther notices, is drawn by the "gaunt pale horse" of death in the Apocalypse – 37: 471). A black-shrouded "Vampire" who defines "immoral" as "unlawful," Mr Vholes is drawn as a demonic shepherd of a hideous pastoral who preys on the young (his office, in "the valley of the Shadow of the Law," smells of "unwholesome sheep"). The narrator comments, "Make man-eating unlawful, and you starve the Vholeses!" The perfectly named lawyer presents himself as a surrogate St Peter for the present age: "This desk is your rock, sir," he tells Carstone; "it pretends to be nothing more." Aided only by his "unclean spirit," Mr Vholes is "a *most* respectable man" (39: 482–5, 488; 60: 721).

If *Little Dorrit* and *Great Expectations* lack the word, they have the offal in ample supply. Pip's dream of London glory turns into the reality of "Little Britain" and its dirt. In *Little Dorrit*'s London, "The name of Merdle [with its root in *merde*] is the name of the age," as Mr Dorrit wisely announces (II: 5: 469). And everyone worships accordingly:

True, the Hampton Court Bohemians, without exception, turned up their noses at Merdle as an upstart; but they turned them down again, by falling flat on their faces to worship his wealth . . . All people knew (or thought they knew) that he had made himself immensely rich; and, for that reason alone, prostrated themselves before him . . . As he went up the stairs, people were already posted on the lower stairs, that his shadow might fall upon them when he came down. So were the sick brought out and laid in the track of the Apostle . . . (I: 33: 380–1; II: 12: 539; 16: 593)

He is another St Peter for the present, "saturating Society" with the blessings of gold. (Esther Summerson uses the same biblical reference, Acts 5: 15, for Vholes – BH: 45: 543.)

Our Mutual Friend baldly consolidates this emphasis on respectability and filth and money. Dickens gives word, emblem, statement. The dust piles, the slime, the ooze are everywhere. A foreigner even thinks that "the eminently respectable" Mr Podsnap means to include horse-dung as one of the "Signs, you know, Appearances" of "our British Constitution in the Streets" of London (I: 11: 178–9; the entire conversation in its *double entendre* has the ring of a morality play). "In these times of ours" in which the novel is set, men and women even read books extolling "The Treasures of a Dunghill" (III: 6: 543). And lest this emblematic portrayal of selfishness and respectability be missed by any dozing readers, Dickens offers the educated Charley Hexam to interpret for us, to "read" it properly: "I am determined that after I have climbed up out of the mire, you shall not pull me down," he says to his sister (II: 15: 461). To his teacher, whom he accuses of selfishness, he announces: "I have made up my mind that I will become respectable . . ., and that I will not be dragged down by others." Hexam is a Podsnap in process. Dickens, offering this young man and his "hollow empty heart" for our evaluation, asks: "What is there but self, for selfishness to see behind it?" (IV: 7: 780–1).

Evidently very little. Lizzie Hexam has urged her brother to "cut" himself off from his environment and family in order to secure "a new and good beginning" (I: 3: 73); and she has, ironically, started him on his journey towards being a Cain, and a very respectable one. Lizzie herself encounters people, conventionally good and decent, who urge her to sever her natural ties to her father in order to get out of the mire. Miss Abbey Potterson, of the Six Jolly Fellowship Porters, has very precise notions of "fellowship": "You needn't break with him [Gaffer Hexam] altogether, but leave him . . . Don't fling yourself away, my girl, but be persuaded into being respectable and happy" (I: 6: 113). Lizzie sees that to make respectability her goal is to damn her father to certain criminality. The horror of her life is that her own genuine goodness cuts her off from what are the commonly accepted signs of civilized life. She sees that she dare not try to have an education because "want of learning" is the only "tie between me and father," the "stay" that keeps him from becoming "wild and bad" (I: 3: 72–3). No wonder she stares so often into the fire or the river; they are, as her brother rightly perceives, her "books," the single images that can allow her, in her "meditation," to escape the dunghill environment. And yet these sources of meditation give her no spiritual freedom. Looking into the river, she sees the "misery" of the lives about her and sees too that the river stretches "away to the great ocean, Death" (I: 6: 115). She sees no promised help for the shipwrecked souls like her father (there is only herself), she sees no promised land at all. She never sees Nell's heavens. (Indeed, Lizzie leaves off her meditation by suddenly thinking she must "do the thing that could be done" rather than dream – certainly a Carlylean note!)

Living amidst such unreality and disorder, Dickens' decent people inevitably find death attractive, a release from the dunghill earth. Thus the emblem partially carries a Bunyanesque quality. It is this traditional meaning which Little Nell shares; she gazes out of the window up at the heavens because she knows what is there. And as her conversation with the sexton about the well illustrates (as does Maclise's drawing), she knows how to read men and images as "types" (OCS: 53: 493). But Bunyan glosses Christian's experience at the river Death with the comment that "Death is not welcome to nature though by it we pass out of this World into glory" (B: 266). Staring at the river, Lizzie sees it only as a place of death, nothing else. And Jenny Wren expresses vividly Dickens' sense of death as a welcome escape from the labyrinthine web of nature.

> "How do you feel when you are dead?" asked Fledgeby, much perplexed.
> "Oh, so tranquil!" cried the little creature, smiling. "Oh, so peaceful and so thankful! And you hear the people who are alive, crying, and working and calling to one another down in the close dark streets, and you seem to pity them so! And such a chain has fallen from you, and such a strange good sorrowful happiness comes upon you! . . . Come up and be dead! Come up and be dead!" (OMF: II: 5: 334–5)

Death is not envisioned here as the passage from a dunghill world to glory; it is simply an escape from life in a "hopeless city" (OMF: I: 12: 191). Death is very welcome to Jenny or to the natural "birds of prey" like Rogue Riderhood. Dickens' comment on Riderhood's death-struggle reveals how far he has transmuted the traditional meaning of the dunghill emblem: "like us all, everyday of our lives when we wake – he is instinctively unwilling to be restored to the consciousness of this existence, and would be left dormant, if he could" (III: 3: 505).

Dickens thus bases his rendering of the Victorian social land-scape in the images of the popular religious tradition which Bunyan and so many others had perpetuated. But he does so only to register his despair that the Romantic vision of nature is no more possible in his city than Bunyan's vision of God. The world of biblical romance and its communally shared emblems of spiritual freedom is as infected as nature – human and natural. Only the dunghill part of these emblems remains as reality, only the literally demonic. Esther Summerson may be able to speak with belief in a "world that sets this right," but there is always the unseen beggar Jo to challenge her:

And there he sits, munching and gnawing, and looking up at the great Cross on the summit of St Paul's Cathedral, glittering above a red and violet-tinted cloud of smoke. From the boy's face one might suppose that sacred emblem to be, in his eyes, the crowning confusion of the great, confused city; so golden, so high up, so far out of his reach.   (BH: 19: 243–4)

The cross (which also appears in similar contexts in *Little Dorrit* and *Great Expectations*) registers the spiritual need. The paragraph's end reports the reality: "There he sits, the sun going down, the river running fast, the crowd flowing by him in two streams – everything moving on to some purpose and to one end – until he is stirred up, and told to 'move on' too." Jo is no Romantic child. God and nature are at strife here, as is the "emblem" with the reality. And for Jo, reality is all.

That God and nature are so at strife in Dickens' later novels tells us how unRomantic, untraditional, and totally Victorian he is. Tennyson's question, "Are God and Nature then at strife?", Michael Timko has written, is the quintessential Victorian query:

the consistent use of bestial imagery serves to emphasize the awareness of the Victorians of the need to find irrefutable evidence to prove the humanity – since no longer was divinity possible – of human beings . . . No longer was it a question of man's divine strivings pitted against his bestial predisposition, a struggle that always took for granted God's concern for man and assumed that man's bestiality was an aberration that could be overcome with time, effort, and faith . . . The questions were now strictly Victorian in the sense that the old problem was exactly reversed . . . All of this was made more complex by [man's] questions concerning his ability to know for certain anything about himself, his world, or his God.[19]

Carlyle, as we have seen, provides the paradigm for Victorian man's effort to prove his humanity. Teufelsdröckh, finding himself a Cain, a dunghill slave, discovers his godborn nature through work that takes him out into the genial world of human fellowship, away from his preoccupation with that "Demon-Empire" within. He thus finds his humanity.

Dickens shares this belief in the absolute necessity of working and living with feeling amongst one's fellows if any personal and social order is to prevail. But he finds quite impossible Carlyle's assertion that "God lives," that there is a transcendent reality behind the world of appearances. His mature novels try to come to terms with these issues, but he never finds anything beyond the human except the bestial: no order, no nature, nothing conquers his doubt. In Pip and Wrayburn he presents profoundly divided human beings who do discover something of the godborn within their Cain-like natures. But he can never extend this discovery to the social order, or to any transcendent order. In *Bleak House* he tries to come to terms with the Romantic belief in man's godlike nature, and with his need to see a God above St Paul's cross who will transform all at "The Appointed Time." But the very opposition between a voice which sees all *sub specie aeternitatis* and one gasping in the pestilential air exposes the uncertainty. *Little Dorrit*'s ending, amidst the "noisy" and "eager" of one of Bunyan's "lusty fairs," and *Great Expectations*' final tableau of an illusionless Pip and Estella, stunted and tired, point the narrowing of "natural supernaturalism" to what can be imagined amidst unreality and dunghills. In *Our Mutual Friend* all effort to suggest a God above "the prison of this lower world" has been abandoned. This novel has all the imagery of the *Latter-Day Pamphlets*, and many of their ideas; it has a modern Teufelsdröckh in Wrayburn and Headstone. But it lacks utterly any God of Wrath who will destroy the erring self-idolaters on the dunghills; and it lacks any voice who believes this is possible. Here Dickens only occasionally manages the pamphlet rhetoric of *Bleak House*.

My lords and gentlemen and honourable boards, when you in the course of your dust-shovelling and cinder-raking have piled up a mountain of pretentious failure, you must off with your honourable coats for the removal of it, . . . or it will come rushing down and bury us alive. Yes, verily, my lords and gentlemen and honourable boards, adapting your Catechism to the occasion, and by God's help you must. (OMF: III: 8: 565)

But the prophet's apocalyptic furor that inspired the narrator's tone in *Bleak House* has vanished, replaced by shrill assertion backed by no knowable authority.

II

Quarles' snare emblem and its epigram bring together the emphases of Dickens' emblematic art (fig. 12):

Be sad, my heart, deep dangers wait thy mirth:
Thy soul's waylaid by sea, by hell, by earth:

Hell has her hounds; earth, snares; the sea, a shelf:
But most of all, my heart, beware thyself.

(III: 9)

Dickens' pilgrims who attempt to make spiritual progresses must confront at once the web without and the snares within if they are to attain any release from their burden. The conversions are always more like Teufelsdröckh's than Christian's. "Fool! the Ideal is in thyself, the impediment too is in thyself," Teufelsdröckh learned, finding the source of essential vision anywhere but in the traditional formulas. "Till the eye have vision," he added, "the whole members are in bonds" (SR: 196–7).

Teufelsdröckh's wanderings provide the model for Dickens in his rendering of a *Bildung* story. But the details, and in the end even the essentials which give this model life, gradually vanish, leaving in *Our Mutual Friend* a kind of macabre parody of any spiritual

PSALM XVIII. 5.

The sorrows of hell compassed me about, and the snares of death prevented me.

Fig. 12.   Quarles, Emblem, III: 9

111

rebirth, for "Conversion" isolates man that much more. In the early novels, whatever conversion experiences there were – young Chuzzlewit's, Dombey's – led to the "Dickensian" fêtes that his contemporaries loved (and found lamentably absent later on). From *Hard Times* on, quiet resignation, at best, marks the final paragraphs. *Bleak House* is the great balance point. Esther Summerson's autobiography proves the possibility of genuine goodness having a lasting effect on those around one. But the doom-saying narrator whose words constantly interrupt her progress reports sees none of the triumph of sacred romance, but instead demons cavorting in an "infernal gulf." *Our Mutual Friend*, in which Dickens uses Carlyle more overtly, I think, than in any previous novel, gives us spiritual progresses, demonic progresses, and Vanity Fair prevailing. And Vanity Fair is so oppressively triumphant that the possibility of any romance – or any Teufelsdröckhean vision – actually establishing itself seems absurd.

Bleak House's two narratives – one an autobiography, the other a prophet's curse on a whoring generation – turn on three questions: "Who am I?", "What is my inheritance?" and "What is Justice?" The first two come from Bunyan and the Romantics, the third from Carlyle (PP: 18, *et passim*); and it is the only one shared by both narrators. As we have seen, Carlyle named injustice as the cause of England's internal disorder, adding: "The real smart is the soul's pain and stigma, the hurt inflicted on the moral self." But protesting always this intolerable condition, he asserted, was that "small still voice intimating that it is not the final lot; that wild, waste, incoherent as it looks, a God presides over it" (C: XXIV: 145). Esther Summerson explores this problem of injustice from a perspective within that world of England's Chancery "justice"; the other narrator explores it from the perspective of Heaven's Chancery. Their conclusions are not the same.

Esther Summerson and Amy Dorrit are the greatest of Dickens' good women, for their goodness is not sentimentalized as Nell's is. It is maintained in the face of horrid forces from within and without that do stunt them. The "hurt inflicted on the moral self" in Esther's case originates in her birth in sternly Calvinistic sinfulness. Her first consciousness is of nothing, no family, no love, no real name. (In the opening paragraph of her narrative, she tells us that her wooden doll, her only confidante, sat "propped up in a great arm-chair . . . staring at me – or not so much at me, I think, as at nothing" – BH: 3: 17.) And she is told that she is basically a Cain:

"You are different from other children, Esther, because you were not born, like them, in common sinfulness and wrath. You are set apart" (3: 19).

Her autobiography, then, is written in the same spirit and with the same intention that prompted so many spiritual autobiographies of the seventeenth and eighteenth centuries. Like Bunyan, Esther too will recount the "Grace Abounding to the Chief of Sinners." Victorian reviewers complained that there was in Esther's narrative "an artificial tone, which, if not self-consciousness, is at any rate not such a tone as would be used in her narrative by a person of the character depicted."[20] This misses the point entirely. Again the vanity-glass emblem (and there are glasses all over *Bleak House*) directs us: "First, thou must see the visible things of thyself, before thou canst be prepared to know the invisible things of God" (Quarles: II: 6). Bunyan gives the mirror the same use: "Now the glass . . . would present a man, one way, with his own Feature exactly, and turn it but an other way, and it would shew me the very Face and Similitude of the Prince of Pilgrims himself" (B: 378). Esther begins her narrative, birdcage in hand, as a record of her movements away from the "shadow" of her birth, her account of her efforts "to do some good to some one, and win some love to myself if I could" (BH: 3: 20). Throughout she credits her successes to that "Father who had not forgotten me," to "the goodness and the tenderness of God" (3: 27; 67: 767). Her retrospective account – written to an "unknown friend," to us – assumes the shape of all exemplary pilgrim's progresses, for Esther finds in her experiences God's hand working, his grace abounding. And she finds correspondences in her memories to Christ's journey. Her constant recording of the praises of others may sound coy (or worse), but those praises and that tone are necessary for a woman exorcising the dunghill of her birth by doing her duty (the word is everywhere) to others; to see in the goodness of others and in her own progress a "looking-glass" of her own self's "growth and change" is already an exorcising of that putrid self of Miss Barbary's cultivation (3: 27). She must exult in names like Dame Durden because they prove her developing soul, her progress from the degradation, guilt, and "shadow" of self-indulgence associated with her own name. As Bercovitch reminds us, for the Puritan "the advantage of self-knowledge" is that "the terror it brings may exorcise our individuality," may get rid of our unique "self."[21] Esther in her self-scrutiny is writing about herself within the tradition in which she was brought up. She is showing how she exorcised what set her apart.

But one phrase in her initial account of her early life quite separates the autobiography from its religious predecessors and links it strikingly with Teufelsdröckh's and Jane Eyre's. Speaking of "the fault [she] had been born with," Esther adds parenthetically: "(of which I confusedly felt guilty yet innocent)" (3: 20). Bunyan knew he was not innocent; Christian told Ignorance he was not, that belief in one's good heart was foolish. That Esther cannot assert her utter depravity underlines the paradox Dickens uses in his creation of her. Her progress towards Romantic wholeness, represented by a knowledge of one's original innocence, is told in the form of a Puritan autobiography, a journey to *self*lessness. Implicit in that "yet innocent" is the scrutiny of her guilt which is her autobiography's focus. She sees God's hand in all of her affairs, even as Dickens shows her own strong sense of duty towards others as redemptive. "Divine creation" and "human recreation" (Frye's definition of a secular scripture) come together in Esther's memoir.[22]

The direction of her narrative at the outset – her first chapter is called "A Progress" – is very clearly that of Bunyan's pilgrim. Both the impersonal narrator and Esther pass into the law courts, underlining the centrality of Chancery justice in English life, and recalling too Christian's encounter with Mr Legality. This Bunyan echo indicates Dickens' subtle handling of his allegorical subtext. Men in this society have set up Chancery as their "eternal bar" (Gridley's phrase for his source of ultimate justice) and thrive or perish according to its favor, as Richard Carstone's story illustrates. Evangelist's words to Christian state precisely Esther's interpretation of these legal doings: "This Legality . . . is not able to set thee free from thy burden. No man was as yet ever rid of his burden by him, no, nor ever is like to be: ye cannot be justified by the Works of the Law; for by the deeds of the Law no man living can be rid of his burden" (B: 157–8).

Yet as Esther continues her memoir, its essentially Romantic nature becomes evident. The movement of that narrative is, finally, a descent into a Dantean Hell, at the center of which is the "infernal gulf" of Tom-all-Alone's, where crowds which seem "like a concourse of imprisoned demons" flit, whistle, and yell (BH: 22: 277, 281). Esther's history is a record of her confrontation with the demon-empires of self and with those unknown sources of herself whose deaths come in that "infernal gulf." In the process of this journey she will throw off forever her "inheritance of shame" (44: 538).

She does, of course, constantly seek – and find – an arbor to rest in, a place where that "shadow" seems lighter – thus the pastoral descriptions of *Bleak House*'s "green landscapes" (6: 57) and of the peaceful country around Chesney Wold, which seems to Esther "like a glimpse of the better land" (18: 228). Yet the demonic infections of Tom's come into the Jarndyce paradise with Jo and the smallpox. And in the Romantic setting of the Dedlock lands Esther faces her unknown mother and confronts her real history and the sources of her stunting.

The first sighting of Lady Dedlock begins in the village church, as the service begins: "Enter not into judgment with thy servant, O Lord, for in thy sight –" (18: 224). The scene, in the subtlest and profoundest way, asserts through the Prayer Book text the relationship of Lady Dedlock's and Esther's histories to the Chancery suit – and reveals the way Dickens relates Christian's journey to the Romantic quest. Throughout the novel, in both narratives, lawyers appear as malign priests and the Lord Chancellor as some surrogate Heavenly Father. Esther pays these representatives of Legality no heed; Lady Dedlock – with no belief in anything or anyone beyond herself – also ignores them, but is hounded by Tulkinghorn. Judgment which burdens both women, Esther from birth and Lady Dedlock in marriage, has utterly nothing to do with God or with justice – as judgment in English courts has nothing to do with Justice, either.

The Prayer Book verse which introduces mother and daughter comes from a Psalm (143) which is a supplication for God's help; its verses foreshadow the future histories of both Esther and her mother (I quote from an 1841 edition of the Prayer Book):

For the enemy hath persecuted my soul; he hath smitten my life down to the ground: he hath laid me in the darkness, as the men that have been long dead . . . Yet do I remember the time past; I muse upon all thy works . . . Hear me, O Lord, and that soon, for my spirit waxeth faint: hide not thy face from me, lest I be like unto them that go down into the pit. O let me hear thy loving-kindness in the morning . . . shew thou me the way that I should walk in, for I lift up my soul unto thee.

Looking at Lady Dedlock for the first time, Esther wonders why the woman's face "should be, in a confused way, like a broken glass to me, in which I saw scraps of old remembrances": "And yet *I – I*, little Esther Summerson, the child who lived a life apart . . . seemed to arise before my own eyes" (18: 225). When she next sees this woman, she will see her old self rising with even more ".terror," for in the interval she has been disfigured and even blinded for a time by smallpox. And she will again think of "the time past" and the guilt she then had to bear (36: 453). But learning that this woman is her mother forces Esther to see someone even more an outcast than she has been since Miss Barbary's death; she sees a woman who can trust and love no one, who can neither accept her daughter's "natural love" nor turn to God for help, a woman whose own self has always been her only resource.

The daughter through all her trials feels the "loving-kindness" of God; the mother feels only the "earthly punishment I have brought upon myself." "The dark road I have trodden for so many years will end where it will," and Heaven never can forgive her (36: 450-2). Lady Dedlock, in "the clutch of Giant Despair" (12: 139), will end there, in the pit of Tom-all-Alone's, because she lacks all remembrance of God's grace or a daughter's "natural love" (and we should notice that Esther offers only her own love; in her humility she never urges God on anyone, thinking the charity ladies have quite taken into custody those urgings). Lady Dedlock has so long suppressed all "natural feelings of the heart" that she has become completely isolated. "I flee unto thee to hide me," the Psalmist wrote. To her husband, the fleeing woman writes: "I have no home left . . . May you . . . be able to forget the unworthy woman . . . who avoids you, only with a deeper shame than that with which she hurries from herself" (55: 667). Hurrying from her Dedlock world, she ends where Esther begins, identified as "nothing": lying in an "infernal gulf" dressed in a pauper's filthy rags.

Lady Dedlock's "sin," Dickens very carefully urges, has not been her love for Esther's father, but the smothering of "natural feelings" (55: 663), and thus of reality, in her pursuit of the Dedlock world of "Dandyism." The worship of surface, where putting a respectable "uniform and dreary gloss over the good and bad, the feeling and the unfeeling, the sensible and the senseless," is the constant work, has suffocated her; she has lost all "wonder" (12: 145; 55: 663). Thus, "in the only natural moments of her life" (36: 450), when she acknowledges her daughter and when she writes her husband the farewell, she refers to herself in the third person. The self of feeling is one she has rarely allowed expression. In becoming Lady Dedlock, she has killed that part of herself where feelings lie.

Her life-history has indeed been, as Teufelsdröckh said of Dandies, one of "Self-worship," or even "Demon-worship" (SR: 276).[23]

In Quarles' emblem for the Psalmist's verse on judgment, there is a dialogue between Jesus, Justice, and Sinner, the latter of whom says: "I quite renounce myself, the world, and flee/From Lord to Jesus"; when Christ intercedes, Sinner adds: "O Love beyond degree!/Th' offended dies to set th' offender free" (III: 10). Lady Dedlock flees, but only to death, not eternal life; there is none of the renunciation of self that is the substance of Esther's progress. As for most of those who go on living, their lives show how the emblematist's idea has been reversed: in this bleak world, the offenders live and prosper, those offended die or are stunted in the "labyrinth" (51: 612).

Esther does get free by facing, honestly and "naturally," the horrid reality about her, and by renouncing self in a way that Lady Dedlock cannot do. In each crisis – the smallpox, her sighting of her mother, their conversation – Esther remembers "the time past," the time of her guilt. Learning her mother's identity, however, precipitates the great meditation of her autobiography; and the result is her conversion – in the Romantic sense of that word. At first there is the "terror of myself," the terror that she will bring "disgrace" on her mother, and that Miss Barbary's prophecy that "the sins of others [would be] visited upon [her] head" is true. But then letters come from Ada and Jarndyce telling her that she is loved. In meditation she sees God's blessings on her life, his providential pattern at work:

That made me think of all my past life; and that brought me, as it ought to have done before, into a better condition. For, I saw very well that I could not have been intended to die, or I should never have lived . . . I saw very well how many things had worked together, for my welfare . . . I knew I was as innocent of my birth as a queen of hers; and that before my Heavenly Father I should not be punished for birth, nor a queen rewarded for it. (36: 454–5)

The pattern of felt grace is on this meditation. Esther discovers in the random happenings of her life a divinely ordained pattern; she sees the hand of God in her history and feels his grace abounding.

Yet Esther's knowledge of original innocence identifies her quest with the Romantics (even as her traditional religious sense prevents her from Jane Eyre's identification with nature; Esther, talking to her mother, is very conscious that their "troubled minds" quite contrast the peaceful beauty around them, a peaceful beauty which is never a thing in itself but a quality she ascribes to Providence). Her coming to awareness of the "visible things" of herself (in the emblematist's words), her knowledge of the relationship of past and present, frees her of the burden she has carried since birth. Her individuality, that which had set her apart as "different," is now exorcised once for all: by the smallpox superficially, but signally by that knowledge of innocence which exorcises the "shadow" over her life as no disfigurement could. When she goes with Bucket to save her mother, she thinks she sees, in the "infernal gulf," "the mother of the dead child" from the bricklayer's cottage. She sees of course Lady Dedlock – figuratively "the mother of the dead child" who vanished in Esther's rebirth. The "conversion" scene closes with: ". . . the darkness of the morning was passing away" (36: 455). Except for the close of *Little Dorrit*, there is nothing in Dickens to equal the rightness of this prose.

Esther's narrative does precisely what meditative prose tradition-ally did; it shows God operating in one's life, caring for his creature who is able to forget self and its desires. Esther's story must move to that happy Bleak House and end with her celebration of the goodness of God and the "world that sets this right" because she has witnessed a divine pattern working in her life and directing her steps. That final flower-encircled home may not satisfy us, it may seem a poor response to the issues the novel has raised. But in Esther's spiritual autobiography, it is right, earned by work, duty, selflessness, love.

Although Esther sees her life as a reflection of God's goodness, that discovery of innocence points the Romantic revision of traditional religion that Dickens intends us to read in her story (as does the "pleasant arbor" nature of her final home: it is very much of this earth; Esther is never Nell, moving towards death). In the community around her, "natural feeling" – not Dedlock formulas, Chancery justice, modern charity ("covering a multitude of sins"), Smallweed greed – does indeed generate "a true region of the Supernatural," a Carlylean society. Dickens has carefully used the traditional pattern of spiritual autobiography to lead readers to a sense of the "natural supernaturalism" possible "in this poor, miserable, hampered, despicable Actual" (SR: 196). Esther be-lieves in traditional religion, she *knows* God works in man's life; and she is justified by her faith. (The law, in *Bleak House* as in Bunyan, only entraps: "the just shall live by faith.") But to her belief in seeing everything *sub specie aeternitatis*, Dickens adds his sense that modern man can not know God except through the "natural feelings of the heart." To see one's original innocence is to free one's feelings and one's life for duty and love amongst one's fellows.

Dickens expresses his own inability to know as Esther knows through the voice of the impersonal narrator who constantly interrupts her narrative with visions of apocalypse to be visited on a whoring people. His words constitute a prophet's anathema. If the supernatural triumphs in Esther's vision, a natural demonism pervades the world this prophet gazes on (he is responsible for the description of that "infernal gulf" which draws all towards it). In his voice – cast in the language of the biblical doom-prophets and Apocalypse writers, and of Carlyle in *The French Revolution* and the *Pamphlets* – we hear anything but the vision of order that Esther records. We hear instead that "the appointed time" is at hand, that the sixth seal of Miss Flite's expectations is opened (Rev. 6: 12–17): "For the great day of wrath is come; and who shall be able to stand?" Who shall be able to defend the injustices and usuries and natural and human degradations of this deadlocked world? This narrator represents that perspective announced by the Prayer Book verse which introduces Lady Dedlock to Esther: "Enter not into judgment with thy servant, O Lord; for in thy sight shall no man living be justified." In this prophet's narrative, wellnigh none is. It is he who sees the offal of London, the varnishing Dandiacal Body at Chesney Wold, the Mammon-worshipping hideousness of the Smallweeds, the "vaporous Babylon" of chimneys in Rouncewell's "Iron Country"; he even qualifies Esther's sense of Chesney Wold's "peace" and "undisturbed repose" by perceiving it as stagnant and decaying.[24] Like Esther, he speaks from a remembrance of God's words. But unlike her (whom he rarely sees, and never "knows" as he does the Dedlocks and Bucket), he sees little of God's mercy and justice influencing human lives; he sees little remembrance of God amongst this crowd of demons – and he sees cause everywhere for God's vengeance.

The England of his narrative is in the "valley of the shadow of the law" (32: 391), in Job's "valley of the shadow of death," in the Psalmist's, and in Bunyan's (where is also the "mouth of Hell" – B: 190). The "stranger's wilderness of London" (48: 584) has only one clear if fouled path, towards the demon-peopled "infernal gulf" of Tom's. And along the wayside is victim after victim of the leave-it-alone Dandiacal "justice" of the Lord Chancellor and his legions. The people in the prophet's narrative who seek an inheritance, their own and others', do so with completely self-centered motives. And their "What shall I do?" is, unlike Esther's, a question of how to gain one's worldly goals – victual and pounds. As for "Who am I?" – who cares?

What gives this prophecy even more awfulness is Dickens' use of the present tense. As we have seen, Carlyle chose the present tense because it forced the reader, he said, to experience "the haggard element of Fear." A past tense put everything, no matter how terrible, in the "moonlight of Memory." Not in the past, Carlyle wrote, "does Fear dwell, nor Uncertainty, nor Anxiety; but it dwells *here*; haunting us, tracking us; running like an accursed ground-discord through all the music-tones of our Existence" (FR: IV: 81). Dickens casts his narrator's stance precisely as Carlyle did his in *The French Revolution* (which Dickens read, "for the 500th time," the summer before beginning *Bleak House*).[25] "Glancing reluctantly in" (FR: III: 113), each narrator charts the bits of chaos that come into his view and the apocalypse that threatens. The nervousness of the voice of Dickens' narrator almost undercuts the comfort of Esther's "progress," her sense of order to events, because it emphasizes all the more England's chaos. Esther, writing seven years after the facts of her history, knows her narrative's conclusion and sees its providential shape; she sees cause and effect in the chaotic events about her; she lives inside time. The doom-prophet moves outside of time and gazes like Blake's God down on the prison-house world. He sees nothing there of order, no sense of past and future, just the on-going world of chaotic action where spiritual progresses simply do not occur. That action he witnesses is horribly stagnant, an action where past, present, and future are terrifyingly alike: Lady Dedlock, "bored to death," is not far removed from Richard Carstone, "the portrait of Young Despair" (39: 484). These men and women are trapped in a cycle that denies completely any idea of spiritual progress (or, in the case of the Dedlocks, any progress at all).

Thus the prophet's voice in *Bleak House* can give us no progresses, no hint of ascensions (except in and out of Tom's itself). And only Esther *can* tell of Bucket's flight after Lady Dedlock, for there is pattern and progress in his movements, whereas the impersonal narrator sees only Bucket's disconnected actions. Vernon Lee, discussing Carlyle's present tense, noted that "it gives continuity not to the things he speaks about, but to what he says about them."[26] That is also the reason Dickens uses it. For the prophet in *Bleak House*, as for Carlyle in the history, there is no other continuity except in the unchanging indictment, evidence for which comes from all directions. No Romantic view of man or nature is possible in a world so bestial, where children are never children and the law never just, and the "still small voice" nothing more than Reverend Chadband's "light of Terewith" (25: 321). St Paul's cross is indeed, to the narrator as to Jo, the "crowning confusion of the great, confused city." No wonder his cry at Jo's death is so damning in its irony: "Dead, men and women, born with Heavenly compassion in your hearts" (47: 572). It is the great anathema of the novel. The Romantic belief in man's godborn nature, in man's essentially good heart, has been destroyed by proof of his bestial actions. "Tom has his revenge."

Bleak House's two movements synchronize chaos and order, a prophecy of doom and a vision of promise, Bunyan's definition of "natural" and the Romantics'. They juxtapose the apocalyptic vision of sacred scripture and the demonic wilderness world of secular romance. They allow Dickens to assert to an age in which the idea of God as knowable has become increasingly remote the survival of Romantic *feeling* – the "natural feelings of the heart" – in a world warped and stunted by injustice and selfishness masked as respectability. Esther Summerson and the narrator come together in their belief in a God governing all, a justice beyond man's. And Esther's vision of justice, incorporated into the prophet's curse – and indeed concluding it – gives to his present-tense vision of doom deserved a ringing declaration that the godborn may survive in this demonic world. Esther's narrative does not answer the prophet's indictment – what can, finally? – but it is a "still small voice" of "natural supernaturalism" surviving amidst a song of doom: "Enter not into judgment with thy servant, O Lord . . ."

III

By the time of *Our Mutual Friend*, any voice witnessing God's loving-kindness in the morning is almost certainly "playing dead," trying to escape all consciousness of the "birds of prey" and of the dunghills on which they feed. The landscape of *Our Mutual Friend* is demonic; like Bunyan's Enchanted Ground, it is a place "where the air naturally tend[s] to make one Drowzy," and where "Dirt and Slabbiness" suffuse everything and render any earnest effort at spiritual progress absurd (B: 386). The journeys that marked *Bleak*

House, *Little Dorrit*, and *Great Expectations* survive in this novel only in the horrible flight of Betty Higden away from the parish and its poor-house towards death. The bird emblem that Dickens used so often in the previous novels, and which in *Little Dorrit* became an emblem of nature perverted ("Bird, be quiet!"), here becomes, in "birds of prey," a "real" picture of cannibals eager to feed off anyone in *their* prison.

The narrative voice echoes this horror in its nervous switching between past and present tenses. The two voices of *Bleak House* come together in one narrator, and the result is a schizoid representation of hope coexisting with despair and damnation. The past tense of biblical romance and the present tense of fear exist together uneasily in this speaker; and his report ends, or rather stops, ominously in a present tense. The past tense appears when men and women not completely bestial, but with some human decency at least latent in them, are on the scene; it also appears when utterly depraved Cains are about their business. Thus the past tense offers the possibility of the order of romance, or else depicts its utter disorder: progress (or hope of it) towards something better, and regressions towards the demonic. The present tense always describes "Society," the members of which do not recognize either the demonic or the idyllic of romance (their mirrors show only their own surfaces, not a way towards salvation), but who instead think themselves living in a "Golden Age" in utter harmony with a Providence who always agrees with their wishes and supports their position. This present tense expresses at once the narrator's disgust and fear, and the everlasting circle of ennui which marks the days of these "respectable" satisfied cannibals in Vanity Fair whose idols are themselves. In the Podsnap world, where everything is done according to pattern – "always getting up at eight, shaving close at a quarter past, breakfasting at nine, going . . ., coming . . ., and dining at seven" – spiritual progresses or any forward movement is out of the question (the present participles in this famous passage dissipate all the energy the verbs contain). Mr Podsnap simply does not acknowledge it.

Our Mutual Friend is as much a *Latter-Day Pamphlet* as a novel, and it is, I think, the most Carlylean of Dickens' novels. Not because of its themes and ideas – they had been in the air for decades and were constants in the work of both men – but because these ideas and themes are rendered in the desperate configurations Carlyle had given them in the *Pamphlets*. The challenge hurled at

Benthamite radicalism in an Age of Machinery, the assertion that men must not be Cains though we all have the Cain-like within us, and the stress on the drugged state which seeking after Mammon and respectability induces are cast by Dickens in an undeniably Carlylean framework. And he illustrates them with a Carlylean cast of characters: the dilettante, the respectable mammonite, the varnisher, the logic-chopping soul-denying rationalist, the biped-of-prey, and the poor woman who cannot prove her sisterhood in a bargain-and-sale world. Yet the novel is not Carlylean without qualification. As far away from *Oliver Twist* and *The Old Curiosity Shop* – with their celebration of the heart's natural goodness – as the *Pamphlets* are from *Sartor Resartus* and Teufelsdröckh's temptation to name nature God, *Our Mutual Friend* yet lacks that Carlylean voice who knows a God will bring vengeance on those who pay no heed to their fellow men. It is Dickens' one novel which comes near Hardy's pessimism; its narrator sees utterly no hope that the "civilized" life of modern society can ever be much more than bestial.

In the Podsnap world – and it is the only coherent world of the novel – "Society" is the true region of the demonic, not much different from that "moral sewage" which resides in riverside slums except in its certainty that it knows "what the intentions of Providence are" (I: 11: 188). This demon-world is populated by Mammon-worshipping, self-worshipping "birds of prey" who wallow in filth and ooze, and feed on the living, the dying, the dead. (Rogue Riderhood even tries to collect money on his own "death.") The novel opens "emblematically" with the modern age's version of a fisher of men, Gaffer Hexam, hunting for dead bodies with coin on them (and asserting his world's "high moralities": the difference between "'Tother world" and "This world," he allows, is that money belongs to this one – I: 1: 47). Before many pages have passed, we are in the drawing-rooms of Society, whose occupants behave precisely as Hexam does: "div[ing] into the same waters," they have "prospered exceedingly" on the gossipy streams of death (in this case, the Harmon murder – I: 11: 180–1). The cannibalism, figurative and literal, defines these people's reality and underlines the incredible moral chaos of a world where Mammon-based respectability has so successfully cobbled together good and evil ("the rights and wrongs" of things, as Hexam would phrase it – I: 1: 47) that each looks precisely, charmingly, like the other.

"Soul, take thy ease, it is all *well* that thou art a vulture soul" – this prayer Carlyle fashioned for Mammon-worshippers and other "bipeds-of-prey" during "hours of mastication and rumination, which they call hours of meditation" (PP: 189, 221). In *Our Mutual Friend*, Podsnap and his crowd, in their prosperous self-sufficiency, have taken the prayer up in an absolutely choral fashion. For them soul *is* synonymous with stomach, and "Spiritual Union" the "Eating together" Teufelsdröckh feared (SR: 116–17).

So it came to pass that Mr and Mrs Podsnap requested the honour of the company of seventeen friends of their souls at dinner; and that they substituted other friends of their souls . . . (I: 11: 176)

These people refuse to consider man as anything more than "a human money-bag and meat-trough" (LDP: 258). The "great looking-glass" above Podsnap's sideboard reflects them precisely as they see each other: not as human (and certainly not as Christ-like), but as wearers of articles valued at so many pounds-sterling ("Mrs Veneering; never saw such velvet, say two thousand pounds as she stands, absolute jeweller's window" – I: 2: 52; 10: 165). As Teufelsdröckh feared, the individual has become a clothes-screen, or else "a mere Work-Machine, for whom the divine gift of Thought were no other than the terrestrial gift of Steam is to the Steam engine; a power whereby cotton might be spun, and money and money's worth realised" (SR: 259). Thus, if someone saves another's life, the question of remuneration is easily handled, according to the "Voice of Society" (here a Contractor, speaking of Lizzie Hexam):

These things are a question of beefsteaks and porter . . . Those beefsteaks and that porter are the fuel to that young person's engine. She derives therefrom a certain amount of power to row the boat; that power will produce so much money . . . (IV: Chapter the Last, 890)

Cash-nexus is indeed the sole relation – of machine to machine. This crowd may think its dinners "worthy of the Golden Age" (II: 16: 478), but the presence of so many scavengers and bone-articulators indicates the "long *Scavenger Age*" of Carlyle's *Pamphlets* (LDP: 329). Enchanted Ground indeed.

Essentially, the one real occupation of these people's lives is "working and rallying around . . . to keep up appearances" (II: 3: 301) and thus to keep reality from consciousness. In his "Hudson" pamphlet, where Carlyle looked at the "Scrip Age" and financiers and money idolatry, he asserted that the financial panics, like the continental revolutions of 1848, announced the "*Bankruptcy of Imposture*" to an age for which "external varnish is the chief duty of man" (LDP: 289). But "these times of ours" in the opening pages of *Our Mutual Friend* require no Mrs General to proscribe wonder and to instruct in the art of varnish. Her work of "emptying the reality out of life" (F. R. Leavis' description of her trade) is quite accomplished in Podsnap, and in the Veneerings it is proceeding apace.[27] These people come together for dinners because they must "work" to sustain their death-in-life; indeed, this collaboration is the only tie binding this drugged crowd together. Like Carlyle's John Bull, in Podsnap's "heavy" rooms they wander aimlessly "in an extinct world of wearisome, oppressive and expensive shadows" ("Hudson," 285); or else remain in that state of "suspended animation" (OMF: I: 11, 181, LDP: 157) Carlyle ascribed to people who deny reality with such determination. Outside the atmosphere cooperates. Over London there hangs an "air of death," and the fog and filthy air throw "animate London" into "blinking, wheezing, and choking" (OMF: II: 15: 450; III: 1: 479). Even the streets of the city seem drugged: "there was a deadly kind of repose on it, more as though it had taken laudanum than fallen into a natural rest" (II: 1: 271). We can hardly be surprised, then, that the Veneerings have bought control in a drug-house (I: 4: 76). They need a business guaranteed to allow them a way to find some soul's-ease.

In such a shadow-world, where life and death are so confused, there is none the less frantic activity to avoid Hell – or, rather, the latest version of Carlyle's English Hell ("the terror . . . of not making money, fame, or some other figure in the world" – PP: 148). These people are terrified of not appearing to have money and the respectability that attends it: "They all spoke of sums of money, and mentioned the sums and left the money to be understood" (II: 4: 313). But theirs is not the working Mammonism of the kind described in *Past and Present*. The present time, in *Our Mutual Friend* and in the *Pamphlets*, is the Scrip Age, with its "Scrip Church" and "Fathers" to expound its doctrines (III: 17: 690). And dashing after Scrip is, naturally, a way of not only avoiding Hell but also of securing another opiate:

O mighty Shares! To set those blaring images so high, and to cause us smaller vermin, as under the influence of henbane or opium, to cry out, night and day, "Relieve us of our money, scatter it for us, buy us and sell us, ruin us, only we beseech ye take rank among the powers of the earth, and fatten on us"! (I: 10: 160)

Cannibalism *in excelsis*. No wonder Carlyle found England's money-intoxication so immense that man's "poor life and all its manifold activities [had been] stunned into frenzy and comatose sleep" (LDP: 206). The respectable Veneerings and Podsnaps and Lammles are about the same business as Silas Wegg, Rogue Riderhood, Hexam and other "amphibious human creatures" by the water's edge: that of getting money and finding some victual in the process without working. Idle Mammonism is here in that "somnambulist state" Carlyle ascribed to Dilettantism. "Praying by Working"? (PP: 230). Well, yes: "Soul, take thy ease, it is all *well* that thou art a vulture-soul."

There are men and women living in this "Dismal Swamp" who are not vultures hungry for respectability and money, who share some of Teufelsdröckh's intuition that "Soul is *not* synonymous with Stomach" (SR: 159). In these people, in Rokesmith-Harmon and Bella Wilfer, in Mortimer Lightwood and Eugene Wrayburn, in Bradley Headstone and Lizzie Hexam, Dickens investigates once again the incredible efforts required of those who would preserve some inner reality in a society of respectable Cains; and he explores in Headstone the psychic damage done to those who are finally unwilling or unable to make the effort. And the horrible irony, which renders the efforts of these few almost absurd, is that their progresses, modelled palpably on Teufelsdröckh's, have utterly no relationship to anything that goes on in the world in which they are made. There is not Esther's relation – metaphorical and literal – to the Chancery suit, nor Clennam's connection to the Merdle world, nor Pip's to Jaggers' justice. The Harmon suit is significant to others only as gossip, not as describing any kind of moral disorder. The social emphasis of *Sartor* and of Dickens' other novels is absent in each *Bildungsroman* within *Our Mutual Friend*. Harmon and Bella Wilfer end in luxury quite unresponsive to the novel's moral atmosphere; Wrayburn becomes a successful pilgrim – and ends in greater isolation than before; Headstone, whose history alone relates to society's affairs in terms of the aspiration towards "respectability," ends a "Brute Beast," drowned. And the novel stops with "the social chorus" labelling as "savages" those who do achieve some health. The freedom that Teufelsdröckh or Clennam or Pip achieves is nowhere in evidence. Dickens does not allow us to feel "victory" in Wrayburn's final assertions of freedom. The "real" world is too oppressively against such "savages."

The pilgrimages in *Our Mutual Friend*, as in *Little Dorrit* and *Great Expectations*, are structured around Carlyle's sense of time as at once man's "seedfield" and prison. Whereas Teufelsdröckh had seen the present growing out of the past naturally, for those in

Dickens' world the present is utterly "trammeled with the Past" (SR: 47), which vampirishly hovers over it. People here are "victims" of their parents or financial benefactors who "pre-arrange" all from the hour of birth (the quoted words are Wrayburn's – I: 12: 193). Lightwood, like Wrayburn, feels his small income has been "an effective Something, in the way of preventing me from turning to at Anything" (IV: 16: 885). Old Twemlow, that rare Dickensian "gentleman" who has some worth, is a parasitic hanger-on to Lord Snigsworth, who has denied him the oppor-tunity, as if by fiat, "to do something, or be something, in life" (II: 16: 467). Lizzie Hexam, confronted by her brother's demand that she leave the riverside in order to obliterate the past, replies: "I can't get away from it . . . It's no purpose of mine that I live by it still"; it is impossible, she feels, not "to try to make some amends" for wrongs done by her father (II: 1: 278).

But the pressure of the past on the inner life is most fully illustrated in Harmon and Wrayburn. Harmon is "the living-dead man" who must ask himself if he should "come to life," so morally timid has he been rendered by his Mammon-worshipping father (II: 13: 430). Those dust mounds he inherits are for him and those about him a reminder of the "shadow" this money has cast over his life: they are the "burden" on his back for which he has no responsibility. Undergoing an emblematic drowning (in a novel where the river insistently yields only the dead, or else a "resur-rected" Riderhood), he is saved ("with Heaven's assistance") to ask the question, "Should John Harmon come to life?" (II: 13: 423). To remain dead, he thinks, is to do away with the curse of the past and to live amongst true friends. It is not until he is recognized by the Boffins, those who gave him love as a child, that the "shadow" of the past begins to lift. When he discovers a way to test Bella and free her from her money-lust, he finally feels free to become again John Harmon. Appropriately, Dickens has Harmon and Bella take up their new house "on the very day when the last waggon-load of the last Mound was driven out of the gates of Boffin's Bower" (IV: 14: 849).

But Harmon's recall to life and Bella's liberation from her belief that "poverty and wealth" are the only "realities" seem, in this death-in-life Golgotha, to come with very little sacrifice (II: 8: 376). Bella sees how morally ugly a "bargain and sale" world can be (I: 16: 244), *and* she has her original desires for wealth satisfied as well, along with the gift of a jewel casket. The victory is rather tawdry (and that jewel casket is vulgar); it is all too easily gained – not earned – and too isolated from that Enchanted Ground where bipeds-of-prey seek their food so diligently. The Harmons and their "doll's house" do not respond significantly to the bleak atmosphere signified by those dust mounds. We do not feel in their confrontation with demonic unreality the pressures Dickens made us experience in the cases of Clennam and Amy Dorrit. There is some welcome drollery (Lavinia Wilfer could issue a tidy volume of her satiric thrusts), but finally only day-dream romance. Dickens is determined to present some relief from the scum and ooze. But these goings-on diminish the significant achievement that marks the remainder of the novel.

The lives of Lizzie Hexam, Eugene Wrayburn, and Bradley Headstone are the stuff of sterner reality; as with the Dorrits and Louisa Gradgrind, we feel in these men and woman a significant exploration of the difficulty of keeping an inner life alive in a mechanical, deadened world. In Wrayburn and Headstone, Dickens explores two quite opposite and yet essentially similar men crippled by the unreality of life around them. By casting each as a conscious demon to the other, he underlines the similar stunting that results when either Dandyism or Mechanism, with their emphasis on the external, controls man's development. And by making the image of Rogue Riderhood, the novel's resident Cain, a *Doppelgänger* to each, Dickens indicates the bestiality that cannot be "civilized" into humanity unless some fellow-feeling redeems.

Eugene Wrayburn is, on the surface, a character straight out of Carlyle's description of the Dilettante who languishes his life away. Pungent, witty, idle, he satirizes all who work, even using the slogan of the Peterloo workers in one of his "ridiculous humours": "A fair day's wages for a fair day's work is ever my partner's motto" (I: 13: 213). Yet Dickens refuses to draw Wrayburn as he did Harthouse in *Hard Times*, as the "One monster . . . in the world" Carlyle proclaimed the idle man to be (PP: 203). Wrayburn is not one of the Lammles or Veneerings or Fledgebys. He and Lightwood attend Society's cookery affairs with disdainful "weariness," despising their "unlimited monotony," but lacking anything else to animate them and needing some opiate. Like Lady Dedlock, they feel their ennui.

Wrayburn's conscious weariness is the first sign of life beneath that dull surface. The second is his refusal to participate in his father's marriage arrangements for him, a "No" which marks his resistance to the "bargain and sale" bazaar of this Vanity Fair world. The final and telling proof that he is more than a mere clothes-screen is his reaction to Lizzie Hexam, whom he glimpses amidst the slime and ooze of the river bank. It marks the turning point of his life; the chance to break into freedom is offered him, the chance to become "earnest" (the word is used again and again) about something. Meeting Lizzie at once gives Wrayburn the opportunity "to be of some use to somebody" (II: 2: 286) and forces him, in Carlyle's words, to look into his "inner man, and see if there be any traces of a *soul* there" (PP: 31). Lizzie understands his needs and recognizes that his failings "have grown up through his being like one cast away, for want of something to trust in, and care for, and think well of" (II: 11: 405).

The process of Wrayburn's discovery of his better self brings him face to face with death and its agent Bradley Headstone. Their scenes comprise Dickens' most subtle attack on the profit-and-loss mechanists who denied value to feeling, to any dynamic element within the human personality. Both Wrayburn and Headstone, as John Lucas has remarked, have identities "which are fixed for them by the social process" and which thus imprison them.[28] The one sees himself as a born idler, the other works earnestly to become a "respectable" man of the middle class. Wrayburn's easy self-possession is a telling psychic contrast to Headstone's "stiffness," and makes the schoolmaster feel that his respectability is merely an acquired veneer, put on like those "decent" clothes which never seem completely adapted to him. Yet Headstone would have been vastly superior to the idle man had he, a pauper's child, not been the product of a Benthamite education; or had he, like Teufelsdröckh, had influences that negated the disastrous effects of such an education. His learning, his musicianship, all of those talents he has so assiduously cultivated, have been acquired "mechanically," and each is performed "mechanically": "From his early childhood up, his mind had been a place of mechanical stowage," and nothing else (II: 1: 266). Like the "mechanically taught" Teufelsdröckh, Headstone loses all possibility of vision, all power of "wonder" which Carlyle had proclaimed "indestructible in Man" (SR: 67). By 1864, however, Dickens finds wonder quite easily destructible in man, indeed perhaps not even possible. Headstone's history charts the process of its destruction.

His education has completely obliterated any sense of the naturalness of human feelings. "I don't show what I feel; some of us are obliged habitually to keep it down. To keep it down" (II: 11: 400). The quietest utterance he makes in the novel comes after Charley Hexam has described Lizzie's "education" (and Charley's disapproving "too much" should not be overlooked):

"Lizzie has as much thought as the best, Mr Headstone. Too much, perhaps, without teaching. I used to call the fire at home, her books, for she was always full of fancies . . . when she sat looking at it."
"I don't like that," said Bradley Headstone. (II: 1: 281)

"I don't like that": the scene is one more forceful dramatization of the suffocating effect the Benthamite-mechanical ideas had on English life. "Undue cultivation of the outward," Carlyle asserted, though "for the time productive of many palpable benefits, must, in the long run, . . . [destroy] Moral Force" (C: XXVII: 73).[29] The benefits of Headstone's education, of rising to a "respectable" position as schoolteacher, finally come to nothing. Wonder, "living Thought," has been a will-o'-the-wisp to him. And because it has, the "truly vital" in him has been suppressed and perverted, and with that gone nothing is left but the satanic demon-empire: "what was animal and . . . what was fiery (though smouldering)" can no longer be imprisoned beneath that veneer of educated respectability (OMF: II: 1: 267).

The light and animal images that Dickens uses to portray the eruption of Headstone's nether self after Lizzie rejects him (he has been attracted to her in spite of all "reason") are identical to those Carlyle uses to show Teufelsdröckh's aimless wandering before the godborn in his nature asserts control and frees him for creative work and for love of his fellows. In *Sartor* Carlyle had written that there lies in everyone "a whole world of internal Madness, an authentic Demon-Empire." Before Teufelsdröckh emerges from the Everlasting No, the balance seems tipped towards that demon-empire. With "a hot fever of anarchy and misery raging within," he walks "in the temper of ancient Cain," and finds the universe "one huge, dead, immeasurable Steam-engine" (SR: 156–64). Similarly, Headstone, "tied up all day with his disciplined show upon him, subdued to the performance of his routine of educational tricks, . . . broke loose at night like an ill-tamed wild animal" (OMF: III: 11: 609). Following Wrayburn in order to glimpse him with Lizzie, he becomes a seething Cain indeed. During these murderous wanderings, he meets Riderhood, that stalking animal who resembles him and whose clothes he will copy. Riderhood is, of course, Headstone's *Doppelgänger*, the concrete embodiment of the demonic energy so suppressed and perverted by his mechanical education. The preying-animal images associated with Riderhood transfer to Headstone; "the passion-wasted nightbird with respectable feathers" becomes "the worst nightbird of all" (III: 11: 618). Then, with the sun down and "the landscape . . . dyed red," Headstone appears at the Plashwater Weir Mill wearing clothes like Riderhood's, and strikes Wrayburn (IV: 1: 701).

This wilderness attack comes at the very moment of Wrayburn's "inquiry into his own nature," an inquiry pitting that part of him which believes in Lizzie, in "her beauty and her worth," against the "Brute Beast" in him which would seduce her. It is a Teufelsdröckhean "Temptation in the Wilderness." The meeting of these two men is essentially Wrayburn's confrontation with his own Cain-like selfishness (imaged perfectly in the Riderhood clothes that Headstone wears). "I am wearily out of sorts with one Wrayburn who cuts a sorry figure," Wrayburn says. And when the battle with his "Brute Beast" is at its most intense, he is struck by Headstone:

In an instant, with a dreadful crash, the reflected night turned crooked, flames shot jaggedly across the air, and the moon and stars came bursting from the sky. Was he struck by lightning? (IV: 6: 766–7)

The imagery parallels remarkably Carlyle's description of Teufelsdröckh's internal battle. Dickens uses elements of that Wanderer's helpless despair to suggest Headstone's nature, and elements of his fire-baptism to suggest Wrayburn's rebirth into freedom.

"And as I so thought, there rushed like a stream of fire over my whole soul . . . The Everlasting No had said: 'Behold, thou art fatherless, outcast, and the Universe is mine (the Devil's)'; to which my whole Me now made answer: '*I* am not thine, but Free, and forever hate thee!' It is from this hour that I incline to date my Spiritual Newbirth . . .; perhaps I directly thereupon began to be a Man." (SR: 167–8)

Teufelsdröckh's wilderness experience brings him an awakening "to a new Heaven and a new Earth," to a sure knowledge that the "Universe is not . . . a charnel house with spectres, but godlike" (SR: 186–8).

These same ideas and images, albeit without the sound of triumph – and with the "godlike" omitted – accompany Wrayburn and Headstone after their encounter. The would-be murderer finds that the "earth looked spectral" (OMF: IV: 7: 770). Wrayburn requests some "fancy" of nature: "Ask [Jenny Wren] if she has smelt the flowers" (IV: 10: 806). But that the image to which Wrayburn awakes is one of imagined flowers and singing birds rather than the real thing (Esther is surrounded by these pastoral elements, Amy Dorrit brings flowers to Clennam in the Marshalsea) suggests how singular and tenuous is his, or anyone's, hold on his humanness in this charnel-house world. Fancies of nature, and of the supernatural, are as close as one comes to the "godlike."[30]

For Headstone the spectral earth is the landscape for his descent into the devil's-dung of an Everlasting No. The chapter following the murder attempt, "Better to be Abel than Cain," underlines his isolation. Headstone may discard the Riderhood clothes for his own "decent" ones, but he cannot elude "the pursuing shadow" of his deed. His existence has become terrifying, and will be more so when Hexam turns on him for selfishness. "A desolate air of utter and complete loneliness fell upon him, like a visible shade . . . he dropped his devoted head when the boy was gone, and shrank together on the floor, and grovelled there, with the palms of his hands tight-clasping his hot temples, in unutterable misery, and unrelieved by a single tear" (IV: 7: 779; 781–2). He is an outcast indeed (though who is the Abel in this scene with Hexam is by no means clear). Headstone's spiritual deadness has made of his life an anti-progress, shadowed by demons he will never elude. Carefully trying to avoid society's snares and become its celebrated "respectable" man, he has ignored completely the snares within (indeed, he thinks them obliterated by his education) – and those snares trap him.

Headstone's death is thus inevitable. Cut off from the one man for whom he can feel an emotional attachment, the animal nature he has stifled bursts out, and he destroys it when he kills Riderhood. Their encounter in his classroom, with the Rogue giving the teacher a lesson (and wiping his name off the blackboard), is grimly comic, a blunt illustration of the horrors that result when natural feeling is totally suppressed.[31] Bradley Headstone, as his surname suggests, pays the price of denying what is dynamic in the self, of perverting moral force to a calculation. It is inevitable that his end be Riderhood's, "lying under the ooze and scum" (IV: 15: 875) amidst the dunghills of Self.

There are "real" pilgrims in this society (and also images of them on the wall of the Veneering study – for meditation!). But spiritual journeys here are isolated – because so isolating. Wrayburn's progress has all the personal elements of Teufelsdröckh's journey, but none of the larger implications. His victory and marriage to Lizzie are not at all comparable to Amy Dorrit and Arthur Clennam's story. Wrayburn and Lizzie may visit the Harmons, they may all find "playing dead" no longer preferable, or needed, as an escape from society's horrors. And their marriages may suggest the continuance, somewhere on this "continent of fetid ooze," of all that is the antithesis of Podsnapian self-interest. But no more.[32] Before the novel's close, Lizzie and Wrayburn and the Harmons vanish from our attention, their "ridiculous affair" reduced to gossip as all other matters of life and death are – and should be, according to the ways of Podsnap's Providence.

In the last chapter, Lightwood has a conversation with Lady Tippins about Lizzie and her friends which indicates how topsy-turvy this world is, and how hopeless is any spiritual renewal:

"Long banished Robinson Crusoe," says the charmer, exchanging salutations, "how did you leave the Island?"
"Thank you," says Lightwood. "It made no complaint of being in pain anywhere."
"Say, how did you leave the savages?" asks Lady Tippins.
"They were becoming civilized when I left Juan Fernandez," says Lightwood. "At least they were eating one another, which looked like it." (IV: Chapter the Last, 888)

"Savages," "civilized," "eating one another": the words resonate through every part of the novel. To civilize savages is, *in partibus infidelium*, to teach them to prey on their fellow human beings. We remember that Charley Hexam is first described as "a curious mixture . . . of uncompleted savagery, and uncompleted civilization" (I: 3: 60). His education, his ascension into respectability, certainly and completely civilizes him, and in the way the Podsnap world defines the world. As for Lizzie and Wrayburn and genuine feeling, "such a ridiculous affair is condemned by the voice of Society" (P. 888). Its way is cannibalism or leave-it-alone. The Podsnap crowd needs the Veneering drug-house desperately in order to preserve their Lethean sleep, quite as Charley needs his political economy. Anything to keep reality out of mind.

"Surely, surely," Carlyle wrote at the end of *Latter-Day Pamphlets*, "this ignoble sluggishness, sceptical torpor, indifference to all that does not bear on Mammon and his interests is not the natural state of human creatures; and is not doomed to be their final one!" (LDP: 335). His own presentation in the eight *Pamphlets* and Dickens' in *Our Mutual Friend* suggest that their "civilized" state is the final "natural state" of Englishmen, precisely as Bunyan would have described it. In this last novel Dickens has even dropped his insistence that man recognize his interdependence with all men. And significantly, he gives no rounding-off to his story, no tying together of plot strands as he had in *Little Dorrit* and the other novels. Instead, *Our Mutual Friend* closes in the present tense, with Podsnap and his hangers-on babbling away. It is a tableau from Bunyan's Enchanted Ground, or from Carlyle's Apes by the Dead Sea in his last *Pamphlet*. Those Apes are, as he prophesied in *Past and Present*, "the enchanted Dilettanti," "with heads full of extraneous noises, with eyes wide-open but visionless, – for the most part, in the somnambulist state!" (PP: 170, 175). "Our poor friends 'the Apes by the Dead Sea' have now no Heaven either; they look into this Universe now, and find it tragically grown to *be* the Humbug they had insisted on its being" (LDP: 334).

Only Twemlow, weak parasite though he is, challenges Society on a "point of great delicacy": he insists that any man can be a gentleman, for the quality of feeling is what tells. In *Our Mutual Friend* his is a significantly life-affirming statement. But hardly a prophecy of the "Golden Age." Dickens' novels until this last one had been structured on an apocalyptic pattern – triumphantly in the early years, hesitantly later, but always concluding with a wedding or some "light." *Our Mutual Friend* stops amongst "civilized" savages because the society the narrator observes reveals anything but the "natural supernaturalism" witnessed earlier. Twemlow may affirm an "aristocracy of Nature" against the bestial "natural" about him. (Carlyle was to do this two years later, in "Shooting Niagara.") But Dickens, ending his novel in the present tense, sees no prophecy in Twemlow. He sees, as the present tense tells us, no pattern to the experiences observed, no "progress," no shared spiritual aspirations. Simply the "revolving funeral" (I: 11: 185) of Society's drawing-rooms. And he is afraid.[33]

Thus he must refuse the last scene to the Harmons and to Lizzie and Wrayburn. The impulse that had caused a rewriting of the ending of *Great Expectations* – and given the readers at least the "shadow" of romance – no longer works for him. Nature – human and natural – is infected in "these times of ours," and the infection halts all ideals of man's interdependence, all notions that any true "region of the Supernatural" is possible. There is no longer any Ideal in the Actual, no Romance – except of the demonic sort – amidst the Podsnap reality: "such a ridiculous affair is condemned by the voice of Society." With one narrator trying to give us both romance and reality, Dickens cannot assert Esther Summerson's sacred romance with any strength. There is nothing here to energize that kind of romance, to make it work towards a validation of "natural supernaturalism" that the histories of Esther and Clennam and Amy Dorrit affirm. Esther's memoir may not respond profoundly to the social issues raised by the doom-saying prophet's anathemas. But the two operate together, metaphorically and spiritually, in their assertion of one final arbitrating Justice having nothing to do with Chancery's Legalities.

Our Mutual Friend lacks both this metaphorical and spiritual coherence. The only shared experience is that of living on the same dunghill, more or less. The novel can assert none of *Bleak House*'s – or Carlyle's – belief that all is finally *sub specie aeternitatis*. Without that frame of reference, no natural supernaturalism is possible, except in dreams and plays. The novel is, then, emblematic of Dickens' closing meditation, after Carlyle, on the Condition of England. It shows honestly, terrifyingly, profoundly, the breakdown of those patterns which Victorians had used so determinedly to make sense of otherwise chaotic experience, the patterns of biblical romance. Dickens' last completed novel is a "vision" of a brave new world of nightmarish, drugged "life." Sacred Romance and its implications are simply obliterated by the demonic, in all its real and respectable clothes: "and I have mentioned," says Mr Podsnap, "what the intentions of Providence are."

"Your homes the scene, yourselves the actors, here!" This epigraph which Dickens wanted to place on the titlepage of *Martin Chuzzlewit* has its fundamental origins in the tradition that shapes his fiction, in Bunyan's "This book will make a traveller of thee," and in the popular emblem books which evangelicals used so often:

> Peruse this little Book, and thou wilt see
> What thy heart is, and what it ought to be.

This is the introductory epigraph to *Scola Cordis*: The School of the Heart. No phrase better describes Dickens' intention, and the emblem book's subtitle aptly defines it: "The Heart of it Selfe, gone away from God; brought back again to him; and instructed by him in 47 Emblems." Dickens would instruct his readers in the "natural feelings of the heart," he would make them see the horrors of a "hollow empty heart"; he would show natural feeling surviving amidst every kind of stunting selfishness possible, and even reviving when it seemed quite extinguished. And to make his instruction tell, he used the emblematic landscapes that were the stock-in-trade of the popular religious literary tradition. That tradition of mixing "literalness and symbolism" Dickens knew from Bunyan, Hogarth, the moral illustrators – and, much later, from Carlyle as well.[34] And he could trust his readers to follow him, even as he re-educated them (thus his Preface appeals to them over the critics); they were used to meeting types and typical landscapes.

His contemporary critics found his work anything but religious. "Not a scrap of religion in it," the Anglican *Christian Remembrancer* huffed of *The Chimes* (while also calling Carlyle in for his share of the blame):

nothing more than morals: the realm of fact, not of grace; the kingdom of the individual will, not of the Spirit and strength of God . . . He wants, because he knows the soul wants, unseen influences and mysterious powers, and he embodies a mixed mockery of German diablerie, and fairies, and Socinianism, because, even while he was not called upon to picture it, he has never realized the Catholic doctrine of the angels; and it is quite wonderful, though significant, how this machinery – to speak according to the card – would have helped him.[35]

The Catholic *Rambler* agreed. Citing, in 1854, the "utterly Pagan and shocking" treatment of Lady Dedlock (she had no conscience!), it moaned that "Dickens is a man to whom the supernatural world is not"; he is "stone-blind to the existence of any thing which eye cannot see, and to an hereafter whose woe or joy is dependent on man's conduct here." Eight years later, the same journal announced the sources of Dickens' "natural religion." Dickens is like "certain Germans of the last century," the reviewer noted; "they made humanity their God, and so made religion simply human, and taught that man was perfectible, but childhood perfect."[36]

And of course there is truth in these reactions. From a traditional theological point of view, Dickens is a very long way from the Christian perspective. Indeed, his good "Christian" often comes speaking the language of Ignorance's "confession of faith" in *Pilgrim's Progress*:

Christian: . . . The Word of God saith of persons in a natural condition, . . . every imagination of the heart of man is only evil, and that continually.
Ignorance: I will never believe that my heart is thus bad. (B: 257)

Ignorance protests Christian's absolute adherence to the Word. For Dickens the revealed Word is no longer potent in the lives of men and women, and thus it becomes all the more necessary to believe in "natural" goodness which survives in the hearts of individual men. In an age where certainty of God's active presence in human life is anything but sure, Ignorance's "faith" offers the only godlike knowable, a natural supernaturalism.

The Romantics' redefinition of nature also contributes to Dickens' presentation of his "Christian." They had given the idea of the good "natural heart" currency by uniting it to the image of the child; the Victorians heard from Wordsworth that children were "quite innocent" no matter what a "distorted religion" taught (Jarndyce's words, BH: 17: 213). But Dickens sees clearly that too much emphasis on the child or on nature can become one more way of escaping or perverting reality – witness Skimpole and Mrs Merdle. And in the Enchanted Ground of Victorian England his quintessential child becomes not Oliver Twist or Nell, but *Little Dorrit*'s Maggie, "naturally" retarded and thus "blessed" to be innocent forever of the varnishing society around her.

Dickens has, then, only one image of the godlike – simply, the good heart. Arthur Clennam, confronted by a world whose "confession of faith" is "We must have humbug" (II: 28: 718), finds in Amy Dorrit's voice "all that great Nature was doing, hear[s] in it all the soothing songs she sings to man," hears in it all that he has never experienced, except in his imagination:

At no Mother's knee but [Nature's], had he ever dwelt in his youth on hopeful promises, on playful fancies, on the harvests of tenderness and humility that lie hidden in the early fostered seeds of the imagination . . . But, in the tones of the voice that read to him, there were memories of an old feeling of such things, and echoes of every merciful and loving whisper that had ever stolen to him in life. (II:34:791)

These "memories" are not Bunyan's, even if both Christian and Clennam share faith in things unseen. Even less are they Lizzie Hexam's "fancies" that bring her relief from the dunghill. Bunyan's Christian calls such imaginations "a fantastical Faith, for this faith is nowhere described in the Word." But for Dickens, such "fancies" which an idea(l) of a goodness entirely human inspires in man's imagination are all that can animate the spirit in a bestial world.

He said that art was "but a little imitation" of "the ways of

Providence."[37] And he uses the demons and angels (the "German diablerie") that Bunyan and the emblem writers and Blake and Carlyle had used to chart those ways. He never locates the "unreal" only in the subterranean levels of his fiction, as Brontë does in *Villette* and George Eliot in many of her novels. If people dream, he gives us demons and fairies; if the soul is diseased, he perceives a dunghill; if man is a spiritual outcast, he sees a prison; if conversion is near, he pictures waters or fires of purgation and cleansing. But his "confession of faith" in a varnishing world must take the form of Florence Dombey's hand, or Amy Dorrit's voice; it must be represented by quiet work and human relationship. His statement is Daniel Doyce's: "You hold your life on the condition that to the last you shall struggle hard for it" (LD: I: 16: 185). Beyond that "last," we know not.

Imagination "had all the terrors of reality," Dickens wrote in *The Old Curiosity Shop* (31: 303). But when reality itself becomes a "revolving funeral," and yesterday, today, and tomorrow form one "inexorable all-encircling ocean-moan of ennui" and bestiality (LDP: 337), imagination of the human heart's "natural goodness," far away from a terrible "reality," is finally all that survives of the godlike. For Dickens, Ignorance's condition is now Christian's.

> Behold, we know not anything;
>   I can but trust that good shall fall
>   At last – far off – at last, to all,
> And every winter change to spring.
> So runs my dream; but what am I?
>   An infant crying in the night;
>   An infant crying for the light,
> And with no language but a cry.

4

Speaking through parable:
George Eliot

In the old days there were angels who came and took men by the hand and led them away from the city of destruction. We see no white-winged angels now. But yet men are led from threatening destruction: a hand is put into theirs, which leads them forth gently towards a calm and bright land, so that they look no more backward; and the hand may be a little child's.

(*Silas Marner*: 14: 190–1)

No passage in Victorian fiction better illustrates the coming together of the biblical and Romantic traditions than this from *Silas Marner*. George Eliot's "sort of legendary tale" (GEL: III: 382) is a Wordsworthian *Pilgrim's Progress*, beginning with a lone individual carrying some "mysterious burden" on his back and closing with that burden gone and the man firmly rooted in a new community of fellow-feeling because of the coming of the golden-haired child. With its image of a journey towards some "bright land," this novel is characteristic of all of George Eliot's fiction. Whether her subjects be the Church people and Methodists of the century's beginning or the very modern men and women surveying a Gwendolen Harleth who has never registered "religious nomenclature" (DD: 8: 95) as part of her inner life, George Eliot needs for adequately exploring her themes the structures that Bunyan and Wordsworth used.

Yet throughout her career George Eliot worries that she will be too schematic in her "teaching," too much a Bunyan. To Frederic Harrison she wrote in 1866 that as a "writer of novels" – "books which the dullest and silliest reader thinks himself competent to deliver an opinion on" – she had always to try to make her ideas "thoroughly incarnate, as if they had revealed themselves to me first in the flesh and not in the spirit."

I think aesthetic teaching is the highest of all teaching because it deals with life in its highest complexity. But if it ceases to be purely aesthetic – if it lapses anywhere from the picture to the diagram – it becomes the most offensive of all teaching. Avowed Utopias are not offensive, because they are understood to have a scientific and expository character: they do not pretend to work on the emotions, or couldn't do it if they did pretend . . . Well, then, consider the sort of agonizing labour to an English-fed imagination to make art a sufficiently real back-ground, for the desired picture, to get breathing, individual forms, and group them in the needful relations, so that the presentation will lay hold on the emotions as human experience.   (GEL: IV: 300–1)

Teaching is her emphasis, as it was for Bunyan and the later religious writers (whom she read during her intensely evangelical early years). And George Eliot constantly searches for the modes of using language which will allow her "to urge the human sanctities" (GEL, ibid.). She wants no diagrams, yet she insists that characters and incident be "typical" in order to "secure one's lasting sympathy" (GEL: II: 86); and she grows more and more attracted to the opera – "a great, great product" (GEL: IV: 92) – and its ways of rendering the emblematic (this interest we see fully used in *Daniel Deronda*).

Her fictions chart her continuing efforts to find a means of taking the novel beyond the level of mere entertainment. In *Adam Bede* and *The Mill on the Floss* she presents "George Eliot" as one who lives amongst the people he observes. Then she becomes in *Silas Marner* a story-teller and writes a romance which openly brings together the traditions of Wordsworth and Bunyan, in all their typicality. From this tale she moves into history, and into the role of historian and poet who, like Herodotus or Virgil, sees the relation of the fictive and the real. Finally, in *Daniel Deronda* she creates again the same "vision" she had offered in the overtly fabular *Silas Marner*. Far more sophisticated in its techniques and ideas, the deep structure of *Deronda* is nevertheless the same as that of the fable; George Eliot is a sacred romancer. Each of her novels, indeed, consolidates the ideas and methods used in the work which has preceded it. But in the consonance of vision which they all share, they underline George Eliot's determination to show her readers the "right road" towards natural supernaturalism.

Late in her career, shortly after *Daniel Deronda* had appeared, George Eliot insisted that "the principles" which went into creating Mordecai were the same as those governing Dinah Morris in *Adam Bede* (GEL: VI: 318). Yet her novels also belonged, as she said in 1861, to "successive mental phases" (GEL: III: 383) because they examined those same "principles" under different lights and from different angles. All were "experiments in life."

But my writing is simply a set of experiments in life – an endeavour to see what our thought and emotion may be capable of – what stores of motive, actual or hinted as possible, give promise of a better after which we may strive – what gains from past revelations and discipline we must strive to keep hold of as something more sure than shifting theory. I become more and more timid – with less daring to adopt any formula which does not get itself clothed for me in some human figure and individual experience, and perhaps that is a sign that if I help others to see at all it must be through that medium of art.   (GEL: VI: 216–17)

"What gains from past revelations and discipline" we need, and the sense of becoming "more and more timid" – the phrases offer a key to her evolving fictions and to her turn in the end towards the Jews with (as Mordecai defines it) their "divine principle" of "action, choice, resolved memory" (DD: 42: 598). Each of George Eliot's novels is a spiritual biography or *Bildungsroman* focusing on Bunyan's question "What shall I do?" and charting the "civil war within the soul" (Mid: 67, epigraph) as answers are sought. From George Eliot's narrative perspective each novel is also a new station in her meditation on English life over a period of seventy years, and thus on a world in such flux that anything "sure" is rarely discernible. She wrote in 1862 that she required "freedom to write out one's own varying unfolding self" (GEL: IV: 49). Barbara Hardy has noted her "process of rewriting one novel in the next."[1] Each novel, as it focuses on the myths, fictions, histories – on the art – that human beings require to live, is a meditation intended to make its readers share the process of *seeing* that foundation in memory of action and choice. This chapter is an examination of those themes, situations, and narrative devices that constitute George Eliot's meditation on nineteenth-century English life.

I

"In the old days": the phrase from *Silas Marner* calls attention to the setting of all of George Eliot's English novels except the last. Each looks back to a time before any reader had been "to Exeter Hall, or heard a popular preacher, or read *Tracts for the Times* or *Sartor Resartus*" (AB: 52: 429); each recalls a time of "history" set in "what we are pleased to call Merry England" (SM: 1: 53). Yet the voice which places and focuses our attention always speaks out of an intense awareness of *Sartor* and of Darwin, and with a sense that "Merry England" is part of the religious *myth* that we – readers and author – need to confront the modern world. Like Carlyle's, the voice is constantly concerned to discover the filaments uniting past and present and tying them together in a community's life and in an individual's. Five years before *Silas Marner*, in her review of W. H. von Riehl's *Natural History of German Life* (*Westminster*, July 1856), George Eliot had stated her sense of developing English society. The ideas in this essay govern her representation of the cultural scene in all of her work:

Language must be left to grow in precision, completeness, and unity, as minds grow in clearness, comprehensiveness, and sympathy. And there is an analogous relation between the moral tendencies of men and the social conditions they have inherited. The nature of European men has its roots intertwined with the past, and can only be developed by allowing those roots to remain undisturbed while the process of development is going on, until that perfect ripeness of the seed which carries with it a life independent of the root. This vital connexion with the past is much more vividly felt on the Continent than in England, where we have to recal it by an effort of memory and reflection; for though our English life is in its core intensely traditional, Protestantism and commerce have modernized the face of the land and the aspects of society in a far greater degree than in any continental country.[2]

George Eliot urges, as Carlyle had in *Heroes and Hero-Worship* and in *Past and Present*, that English society strive to be what von Riehl saw European society to be, *"incarnate history"*; "any attempt to disengage [society] from its historical elements," she warns, "must be simply destructive of social vitality."[3]

George Eliot wants her fictions to incarnate history imaginatively and concretely, to show – as the phrase itself suggests – the transformation of the natural through the workings of the super-natural. Her novels present, in fact, the most incisive "natural history of English life" available. The metaphors of seeds and roots from this early essay resonate throughout her career (*Deronda*'s last book is called "Fruit and Seed"). Indeed, in her early novels she wellnigh insists that the way to the Celestial City is through the country (if not up the Delectable Mountains). But that "natural history" she writes is more a portrayal of dissociation and dislocation than any depiction of the "vital connexion" of past and present that she believes in. Her writing shows us the increasing severance of an individual from his heritage and of a community from its past. George Eliot cannot find, in a *real* English setting, a "Merry England" which will allow her questing protagonists to relate the community's evolving life to their spiritual needs, or to realize the place of the supernatural within the natural processes of their own lives or in the natural world itself. Dislocations, uprootings kill all possibility for incarnating history – except in a very individual and private sense. Only the fairy-tale structure of *Silas Marner* allows her to present a "history" where any "fruit," any resolution, occurs – and that tale begins with a slashing of past and present which is never reconciled.

George Eliot's first novel tries to deal with a community where dislocations look impossible. *Adam Bede* offers us in Hayslope a "Merry England" where there is "no rigid demarcation" (9: 84) between classes or sects within the community. But central to this novel is the problem of discovering roots which while natural are not merely natural. The two women protagonists embody at once two sides of the dilemma and underline George Eliot's inability to resolve it within the world of the novel. Hetty Sorrel's frightening inability to conceptualize beyond the narrow range of her egoism suggests the terrible limits of a nature which is merely natural. "There are," George Eliot says of Hetty, "some plants that have hardly any roots" (15: 132); and the sorrel plant is associated with bitterness and acidity. Hetty has utterly no sense of community, relationship, or God; she sees nothing beyond her image in a mirror.

But Hetty's opposite in this novel, Dinah Morris, is for George Eliot equally limited in her sense of having only heavenly roots rather than those firmly tied to the earth. Dinah's Methodism and her insistence on seeing a community as irrevocably divided between "the children of light" and "the children of this world" (10: 97) clearly bind her to the Bunyan tradition (and *Pilgrim's Progress* begins with a denial of earthly spiritual community). She calls the Hayslope area the "land of Goshen" (3: 32), comparing its life to Israel's contented home in Egypt before the Exodus became a necessity.[4] And she renders a Bunyanesque judgment on the "comfortable" world Mrs Poyser happily attributes to communion in the Established Church: "I've noticed, that in these villages where the people lead a quiet life among the green pastures and still waters . . . there's a strange deadness to the Word," Dinah tells the Reverend Irwine (8: 80). George Eliot does not endorse the judgment, finding instead that those "select natures who pant after the ideal . . . are curiously in unison with the narrowest and pettiest" (17: 157).

She also develops a contrast between Dinah's Methodist ministry and that of the Established Church's Reverend Irwine to show the unnatural severing of past and present which sectarianism – and later commercialism – will inflict upon English life. Christopher Herbert, examining the "Schemes of Nature" in *Adam Bede*, has argued that Eliot in her two preachers is juxtaposing two "differing interpretations of the idea of Nature."

Dinah's Methodism rests ultimately on the doctrine that Nature in all its aspects is corrupt, by virtue of Adam's sin; for her the goal of religious faith is to renounce and to overcome, therefore, whatever is natural (starting with all human instincts) . . . In contrast to this otherworldliness Mr. Irwine stands principally for a grateful acceptance of Nature, including human nature with all its imperfections.

The contrast is, essentially, between the Calvinistic and the Wordsworthian ideas about the natural world.[5] And what we notice most strikingly in this novel is the destructive consequences for English society of the split between these two traditions; religion itself threatens to become a dividing force. The awful case of Hetty sufficiently refutes the Wordsworthian idea of the beneficence of nature without human connection and concern (and we might remember that Hetty's journey has striking affinities with Wordsworth's "The Thorn"); and the miserable death of her child undermines Mrs Poyser's pious notion that "there's One above 'ull take care o' the innicent child, else it's but little truth they tell us at church" (40: 348).

But while George Eliot can, in *Adam Bede*, adequately diagram the problem, she cannot convincingly project an image of its solution. She tries with Dinah and Adam, who ostensibly provide the book's central focus. In presenting them she is very concerned to shape their histories on models that her readers will recognize. We do not need to know of her wish to give Carlyle pleasure with her novel (GEL: III: 23) to see the Carlylean emphasis in the portrait of Adam himself: this "Saxon" (1: 6; he also appears as a Celt) is a spiritual son of Abbot Samson. He has no patience with Methodist self-scrutiny ("But t' hear some o' them preachers, you'd think as a man must be doing nothing all's life but shutting's eyes and looking what's a-going on inside him" – 1: 9); his work has "always been part of his religion" (50: 407); and when his own suffering comes, it brings a "baptism of fire" which yields "a soul full of new awe and new pity" (42: 357).

If Adam's ideas and suffering suggest a Carlylean background, Dinah Morris' sermon and her account of her "Calling" to the Reverend Irwine (chapter 8) are straight out of Methodist memoirs and testimony (even to Dinah's being an orphan). And the entire prison experience of the novel, as Valentine Cunningham has shown, is a central image of Methodist confessional literature and hymns, which reflected the Methodists' "awareness that conversions effected in prison were an appropriate acting out of New Testament metaphor: salvation was a release from the bondage and captivity of sin."[6] Hetty, of course, experiences no religious conversion; her sense of the godlike is nonexistent. But George Eliot appeals to the typical, and to the readers' recognition of it, even as she varies its resolution to make her *human* case.

Dinah and Adam provide two modes of existence in this world, modes which may be modified as the novel progresses but which are formed when we meet them. Dinah's work is to try like Bunyan to help others see the rewards of the next world; Adam is determined, like Teufelsdröckh, "to do my work well, and make the world a bit better place for them as can enjoy it" (48: 394). Their union, in a fine pastoral scene, is meant to tell thematically. But it never makes the human case of the novel as do the stories of Arthur and Hetty.

In these two unformed "children" we have the true *Bildung* possibility, and its thwarting. Each begins life with little sense that the world is not an extension of his or her own personality. Arthur Donnithorne constantly announces his concern for others, but his alliance with Adam, in its superficiality, underlines the ease with which he utters his concern. His education will simply burn into his soul the meaning of those words he so glibly utters. But Hetty, as the famous mirror scene suggests (chapter 15), never sees anything beyond her own self, and never sees that very adequately. Her journey is so horrifying because it so darkly parodies Dinah's vision of her salvation and Calling. It is an egoist's journey into a self where there is only a vacuum (Christopher Herbert calls it "an allegorical journey to the core of human nature, stripped of all its lendings"),[7] a "journey in despair" rather than hope, a cruel inversion of Israel's or Christian's march towards some promised land. She is without a sense of the past (the plant with no roots); she has never read a novel and cares not a whit for what the pictures in *Pilgrim's Progress* signify. Her lack of response to words is part and parcel of her lack of response to human beings: in George Eliot the two are inseparable (thus we know from Dinah's language what she reads, we see Adam reading Bunyan and Baxter, we hear Arthur on the "twaddling" *Lyrical Ballads*). Hetty's lack of education has left her no "shape for her expectations" (13: 116). Her final journey is such an awful inversion of a pilgrim's progress because it is an "objectless wandering" (37: 326). Hetty, like the malign Grandcourt later, terrifies because she is so utterly – and unknowingly – soulless: she has no models, no myths of *living* which pull her beyond her own vision in the mirror and force her to acknowledge her connection with her fellows. As the animal imagery associated with her suggests, she has only an empty human self.[8]

Maggie Tulliver's journey is "objectless" too, but she has fictions, words, that animate her, that give some "vision" even if limited and finally without sustenance. Indeed, *The Mill on the Floss* reworks an emphasis begun in *Adam Bede*: a focus on the way the mind works with the myths – religious and Romantic – available to it, on the way it accepts or alters or rejects them as it tries to find a *ground* for belief in the modern world. A passage of commentary states this explicitly. George Eliot is discussing the needs of working men and women, of those who form "a wide and arduous national life" which supports a nation in its well-bred ease:

This wide national life is based entirely on emphasis – the emphasis of want . . . Under such circumstances, there are many among its myriads of souls who have absolutely needed an emphatic belief . . ., something that will present motives in an entire absence of high prizes, something that will give patience and feed human love when the limbs ache with weariness, and human looks are hard upon us – something, clearly, that lies outside personal desires, that includes resignation for ourselves and active love for what is not ourselves.   (MF: IV: 3: 255)

The passage, with its Carlylean emphases, at once summarizes *Adam Bede*'s conclusion and urges us to see the new ways *The Mill* explores the same issues. In this second novel there is no golden pastoral Hayslope, nor any Reverend Irwine to make life whole and "comfortable." St Ogg's is a perfect town of Carnal Policy, and it illustrates the wedge between past and present and between classes which the combination of commerce and Protestantism has forced into community life. Its Protestantism is not evangelical, but the much more deadened and deadening religion of "respectability" (and George Eliot adds Carlyle's notation – "proud respectability in a gig of unfashionable build" (IV: 1: 238) – to illuminate her point about the "pagan" nature of this "variation of Protestantism unknown to Boussuet"). The narrator warns the reader that in the Dodsons and their St Ogg's peers we find "a kind of population out of keeping with the earth on which they live" (IV: 1: 238). There is an "oppressive narrowness" about the "religion" where no real harmony exists between man and nature. The ineffective Reverend Venn, with so little aid to offer Maggie, notes the dislocation: "At present everything seems tending towards the relaxation of ties – towards the substitution of wayward choice for the adherence to obligation, which has its roots in the past" (VII: 2: 435). It is a truth which we have, under a different rubric, seen enacted in the lives of Hetty and Arthur Donnithorne, and which we see once again in Maggie's history. To Stephen Guest's assertion that "natural law surmounts every other," she replies: "If the past is not to bind us, where can duty lie? We should have no law but the inclination of the moment" (VI: 14: 417). This statement suggests how much Maggie's history is a rewriting of Hetty and Arthur's story.

Maggie's quest is for some sense of what this *past* is, what its structures and foundations are. She wants an "emphatic belief." Her frustrated efforts to find some creed to live by, to make what Deronda will call "that hard unaccommodating Actual" (DD: 33: 430) sensible and bearable, provide the novel's focus. And the narrator dwells on Maggie's use of fictions to explain her world, or to provide grounds for hope: the eight-year-old girl amongst the gypsies wants her father to rescue her, but if not him then "Jack the Giant-killer, or Mr Greatheart, or St George" (I: 11: 98). The Maggie who at thirteen sees her father in despair finds that the "world outside the books was not a happy one" (III: 5: 205), and turns to Thomas à Kempis' words to make it bearable. Then, as a young lady in Lucy Deane's "fairy tale," Maggie finds herself "in her brighter aërial world again," in "a world of love and beauty and delight, made up of vague, mingled images from all the poetry and romance she had ever read" (VI: 3: 338). Her internalizing of the images and languages of books is an expression of her "blind, unconscious yearning for something that would link together the wonderful impressions of this mysterious life, and give her soul a sense of home in it" (III: 5: 205). The Word gave Bunyan one home; words give Maggie many, but no permanent one.

The book titles within the novel call our attention to the sources of George Eliot's presentation of Maggie's progress. The first two – "Boy and Girl" and "School-Time" – suggest a Romantic childhood, with its *Bildungsroman* emphasis on education and its Wordsworthian glow around Maggie and her brother at that age when still "the outer world seemed only an extension of our personality" and they had not "known the labour of choice" (II: 1: 133). But then come titles – "The Downfall," "The Valley of

Humiliation" – that invoke Bunyan and man's fall, and underline Maggie's metaphysical homelessness. The naming of the novel's central book "The Valley of Humiliation" places Bunyan's pilgrimage firmly in the novel's texture – for counterpoint. Here we see the consolations available to Maggie as she seeks "some explanation of this hard, real life" (IV: 3: 250). Significantly, the book opens with Dodson Protestantism, which Maggie's brother embraces without question, but it closes with Thomas à Kempis. Or rather, with Maggie's version, for George Eliot warns us (in Carlyle's language) that Maggie's celebration of "renunciation" as a key to "happiness" mistakes what renunciation centers on: "sorrow borne willingly" (IV: 3: 254). For Maggie, Apollyon assumes no certain shape except that of the absence of "established authorities and appointed guides" (IV: 3: 255). Bunyan's Christian survived the Valley of Humiliation only to face the Valley of the Shadow of Death, and then Vanity Fair. Maggie seems to escape the Humiliation (with Philip Wakem's aid), then survives her father's death, only to arrive in Vanity Fair ("Duet in Paradise") – and get very little beyond. Her final prayer, "O God, what is the way home?" is her hard and unflinching acknowledgment of her failure (even Philip's offer to be her Hopeful will not serve). There is, in the end, a Wordsworthian reunion with her brother and a pastoral frame supplied by George Eliot's commentary. But they do not efface the futility of Maggie's effort to break from her imprisonment, to fuse the world of words and the world of hard and harsh living.

George Eliot does not, however, intend us to see *The Mill* as only Maggie's biography. Two other figures share her pilgrimage, and make their own as well, and together their three *Bildungsromane* make the novel's emphasis. Tom Tulliver, in the "Valley of Humiliation," takes up Dodsonism and never looks back. He becomes a "character at unity with itself," one with "no visions beyond the distinctly possible" (V: 2: 272–3). His is the Utilitarian answer, a worldling's knowledge of "what is right and respectable" – and the answering "faith" in a world of change. "I don't find fault with change," says Mr Deane; "Trade, sir, opens a man's eyes" (VI: 5: 347). It is the modern *vision*. And Tom Tulliver's.

It is Philip Wakem, Tom's schoolmate and Maggie's Greatheart (the "opening in the rocky wall which shut in the narrow valley of humiliation" – V: 3: 285), who gives us the novel's one real – because living and practicable – definition of vision. From his first appearance, this hunchback is seen as even more isolated than Maggie. Yet he breaks out of that isolation. His final letter to Maggie, though it cannot save her from being forever the "lonely wanderer" (VII: 5: 451) she feels condemned to being, narrates his battle with his own Apollyon:

> In the midst of my egoism, I yet could not bear to come like a death-shadow across the feast of your joy . . . The new life I have found in caring for your joy and sorrow more than for what is directly my own, has transformed the spirit of rebellious murmuring into that willing endurance which is the birth of strong sympathy. I think nothing but such complete and intense love could have initiated me into that enlarged life which grows and grows by appropriating the life of others; for before, I was always dragged back from it by ever-present self-consciousness. I even think sometimes that this gift of transferred life which has come to me in loving you, may be a new power to me. (VII: 3: 442–3)

This "new life," "that enlarged life": it is Teufelsdröckh's language when he has broken into freedom. We do not read *The Mill* as George Eliot guides us to read it – with Philip's consciousness closing the novel at the point of *his* vision, his apocalypse – unless we see his education, his passage from the narrowness of egoism into "transferred life," as central to the meaning of the novel.

> His great companionship was among the trees of the Red Deeps, where the buried joy seemed still to hover – like a revisiting spirit. (VII: Conclusion, 459).

What George Eliot means by memory, by choice founded in "the deep immovable roots in memory," is in that phrase "buried joy." Certainly words have been part of its formation, but they have been animated – incarnated – by human relationship. The conjunction tells in the most liberating way.

But still the ending of *The Mill* does not resolve the issues of the strife of nature and God and man that Maggie's case raises any more than does the marriage which concludes *Adam Bede* (indeed, the cleansing flood touches the questions even less). The next year's *Silas Marner* does satisfactorily resolve them, and in precisely the way the case of Philip Wakem had pointed to. In this novel the words of supernatural creeds find illustration and confirmation not in religious worship but in the appearance of a child. The motto, from Wordsworth's "Michael," announces the theme:

> A child, more than all other gifts
> That earth can offer to declining man,
> Brings hope with it, and forward-looking thoughts.

Wordsworth and Bunyan are united in this "legendary tale." In the history of the weaver of Raveloe George Eliot juxtaposes – and reconciles – the Poysers' "comfortable" world and Mr Tulliver's "puzzlin'" one, Dinah's "prison" and the Dodsons' solid world.

The novel is something of a *jeu d'esprit* (it was done in a moment of inspiration while she labored on *Romola*), and it is a perfect construction. George Eliot's pilgrim is Israel outcast (men of his type "looked like the remnants of a disinherited race" we hear in the novel's first paragraph). The burden on the back of this poor nineteenth-century Christian is not, however, original sin; as Q. D. Leavis notes, it is the "loss of faith and of a community," a particularly Victorian dilemma.[9] The pilgrim comes to his promised land from a place where "the currents of industrial energy and Puritan earnestness" (3: 71) are strong indeed, even as they are quite foreign to a Raveloe that becomes "home" in a very Old Testament way; it becomes a "land of milk and honey" for Marner. (We note the characteristics of the novel's "Egypt" – its linking of Protestantism and commercialism – even to the factory standing where Lantern Yard's chapel once did.) In his new environment – "Merry England" – Marner is forced to see that the sources of "emphatic belief" are placed quite differently from what his early religious training had indicated. Starting out amidst the most emphatic of religious sects, he has his faith in God and his fellow-feeling shattered by a magical – and Bible ordained – drawing of lots; the Bible will never again be a source of literal truth for him. Going into exile, weaving for the gold which commands his only worship, Marner's life "narrow[s] and harden[s] itself more and more into a mere pulsation of desire and satisfaction that had no relation to any other being"; it reduces "itself to the functions of weaving and hoarding, without any contemplation of an end towards which the functions tended" (2: 68). The mechanical and animal language describes his state: he seems another Hetty, on an "objectless" journey and reduced to satisfying only "natural" needs. But unlike her and like Maggie, he has known – felt – in that Lantern Yard sect the structures and the language and the situations that some "far-echoing voice" existing beyond the self can suggest. Thus, he never hesitates to think of the "golden" child who comes to him as Providentially sent; he has never been able to cut himself off from the biblical heritage and its supernatural agencies that are the foundation of his memories. And though he is "quite unable, by means of anything he heard or saw, to identify the

Raveloe religion with his old faith" (14: 183), "that new self" (16: 201) to which Eppie's coming gives birth allows him an integration into Raveloe's "communion" (14: 190).

The child's appearance reinstates even as it redefines Silas' supernatural understanding of his natural world – and both natural and supernatural worlds then lose their isolation and terror. His is a redemption underlining the source of Eppie's name, Isaiah 62: 4: "Thou shalt no more be termed Forsaken; neither shall thy land any more be termed Desolate: but thou shalt be called Hephzibah, and thy land Beulah: for the Lord delighteth in thee." The supernatural and the natural join in the child Eppie – and "save" Marner, literally. He recovers "a consciousness of unity between his past and present" (16: 202) and a "presentiment of some Power presiding over his life" (12: 168). It is Carlyle's "new Mythus," and perfectly embodied.[10]

But if Eppie gives palpable life to belief, she does not answer the questions that the severed past has raised. Silas constantly meditates on that past, and uses the Bible's language to frame his experience ("mine own famil'ar friend, in whom I trusted, had lifted up his heel again' me, and worked to ruin me" – from Psalm 41: 9 [16: 203]). This language is Silas' means of bearing the burden of the past. But the very fact that the words can no longer promise an answer as they did for the Psalmist is telling. And we note that the "good" people of Raveloe are quite ignorant of the Bible's language; it is the church service and the songs they have heard there that they respond to (the same response is made by Adam Bede and the Poysers to the communal worship, and by Daniel Deronda in the synagogue). Dolly Winthrop has told Silas, after his gold had vanished, that a carol in church, amidst so many ills in the world, caused one to think "you've got to a better place a'ready" (10: 139). Eppie's coming animates this idea for Silas, and integrates him into the established communion even as he uses "other" language to explain what is happening. The Bible serves him as a source for ordering his experiences, a means allowing him to transcend the natural world of chance and function and to find continuity between his past and present.

If Eppie's coming awakens in Silas "old impressions of awe at the presentiment of some Power presiding over his life," it also forces the same recognition on her father.[11] Godfrey Cass and his wife form the "respectable" (19: 233) part of *Marner*'s history, and their story points the full implications of Eppie's name. Isaiah, in calling the Hebrews Hephzibah, had prophesied: "And the Gentiles shall see thy righteousness, and all kings thy glory" (62: 2). Godfrey Cass is forced to see Marner's "righteousness." This man who had seen his brother's absence and his first wife's death as simply his own luck finds the child's presence with Silas a guarantee of his own future "as a promised land" (15: 192). But that Beulah turns barren when he finds his home childless. He is forced, finally, to acknowledge himself "in no sense free" (Deronda's phrase), and to see in his childlessness a "retribution," an announcement that the past does tell in the present, that no law takes precedence over natural feeling.

"What you say is natural, my dear child – it's natural you should cling to those who've brought you up," [Godfrey's wife] said mildly; "but there's a duty you owe to your lawful father" (19: 234).

The Law – and in so allegorical a book that word carries Old Testament resonances – must give way to the relationships of feeling; Bunyan must give way before Wordsworth even as his idea of a jealous God is softened into a sense of some Power presiding over our lives (the New Testament substitute of Love for Law is part of the novel's "Morality Play"). Godfrey's recognition involves his own resignation to lifelong sorrow. The Gentiles *do* see Israel's righteousness, and Christ's love.

All ends then with "emphatic belief" defined as that "something, clearly, that lies outside personal desires, that includes resignation for ourselves and love for what is not ourselves." For Silas Marner and Godfrey Cass, as for Dolly Winthrop, this involves the Judeo-Christian promise of a "better place"; for George Eliot and her readers, this place seems quite established with Silas and Eppie in the Actual. But the point is that the human beings of this "legendary tale" need the words and structures of myths they know if they are to find meaning in their everyday experience (and to break out of personal selfishness and isolation). David Carroll has said that "the subject of the novel is the different ways in which we create myths, valid and invalid," to help us to understand "the mystery of the worlds in which we live." The two plots of *Silas Marner* allow George Eliot to explore two modes of living: one which sees nothing but what the eye focuses on; the other which acknowledges the power of the unseen, for good or ill. This "structural division" of the novel, Carroll notes, "creates an area of mystery which George Eliot says is an inescapable condition of human existence."

This area is the testing-ground of the protagonists' myth-making faculties and within it George Eliot demonstrates that valid myths of order are a direct expression of love, while invalid myths of chance result from an absence of love. The former act as intermediaries between the individual and the realities of life, and the latter seek to deny these realities.[12]

Importantly too, these plots together incorporate those worlds of "above and below" (16: 203) which Silas had found so indifferent to him. They incorporate the worlds of romance and of history.[13]

II

Without the fairy-tale wonders of *Silas Marner* or its Words-worthian nature, George Eliot's next two English novels do precisely what that book did: though set during the period of the first Reform Bill, both *Felix Holt* and *Middlemarch* explore the myths, fictions, and lies that men and women create or expropriate in order to confront and survive change. Nothing in the early 1830s offers the soul's-aid that a tradition-centered community had in the earlier novels. Indeed, religion and its ministers have become one more of the controversies of the day, a very obvious source of division and contention ("But now, if you speak out of the Prayer-book itself, you are liable to be contradicted" – Mrs Farebrother, Mid: 17: 126), or else a supporter of worldly comfort (a "way of conciliating piety and worldliness, the nothingness of this life and the desirability of cut glass, the consciousness at once of filthy rags and the best damask" – *Middlemarch*, with Bunyan's language, 27: 198). By the time of *Deronda*, set in the readers' present, religion for the English ceases even to be controversial; "religious nomenclature" becomes an unnoticed part of secular language. And because of this deforming of mythic language, George Eliot returns in this novel without hesitation to the overt "romance" structure of *Silas Marner*, with its basis in Israel's history. She has, indeed, "become more and more timid" in insisting that the myths which offer a basis for action and choice be anchored in the chief narrative of western man's religious experience. But she is bolder than ever in garbing this traditional religious myth in the forms of romance.

To understand why *Daniel Deronda* had to be centered in Hebraism and the Zionist revival, we need to trace George Eliot's evolving narrative voice and to view that voice as the chief indicator of her "successive mental phases." As we have seen, she conceives of human life in the pattern of Carlyle's *Bildungsroman* with its emphasis on the possibility of visionary experience even when life seems trapped in an Everlasting No. Like *Sartor*'s Editor, she constantly guides the readers' interpretation of the words at hand even as she urges them to acknowledge how much a part of their own lives these fictions are. "Art is the nearest thing to life," she had written in the essay on von Riehl; "it is a mode of amplifying experience and extending our contact with our fellowmen beyond the bounds of our personal lot," of "surpris[ing] even the trivial and the selfish into that attention to what is apart from themselves, which may be called the raw material of moral sentiment." [14] Through her changing narrative voice, George Eliot searches out ways to effect this self-extension in her readers. In effect asking herself again and again "What shall I do?" she grows into that final guiding voice which we think of as George Eliot's. From *Adam Bede*'s remembrancer, settled amongst the characters he is describing, George Eliot moves to the historian and then to the romancer. The "strong terrible vision" that forces attention to what is apart from ourselves is, finally, effected only by that guide who is also prophet or seer.

Silas Marner is her first experiment with sheer romance. The fairy tale that the characters themselves experience is the medium for rendering the "history" (2: 69). Indeed, this story of "Merry England" is so wonderfully successful because it is so spare in its narrative techniques. Its narrator is George Eliot's most repressed – no fireside chats, no historical comparisons and speculations, few allusions beyond Bunyan, Wordsworth, and the Bible, beyond the common literary possession of readers. The mythic nature of the story relieves George Eliot completely from any need to insist on the reality of her common people, or from any need to supply titles and epigraphs to guide us. The belief of the "you" so often referred to is assumed – as in any Puritan allegory where the real and the symbolic are so inextricably connected by means of familiar biblical correspondences.

But what anchors this "Merry England" tale in the probable is its double plot, George Eliot's "device for telling the same story twice, with different endings" (Hardy, p. 137). It allows her the necessary freedom to use romance without apology, and to juxtapose it with the real in order to show their resemblance and the necessity of each for the "truth" of the other. The tale of Silas Marner and his golden child is romance; the history of Godfrey Cass is petty reality. Cass's life is inseparable from Marner's, the weaver's inseparable from

Cass's. The landowner's story toughens Marner's and grounds it in the real; Marner's "history" forces Cass – and us – to acknowledge the place of visionary experience in man's life, whether he would see it or not. We see that "in these hard, unbelieving utilitarian days," the "Unseen but not unreal World" exists, that "the Actual and the Ideal," the real and the romantic, are not separable if we are to live wholly, adequately (C: XXVI: 208). Indeed, to sever them is to make life sterile and barren.

The novels before *Silas Marner*, told by solidly characterized narrators insisting on the "real" nature of their narratives, do not so easily or successfully render the path towards the visionary. Dinah Morris through her sermons and meditations gives this element to *Adam Bede*. Maggie and Philip in *The Mill* discuss the need to acknowledge "the divine voice within us" rather than "indulge ourselves in the present moment" (VI: 14: 418–19). But next to these pleas for recognizing the need of vision in one's life stands George Eliot's voice – and it curiously qualifies the assertions of the novels' protagonists, even as it makes the same plea.

Because each "story is told as the thing remembered, not the thing invented" (Hardy, p. 157), George Eliot talks directly to the reader, much as Bunyan or the overtly religious writers had done as they recounted their experiences and instructed their readers.[15] Yet this explicitly didactic voice, which by its very nature implies that "art" is not its purpose, is forced again and again to discuss "art," to claim the "real" as its province and to defend fiction as its means of rendering truth. In *Adam Bede* George Eliot's belief that "Art is the nearest thing to life" is stated overtly in the invoking of Rembrandt, in the requests that we sympathize with plain Methodists and "old women scraping carrots" at least as readily as we would with "heroines in satin boots" and "heroes riding fiery horses" (3: 34), and in the interview with the title protagonist (chapter 17). George Eliot is concerned that we know that she moves amongst – not above – her men and women. In *The Mill* she is again the remembrancer, but she also emphasizes that she is a dreamer (and her characters are oblivious to her). Art itself – literature, music – is not part of her commentary here, though it is part of the lives of her characters: George Eliot simply notes their (mis)interpretations.

Yet in working with her narrative voice in these first novels, George Eliot discovers how hard it is to extend sympathy to those whose aims and feelings are utterly opposed to her own. In her first novel she is imaginatively devoted to a "Merry England," a fiction that allows her to present a "comfortable" world where nature and man *seem* at strife neither with each other nor with God. In *Adam Bede* George Eliot so loves the community around the Reverend Irwine and Mrs Poyser that she tries to keep at bay all disturbing elements. She energetically defends them against her sense that modern (1859) readers will see them as "pagans." And she even more vigorously defends them against the onslaught of the self-centered Arthur and Hetty. Hetty receives almost no sympathy. We get harsh analogies ("One begins to suspect at length that there is no direct correlation between eyelashes and morals" – 13: 131) and little acknowledgment that Mrs Poyser's "comfortable" environment might have warped this woman's development. (There is surely some indictment in the question raised after Hetty's inability to read is mentioned: "How then could she find a shape for her expectations?"; the community has participated in her isolation.)[16] George Eliot's voice is one quite at odds with Dinah's damnation of the natural self, yet her very harshness of tone when Hetty appears makes us doubt her judgment of Dinah (Dinah would make the same analysis of Hetty). Even the epigraph for *Adam Bede*, from Wordsworth's *The Excursion*, finally tells against her:

> And when
> I speak of such among the flock as swerved
> Or fell, those only shall be singled out
> Upon whose lapse, or error, something more
> Than brotherly forgiveness may attend.

Adam and Dinah do come together in extending this forgiveness to Hetty – and in their own resulting recognition and abandonment of pride in their ways. George Eliot tries to focus her emphasis on their conversion, on their education for daily living with awe and pity amongst their fellows. The closing marriage and the verbal Constable accompanying it are meant to underline this. But her interest in Arthur and Hetty, her often arch irony towards them, and her resort to melodramatic contrivances to get them off the stage undercut this focus – and show us the problems she has with "Merry England." That devotion to the memory of Mrs Poyser's England – to the country in all its Wordsworthian significance – sits uneasily beside the story of "natural" lives like Hetty's and Arthur's.

In *The Mill on the Floss* George Eliot faces the ways memory distorts, and the ways she has used it for comfort rather than truth or vision. Within the story itself Maggie insists on the sacredness of the past and of the community that has grown out of it, and she damns a life lived completely for itself: "If the past is not to bind us, where can duty lie? . . . but I can't believe in a good for you, that I feel – that we both feel is a wrong towards others" (VI: 14: 417–18). But beside her voice emphasizing the "sanctity" of memory is George Eliot's, and there is a tension between its perceptions and Maggie's emphatic beliefs which emphasizes their transitoriness. George Eliot simply does not care about the St Ogg's community as she did about Mrs Poyser's world. As a result she is able to examine through Maggie that belief in memory which had been so signal a part of *Adam Bede*.

She constantly evokes memory, reminiscing again and again. In the opening pages she pronounces the river "a living companion," "the voice of one who is deaf and loving." But suddenly the reader finds this only a dream. Then he is launched *in medias res*, into Mr Tulliver's talk (a talk singularly devoid of any idea of harmony) and into Maggie's life. And in that life the river is anything but a companion; from her earliest days her mother predicts her end will come in those waters. (George Eliot throughout acknowledges nature's unreliability: she is "cunning," "not unveracious, but . . .") Constantly, George Eliot's voice interrupts the action to place the events in some frame that will extend their meaning beyond the specific instance and make them a part of some larger order where suffering did have significant meaning (thus the references to Bunyan from the middle of the novel onward, even though George Eliot admits that Maggie's journey towards the "Promised Land" is "thirsty, trackless, uncertain" – MF: IV: 3: 251). But these allusions only underline Maggie's needs – *and* George Eliot's. She needs Bunyan to make sense of – and even to elevate – Mr Tulliver's "puzzlin' world"; she requires Wordsworth to mark the end of childhood and preserve it as a resource of memory: "They had entered the thorny wilderness, and the golden gates of their childhood had for ever closed behind them" (II: 7: 168). It is a Romantic recollection of early childhood – except that this is not the way we have experienced what the novel tells us.[17] Indeed, our experience is quite the reverse. From the time we meet Maggie she is different, and aware of her difference. Like Jane Eyre and Lucy Snowe, she never enjoys a state of innocence. Maggie is a "wild thing," her black hair and her reading do set her apart – really and imaginatively – from the Lucy Deanes of her world (and from their fictional counterparts; Maggie notices that black-haired heroines do not live happily ever after! – V: 4: 292). No hazes of memory nor natural imagery can obscure her isolation.

What happens to George Eliot's handling of her narrative voice in *The Mill* is that she herself is questioning the value of memory and the value of the memories. The concern about what memories afford us elicits those often shrill apologies for this "history of unfashionable families" and the efforts to share the readers' attitudes even as she seems uncertain what those attitudes are: "I share with you this sense of oppressive narrowness; but it is necessary that we should feel it, if we care to understand how it acted on the lives of Tom and Maggie – how it acted on young natures in many generations, that in the onward tendency of human things have risen above the mental level of the generation before them" (IV: 1: 238). Surely no one thinks Tom Tulliver above the "mental level" of the previous generation, surely the only "onward tendency" we see in *The Mill* is the rush of business and of Maggie's hopes. There is confusion here, between George Eliot's beliefs and perceptions (as there is in Maggie's). This confusion is focused for us by George Eliot's surprise that readers found the Dodsons "mean and uninteresting" (GEL: III: 299).[18] In their talk and action they certainly are not; indeed they are great fun even as they register quite thoroughly the indictment. It is George Eliot's apologetic labelling, her "unfashionable families" versus "good society," that blurs the emphasis and creates the negative impression. She is herself unsure about the Dodsons, and about the readers who will react to them. She is even more uncertain of what Maggie's sense of the past is, for she finds it unattractive in all of its "respectability." The respectable people do not care a whit for this past, except as it supports their position. Maggie believes in it as she does in the God she calls on: it is sanctified by the fictions she knows if not by the chaotic experience she has suffered.

Although George Eliot acknowledges at the "Conclusion" that "To eyes that have dwelt on the past, [Nature makes] no thorough repair" (VII: 459), she avoids facing what the epigraph with which she begins and ends Maggie's story actually means. Surely, "In their death they were not divided" implies no victory over death for Maggie and Tom (even though the dwelling on Tom's "Magsie" and on the "new revelation to his spirit" urges us to accept their end as visionary apocalypse). The epigraph is from David's elegy on Saul and Jonathan, father and son divided in life by questions of familial loyalty; David speaks in sadness of the irony of death. Only

Philip Wakem has gained this Davidic understanding by seeing the effect Maggie's life and its close have had on his vision. He sees that the unity of the end, in the mythic history or in the specific lives, is real only in that it gives the seer (and Philip is an artist) perception of "enlarged life." His story, completed, allows the reader to see. But Philip Wakem's victory is too private, too "inward" for George Eliot's purposes here. She is too devoted to an "enlarged life" that is community-centered. And not until *Felix Holt* and *Middlemarch* will she fully chart the separation of personal vision and communal life which Philip Wakem's case first illustrates.

In *The Mill on the Floss* George Eliot displaces the unpleasant past (which Philip accepts, with resignation) through memory; she renders "respectable" life bearable by fictionalizing it, by putting it in the shadow of larger myths that have told on experience. Maggie never comes to the vision she has sought, and which books have promised her is possible; she never sees how the past can "bind" one in a liberatingly human way. George Eliot, with hesitation and certainly with regret, of course sees this. But to her, memory is – in Carlyle's words – "beautiful, sad, almost Elysian-sacred"; there "the haggard element of Fear" vanishes. Memory fictionalizes the past for our comfort; it does not propel us towards strong vision. George Eliot, however, will not create a fiction urging this truth until she considers Daniel Deronda.

The English novels which follow *Silas Marner* (and George Eliot's work with history in *Romola*) underline the narrative discoveries that *Marner* showed. A remembrancer is not necessarily a guide; *vision* can indeed be hindered when devotion to "fictions" – of nature, of community – refracts truth. The question "What shall I do?" can be answered honestly – in life and in art – only by *forms* which acknowledge their fictiveness by telling the reader that the words before him do distort, but that they also show and share his experience – its unity with the past – as at once unique and common. "Wouldst read thy self . . .?/. . . Oh then come hither,/And lay my Book, thy Head and Heart together." Thus, George Eliot gives up the remembrancer figure and begins her search for a voice which is at once historian and seer, an investigator of our communities and of our inner lives – and always our guide.

Finding the appropriate figure for this task in Wordsworth's Wanderer and Dante's Virgil, she devotes the Introduction to *Felix Holt* to discussing their importance as narrators. Her story-teller in this Introduction is a coachman giving a tour of England over a thirty-year period.[19] As we hear him, we know immediately that "Merry England" is not his binding fiction:

The coachman was an excellent travelling companion and commentator on the landscape: he could tell the names of sites and persons, and explain the meaning of groups, as well as the shade of Virgil in a more memorable journey; he had as many stories about parishes, and the men and women in them, as the Wanderer in the 'Excursion,' only his style was different. His view of life had originally been genial, and such as became a man who was well warmed within and without, and held a position of easy, undisputed authority; but the recent initiation of Railways had embittered him: he now, as in a perpetual vision, saw the ruined country strewn with shattered limbs . . . Still he would soon relapse from the high prophetic strain to the familiar one of narrative. (FH: 9)

Vision and prophecy versus narrative – we come here to what for George Eliot art in a shattered age must be if it is to deserve our attention. Not mere narrative, but language forcing us to open our eyes and selves to vision. It must make us see in new ways, expose us – in Klesmer's words – to a "breadth of horizon" beyond ourselves, force onto us, willing or not, a "sense of the universal." This is what the Wanderer does, and Virgil. They guide us beyond that indifference which is "self-satisfied folly"; they show us the "right road" (DD: 5: 79; 23: 297):

> Midway this way of life we're bound upon,
> I woke to find myself in a dark wood,
> Where the right road was wholly lost and gone.[20]

It is the opening of the *Inferno*, but it could as easily translate the beginning of *Pilgrim's Progress*: "As I walk'd through the wilderness of this world, I lighted on a certain place, where was a Denn . . ." There is one signal difference: Bunyan had the Word to show him the right road while Dante needed a Virgil who could show others a Promised Land he himself would never enter. And modern man, as Maggie's case had shown, needs human guides as well in an age when the Word and all words are so many "mere *words*."

For George Eliot, such guides will not be remembrancers who glorify the past but voices which have, Carlyle-like, meditated on past and present unflinchingly, have seen that even in days without machines and rick-burners there was a *"via media* of indifference" in those church-centered communities quite opposite to any sincere fellow-feeling (FH: 6). A narrator must show more than George Eliot's remembrancers have because he sees – he must see – more:

The poets have told us of a dolorous enchanted forest in the under world. The thorn-bushes there, and the thick-barked stems, have human histories hidden in them; the power of unuttered cries dwells in the passionless-seeming branches, and the red warm blood is darkly feeding the quivering nerves of a sleepless memory that watches through all dreams. These things are a parable. (FH: 11)

"These things are a parable" – George Eliot will repeat the line in *Middlemarch*, and she will write her own in *Daniel Deronda*. She will assert that "histories" are parables, not just compilations of "mere *words*" presenting facts. Prophecy springs from narrative at the moment when indifference is replaced by "the pity and terror of men," and by fellow-feeling. George Eliot notes that Sampson the coachman often gossiped of "fine stories," "stories not altogether creditable to the parties concerned."

And such stories often come to be fine in a sense that is not ironical. For there is seldom any wrong-doing which does not carry along with it some downfall of blindly-climbing hopes, . . . some tragic mark of kinship in the one brief life to the far-stretching life that went before, and to the life that is to come after, such as has raised the pity and terror of men ever since they began to discern between will and destiny. (FH: 11)

In a time when sectarian disputes and politics have divided communities, George Eliot's guide must be a Wanderer who sees and shows us the connections of past and present all around us, he must be a Virgil who will lead us into the demon-empires of ourselves and – perhaps – out of them towards health. Her narrator should be the historian of our consciousness and the seer of our unconsciousness, the Wanderer and the Virgil who will show us the way to vision.

And that way, as Dante shows us, very clearly involves the conjunction of the fictive and the real. The chapter epigraphs which George Eliot uses in each of her last three novels constantly and allusively place the "real" people before us in the context of Bunyan, Burton, Homer – in literary contexts which at once generalize experience and make us see connections that the men and women whose lives we are reading can at best only dream about. The *Purgatorio* epigraph to chapter 64 of *Deronda* connects Gweldolen's experience and her victory to Dante's journey. The Bunyan epigraph to chapter 85 of *Middlemarch*, with its picture of Vanity Fair's jury, places Mr Bulstrode's critics even as it offers an inverted parallel to his case. The constant references to Greek tragedy in the *Holt* epigraphs point out the "tragic mark of kinship"

161

even as the characters seem incapable of (and too mean for) real tragic exaltation. The result: our pity and terror are required.

Furthermore, George Eliot asks us to acknowledge that even history and biography, the books Victorian readers accept as truth rather than artful lies, are not fundamentally different from poetry; there are no rigidly separated literary genres. Science and "[h]is less accurate grandmother Poetry" both have to choose a beginning point and then set "off *in medias res*": "Men can do nothing without the make-believe of a beginning" (DD: epigraph, 1: 35). In *Middlemarch*, where Lydgate makes so much of scientific discovery, George Eliot, as the historian–narrator also striving for accuracy, notes: "Even with a microscope . . . we find ourselves making interpretations which turn out to be rather coarse" (6: 44). No wonder she links herself, without apology, to Fielding as well as to Herodotus:

> In fact, much the same sort of movement and mixture went on in old England as we find in older Herodotus, who also, in telling what had been, thought it well to take a woman's lot for his starting-point; though Io, as a maiden apparently beguiled by attractive merchandise, was the reverse of Miss Brooke, and in this respect perhaps bore more resemblance to Rosamond Vincy. (Mid: 11: 71)

The historian begins his history with myth; the novelist begins her tale with history. "Feigned truth and historical truth coalesce" here, as U. C. Knoepflmacher notes in discussing this passage.[21]

George Eliot in *Middlemarch* constantly emphasizes how fact takes on quite another shape entirely once it gets itself lodged in our consciousness; to articulate is to interpret, and to distort:

> There is always a good number who once meant to shape their own deeds and alter the world a little. The story of their coming to be shapen after the average and fit to be packed by the gross, is hardly ever told even in their consciousness; for perhaps their ardour in generous unpaid toil cooled as imperceptibly as the ardour of other youthful loves, till one day their earlier self walked like a ghost in its old home and made the new furniture ghastly. Nothing in the world more subtle than the process of the gradual change! In the beginning they inhaled it unknowingly: you and I may have sent some of our breath towards infecting them, when we uttered our conforming falsities or drew our silly conclusions: or perhaps it came with the vibrations from a woman's glance. (15: 107)

"What is truth?" as Jesting Pilate asked, with "Thick serene opacity" veiling his eyes (PP: 19). For George Eliot modern man has much less chance of discerning an answer. Memory itself, as she discovered in the early novels, is selective, and thus fiction-making. "There's no disappointment in memory," Daniel Deronda says, "and one's exaggerations are always on the good side" (DD: 35: 476). Interpretations too, because they are our means of ordering random experience, also help us relieve disappointment and comfort ourselves.

> We sit as in a boundless Phantasmagoria·and Dream-grotto; boundless, for the faintest star, the remotest century, lies not even nearer the verge thereof: sounds and many-coloured visions flit round our sense . . . Then, in that strange Dream, how we clutch at shadows as if they were substances; and sleep deepest whilst fancying ourselves most awake! . . . This Dreaming, this Somnambulism is what we on Earth call Life; wherein the most indeed undoubtedly wander, as if they knew right hand from left; yet they only are wise who know that they know nothing. (SR: 53–4)

Like Teufelsdröckh, George Eliot in her later novels insists that we see what dream-worlds we require for living; in that consciousness there is vision.

So Virgil's shade takes Dante through his own Inferno, and Christian with the Word's direction encounters the *real* aspects of himself that would keep him off the "right road." But for modern man it requires "a good strong terrible vision" (FH: 27: 224) if he is to escape the "danger of absorption within the narrow bounds of self" and keep to his "best self" (FH: 15: 149). Only such a vision answers the cry of the lost, "What shall I do?" And for George Eliot no novelist can show this vision except by parable, by making "mere *words*" speak *sub specie aeternitatis*. Her multiple plots, as *Silas Marner* illustrates, allow the reality and the Romance to merge into this parable.

Lest we miss the "Morality Play" beneath her narratives (Hardy, pp. 98–9), George Eliot increases her use of the Pilgrim's first question, "What shall I do?" Certainly it is used for expediency, for protecting the self from its mistakes and petty failures. But it is also used for a scrutiny of the soul, for finding a path to take one beyond the trivial and the selfish into "enlarged life," into the typical life. The very commonness of this question – in literature and in our lives – forces us to share with the narrator's men and women, to see how they incorporate themselves into the fabric of our lives. In the novel's Morality Play, George Eliot provides us with the same frame of reference that she uses for valuation. Her epigraphs and allusions, her parallel structuring of the narratives, all take us beyond the surface differences until we see how we – readers, characters, author – participate in fictions for good or ill.

George Eliot knows, says David Carroll, "that the mind in its own defence must create a theory by which to mediate with the outer world."

> But what she demands is that we become sensitive to the exact point where the mind meets the outer world, where the hypothesis comes into contact with the facts it is trying to explain, where the deduction begins to mould the evidence, where for example, Mrs Cadwallader's caustic tongue and sharp epigrams begin cutting reality into the shape she desires.[22]

Silas Marner showed Godfrey Cass moulding the evidence to fit his own happily planned Promised Land. And it showed the vision of the real pushing its way into his self-enclosed consciousness. But for George Eliot this story was too "legendary." It did not correspond to the way we live now, amidst rick burnings, trains, reform bills, Catholic questions, *Sartor Resartus* and Strauss. In *Felix Holt* and *Middlemarch* she makes her narrative voice consciously that of an historian who will chart these signs of the times even as, like Dante's Virgil, he will gaze into those areas of the self where vision originates. These novels and *Deronda* explore that moment when vision comes and we see who we are and what we must do; and they explore the continuing moments when we deny that we "dream" – and thus imprison ourselves.

Felix Holt introduces this concentration on the way towards vision – the word is everywhere – and the self-created prisons which prevent it. Mrs Transome is in "bondage" (8: 99) utterly and forlornly as anyone in Dante's infernal forest. The Reverend Rufus Lyon, minister of the Independent Chapel, sees in his own history an example of a wanderer who for a time left the "right road" for an earthly paradise. A later epigraph (chapter 45) summarizes his experience for us, and the experiences of Mrs Transome as well.

> We may not make this world a paradise
> By walking it together with clasped hands
> And eyes that meeting feed a double strength.
> We must be only joined by pains divine,
> Of spirits bent in mutual memories.

It is an epigraph that marks for us how much George Eliot has matured since the "paradise" she insisted on seeing in those early novels.

The Reverend Lyon's revelation to his daughter Esther that she is not in fact his child begins her progress towards understanding what Felix Holt means by "vision," and how much it is tied to our relation with our fellows ("Very slight words and deeds may have a sacramental efficacy, if we can cast our self-love behind us" – 13: 134). Like Jane Eyre's orphanage, that of Esther begins her journey into the self. In the process this young woman for whom Byron, to Holt's disgust, offered visions of the happy life gives up the poet with Carlylean fervor (22: 197), and more and more finds it "impossible to read": "her life was a book which she seemed herself to be constructing – trying to make character clear before her, and looking into the ways of destiny" (40: 322). In casting his life into the biblical paradigms, Bunyan would have said the same thing. But the guides Esther needs are human: Felix with his kind of vision, her father with his (again, the Carlyle and Bunyan contrast). She is not like Maggie, stymied by books which she cannot see round, but like Philip Wakem: there are human voices to awaken her and pull her forward. Esther has the Dantes to force her towards those "strong visions" which will not be found in the well-bred ease of her daydreams (49: 386).

The importance of the human will be Dorothea Brooke's experience too. This woman whose central concern, "Tell me what I can do" (Mid: 30: 213), has a Bunyanesque resonance far beyond its immediate application, breaks out of her "theoretic" imprisonment, out of self-absorption: "I used to pray so much – now I hardly ever pray. I try not to have desires merely for myself, because they may not be good for others, and I have too much already" (39: 287). And finally, in chapter 80, with its epigraph from "Ode to Duty," Wordsworth and Bunyan come together in her life:

The objects of her rescue were not to be sought out by her fancy: they were chosen for her. She yearned towards the perfect Right, that it might make a throne within her, and rule her errant will. 'What should I do – how should I act now, this very day, if I could clutch my own pain, and compel it to silence, and think of those three?'
It had taken long for her to come to that question, and there was light piercing into the room. She opened her curtains, and looked out towards the bit of road that lay in view, with fields beyond, outside the entrance-gates. On the road there was a man with a bundle on his back and a woman carrying her baby . . . Far off in the bending sky was the pearly light; and she felt the largeness of the world and the manifold wakings of men to labour and endurance. She was a part of that involuntary, palpitating life, and could neither look out on it from her luxurious shelter as a mere spectator, nor hide her eyes in selfish complaining. (80: 577–8)

It is the process of the visionary moment for all who are saved in George Eliot's novels, this breaking out of self-fancy, this understanding of how we dream, and this insight about the burdens that we must all carry and share *here*. Lydgate too may see momentarily, but he is denied the healing vision. He will live and die in the Slough of Despond (epigraph to chapter 79), imprisoned by that early belief in the factual truth of his "scientific views" of tissues and of his romantic views of women. He has no eyes to see that "the vision is all within" (FH: 45: 361), and no guide, finally, to take him beyond the depths of his demon-empire into a higher world of freedom: "He must walk as he could, carrying that burthen painfully" (Mid: 81: 586). His burden is there forever. We note the emblem. He, Casaubon, and Bulstrode, like Mrs Transome, will feel "the fatal threads" about them (FH: 8: 99) and have no more chance of escape than the souls in Dante's trees. "These things are a parable" (Mid: 27: 195).

In directing our attention to the parabolic nature of these *Bildungsromane*, George Eliot ties them to plots that are as conventional as Marner's tale. Only the endings surprise. *Felix Holt*'s plot is as clanking as that in any Victorian melodrama; George Eliot is not adept in using to her story's advantage the theatrical contrivances of the laws of inheritance and entail in the way Dickens often does. But the plot's very conventionality tricks the readers: the expected resolution does not follow the conventions. There is no certain pattern to trust, in 1832 or 1866. The Cinderella of the tale cares not a whit for the prince of *her* palace. Her happy-ever-after life is based on her rejecting that myth of self-fulfillment. Esther's "last vision" has directed her away from this grand material world of fairy-tale comfort towards "the life where the draughts of joy sprang from the unchanging fountains of reverence and devout love" (50: 393–4).

The ending of *Felix Holt* is radical from George Eliot's narrative perspective as well (and has little in common with the conclusions of the earlier novels). There is irony about the prosperity of Treby Magna (accompanied "doubtless" with "more enlightenment") and about the "all-wise" newspapers setting standards, an irony which quite undercuts a Trebian's summation of the effect of Esther's marriage: "It's wonderful how things go through you – you don't know how. I feel somehow as if I believed more in everything that's good" ("Epilogue," p. 398). But the sources of vision – new and old, Felix and the Reverend Lyon – leave the community. As does George Eliot. She tells us that she can not say whether the people are better, or whether "the publicans [are] all fit, like Gaius, to be friends of an apostle – these things I have not heard, not having correspondence in those parts" (p. 399). Although the language is patterned after the Apostle Paul's (see Romans 15: 23), there is the sense of having done no work "in those parts," and this sense is reinforced by the refusal to give Felix's exact residence. George Eliot here seems to hint little belief in the lasting efficacy of her *spiritual* letters or of Felix's work.

It is a profoundly disconcerting close. The plotting and allusions in *Felix Holt* promise that tendency towards apocalypse which George Eliot's previous work had shown, but its ending denies that promise. The great vision is allowed only in an inward and individual sense; there is no reintegration into the community, no (more than momentary) social healing effected at all by Holt's work and Esther's "vision." Reality as George Eliot perceives it does not allow the "reconciliation" between the individual and the world, and between man and the sacred. Like Bunyan, these characters must choose between communal life in all of its constricting narrowness, and spiritual wholeness. Only romance, as *Silas Marner* showed, allowed both together. Israel's exodus towards a Promised Land is not a national paradigm that operates in the real world of rickburners and Dissent. The paradigm applies only in individual cases. And George Eliot, with her Pauline revisions, refuses to gloss over that discovery with pastoral painting.

Middlemarch is George Eliot's great meditation on the resignation that the ending of *Felix Holt* required of her. In this novel the one conventional plot – Bulstrode's – counterpoints and reinforces two biographies which tell the same "history," a history of the necessity of resigning our fictions, our aerial dreams which agree with nothing outside our own fancies and which will paralyze every action in life unless recognized as fictions. Esther gave up her books, and so must Dorothea and Lydgate. They come to the insight of Mary Garth – whose story is the fourth plot and the constant in this "experiment in life" – that "things were not likely to be arranged for her peculiar satisfaction" (33: 232). But they come to this "vision" too late to remain a part of the community. In the significant consonance of the novel, they end along with Bulstrode in exile, uprooted or rootless forever. The old plot exiled the bad; the new and less fixed ones force out the good as well.[23]

And the narrative voice who has told us this "parable" (and that of the pier glass)? George Eliot's voice here is that of an historian resigned to the need to tell of "hidden" lives lived in a "medium" so deadening that the "ardent deeds" of a Theresa or Antigone will never be possible. It is a parable of a very limited "vision" that she has to tell; there is not even the promise of a heavenly community. Fellow-feeling, mutual memories: they are not enough for the "strong vision" that will result in something greater than the "incalculably diffusive." Dante's vision is not possible if his guide is bound to that reality which is always limiting. If a parable is to be effective, it should make its readers feel the world Tennyson "saw" and expressed in those lines which form the epigraph to chapter 43 of *Felix Holt*, and it should allow the men and women who illustrate its meaning the vision too:

> Dear friend, far off, my lost desire,
> So far, so near, in woe and weal;
> O, loved the most when most I feel
> There is a lower and a higher!   (FH: 43: 340)

This world, where the "lower and higher" form a thread that pulls us out of ourselves and unites us with the "enlarged life," is the world of parable, for a parable allows us a vision of the "higher" operating in the simplest "medium." But *Middlemarch*'s historian, even as she notes the fictive nature of history, can find no medium to support such parabolic work. George Eliot turns in *Daniel Deronda* to confront head-on the subject of art and vision. And in sacred romance she finds a means of creating vision out of the meanest reality.

III

Perhaps *Daniel Deronda* is so disturbing because it seems, *ab initio*, like none of George Eliot's earlier works. There is no Wordsworthian glow of memory to displace the fragmented present with a Hayslope, no invocation of a St Theresa to cushion the reader by framing and elevating the often confused and blind doings of a woman and a rural community living in an England with no certain notion of what the signs of the time might portend. Instead, we are placed *"in medias res,"* in the readers' present. And the spiritual values of St Ogg's, Stoniton, Lantern Yard, and Transome Court are combined and become horribly, because unmediatedly, present. A "scene of dull, gas-poisoned absorption" (1: 37), featuring men and women as drugged as any of the Veneering crowd, begins the novel; the Land of Goshen has become a casino. Yet it all ends with Manoa's elegy from the conclusion of *Samson Agonistes* – as if these Philistines had been destroyed and the children of light were quite triumphant in their cleansed Promised Land.

Which they in no way are. Yet we, as readers, have *seen* that land, and seen it in the most clearsighted way because George Eliot, after so many fictions alluding to the Judaic-Christian myth and Bunyan's use of it, constructs this final novel overtly around the chief situations and landscapes that had provided the texture of Puritan and evangelical biography and autobiography, and of Dinah Morris' sermons. The "children of light" are in bondage, to their own psychic heritage of slavery and to heathens "doing as they like" with more fervor than even Arnold's Philistines. And lest any casual reader miss the analogies – the Morality Play beneath the surface – the "children of light" in *Deronda* are not sensitive "Christians" like Maggie and Dorothea, but actual Jews. One is even a Moses as well ("an accomplished Egyptian" – 52: 721). The novel's formal construction insists on our recognition of its epic historical foundation: a beginning *in medias res*, constant allusions to Tasso's *Gerusalemme liberata*, to Handel's *Rinaldo* (itself based on a scene in the Tasso), to Dante's *Commedia*, and to the story of the Exodus and the Dispersion. Furthermore, the titular hero is himself identified as a savior–knight, as Moses and Prince Camaral-zaman, at once the leader of history and a hero of romance. As in all romance, this hero does go off to found a newer world; as in the history, on the final page he stands like Moses glimpsing the promised land – although his sight is the vision and not Moses' reality.

In all of this tale-spinning, as readers since 1876 have been announcing, there is one flaw: the hero leaves the real – because palpably living – heroine behind him in the City of Destruction with no promise of a Greatheart to bring her away towards some happy-ever-after. But in making this complaint we respond more to the hero's failure to satisfy *our* "dreams" than we do to the guideposts George Eliot gives us. The stories of Dorothea and Esther also end with a sense of dissatisfaction, but in each case the narrator shares the readers' letdown, even as together they share Dorothea's or Lydgate's. The narrator of *Daniel Deronda*, on the other hand, feels no melancholy sadness at the failure of youthful hope; indeed, there is wellnigh euphoria. *Deronda*'s narrator is not *Middlemarch*'s historian, nor *The Mill*'s remembrancer. Those narrators had told of the necessity of giving up our fictions if we were ever to live adequately – albeit never heroically – in the "real." But that forsaking of romance – whether Maggie's, Esther's, or Dorothea's – had left the lives of these "substantive and rare" human beings "absorbed" in the lives of others, or in death (Mid: "Epilogue," p. 611). All vision narrows to domestic dimensions.

George Eliot's last "experiment in life" is her meditation on this sense of loss when so much of romance is given up. *Daniel Deronda* asks, more fearlessly than any Victorian novel, what is the place of art in our lives, of the fictions we read and the paintings we see and the music we hear? And it avows that all art, whether of words or colors or sounds, distances and distorts reality: all becomes romantic to some degree.

Perspective, as its inventor remarked, is a beautiful thing. What horrors of damp huts, where human beings languish, may not become picturesque through aerial distance! What hymning of cancerous vices may we not languish over as sublimest art in the safe remoteness of a strange language and artificial phrase! Yet we keep a repugnance to rheumatism and other painful effects when presented in our personal experience. (14: 193)

Within this contrast – between the artificial and the severely real – how is art to function? How are mere words to tell morally? How are they to become a perhaps painful part of our personal experience in the way they burnt into Bunyan? The answer that *Daniel Deronda* implicitly offers is that art must find its sources in the religious myths that form part of man's consciousness, in the archetypal experiences that are innate. Bunyan's way is the only way. Otherwise art is, as Klesmer suggests, sheer idolatry.

George Eliot is not suddenly urging some creed on her readers. Her attitude is the same as Arnold's, and Carlyle's earlier. In 1875 Arnold had noted that "two things about the Christian religion must surely be clear to anybody with eyes in his head. One is, that men cannot do without it; the other, that they cannot do with it as it is."[24] Carlyle had said the same thing in *Sartor Resartus* and thereafter, and had said it through structures and language that formed the central literary and religious heritage of his readers. Yet by the time of the *Pamphlets* he had become so frightened by the "aerial distance" that language seemed to confer on truth that he shrilly defended the *Iliad* and the Hebrew Bible against the "Fine Arts." These epics are not "Fiction" but "histories," he proclaimed, "burning with . . . *belief*," "before all things, *true*" because grounded "on the Interpreting of Fact" (LDP: 322–3).

Obviously, he wants – has always wanted – another language to tell those eternal truths, but there was none available. "My friend, I have to speak in crude language, the wretched times being dumb and deaf: and if thou find no truth under this but the phantom of an extinct Hebrew one, I at present cannot help it" (LDP: 325).

By the time of *Daniel Deronda*, George Eliot has come to this same conclusion. Confronting the "wretched times" of the deaf and dumb men and women of the present day, she turns to the one ground of associations she hopes is still "deeply rooted in [her] readers' minds." Every major character in *Daniel Deronda* except Grandcourt thinks in terms of "genteel romance," fairy tales, or the Bible; and only those who use the latter survive spiritually. Every one of these people looks at the chaotic world around them in terms of old patterns that sort out the confusions of the present by showing their ordering, their beginning and end. George Eliot's men and women seek, or are forced to seek – if they would be alive – that symbolic situation in the past ("where peace and permanence seemed to find a home away from the busy change that sent the railway train flying in the distance" – 13: 167) that will give meaning and understanding to their own lives; they look for some "accustomed pattern" (22: epigraph, p. 278) for ordering the "unmapped country within us" and without (24: 321).

The only past that can provide such a "key" is, finally, the old Hebrew one. It is a memory based in fact. And to insure that no reader misses this idea, George Eliot uses an epic paradigm founded on the histories of the effort to retake Jerusalem from the "heathens." She bases the novel's structure – *its two plots* – on an episode in Tasso's *Gerusalemme liberata* and, very likely, on an adaptation of the episode by Giacomo Rossi for Handel's *Rinaldo*. The opera tells of a Christian knight in love with Almirena, daughter of Godfrey, the Christian leader of forces which will liberate Jerusalem. The opposition to the Christians – and to the heroine's love – is Armida, an enchantress who commands dragons and who loves Rinaldo. Her reward is conversion; his, Almirena; Godfrey's, Jerusalem. The chief difference between the opera and the Tasso episode is the absence of Almirena in the Tasso; there the enchantress takes both forms – helpless maiden in the water and queen of the heathen forces.[25]

George Eliot makes one signal change in this old plot, an exact reversal: her Christians need the Jews for liberation. Otherwise, she exploits all of its romance possibilities. In *Daniel Deronda* she simply becomes, without apology, the sacred romancer – this even as she keeps a firm grip on the narrator's mirror-observer function. What she does is to juxtapose – *not* fuse – the dream worlds of Maggie and Dorothea to the quotidian world of the Poysers and Dodsons and Middlemarchers. In Deronda and Mordecai she gives scenes which seem remote and "romantic" because they center on "visions," on what Mordecai defines as "the creators and feeders of the world" (40: 555). In Gwendolen and "Philistia" (13: epigraph, p. 165) we have Dodson Protestantism hardened and seen in a harsher light. The structures and language that express the teleological ideals of religious experience stand boldly beside language depicting the "puzzlin'" world that Mr Tulliver experienced and Mary Garth accepts, the world of chance and no pattern that Godfrey Cass so easily thought himself born into. A world devoted to visionary experience confronts and affronts a world centered on satisfying its own immediate "natural" desires. And after George Eliot has given us the histories of her two protagonists, she makes the relationship of their lives quite clear. Within Deronda, she notes, "there was a fervour which made him easily find poetry and romance among the events of everyday life."

And perhaps poetry and romance are as plentiful as ever in the world except for those phlegmatic natures who I suspect would in any age have regarded them as a dull form of erroneous thinking. They exist very easily in the same room with the microscope and even in railway carriages: what banishes them is the vacuum in gentlemen and lady passengers. How should all the apparatus of heaven and earth, from the farthest firmament to the tender bosom of the mother who nourished us, make poetry for a mind that had no movements of awe and tenderness, no sense of fellowship which thrills from the near to the distant, and back again from the distant to the near? (19: 245)

It is the question the novel explores, and explores with "the apparatus of heaven and earth" – with the story of the Hebrews and Jerusalem which was first history and then the stuff of epic and romance.

None of this is apparent at the novel's beginning, any more than is its traditional *Bildungsroman* structure. George Eliot's manipulation of narrative time does not allow readers to see, until two hundred pages have passed, that her recountings of Gwendolen Harleth's and Daniel Deronda's histories begin at that moment in each of their lives which initiates all pilgrims' progresses: when the question "What shall I do?" forces itself on the consciousness. Gwendolen and Deronda, seeing each other for the first time, significantly in a casino, are trying to find a "pathway" (*passim*) towards freedom amidst the pressures of what seem intractable circumstances. Daniel "felt himself in no sense free" (15: 202). Gwendolen views "the life before her as an entrance into a penitentiary" (24: 315). Yet all this remains hidden from the readers for fifteen chapters.

George Eliot instead begins her "story" (14: 185) as Bunyan did his dream and Dante his journey: *in medias res*. But that itself is ambiguous. It means at once Gwendolen at the roulette table and Gwendolen "in Daniel Deronda's mind," which is the locus of the novel's opening paragraph. Yet instead of immediately exploring that mind, we enter Gwendolen's case history. Only when we know how and why she got to that casino do we return to Deronda; and then we immediately begin his history, one which seems to have about as much to do with Gwendolen in Philistia as Teufelsdröckh's story has to do with a drawing-room in *Pelham*. Whatever "romance" there is in the story of "the princess in exile" is, her uncle, Reverend Gascoigne, tells her, something quite inferior to the "higher" considerations of money, rank and marriage (13: 180).

On the other hand, everyone (including himself) perceives Daniel's story as "romance"; and *it* centers on "higher" considerations which quite damn the parish minister. In outline it differs no whit from Teufelsdröckh's youthful history: though his childhood is happy, it is also marked by "the first arrival of care" (16: 206), at the age of thirteen, when the question "Who am I?" forces itself on the young boy. The need to know his parents, the shock of questioning his heritage and finding no answer, will mark an epoch for him:

> he was romantic. That young energy and spirit of adventure which have helped to create the worldwide legends of youthful heroes going to seek the hidden tokens of their birth and its inheritance of tasks, gave him a certain quivering interest in the bare possibility that he was entering on a like track – all the more because the track was one of thought as well as action. (41: 573–4)

He sets out to involve himself in a significant action, to know the past – his and others – and to see its connection with the present. He "had a passion for history, eager to know how time had been filled up since the Flood, and how things were carried on in the dull periods" (16: 203).

But that passion cannot be satisfied until he knows his own

heritage. Like Teufelsdröckh he feels himself an "Ishmaelite"; and his "inexpressible sorrow" over his unknown parentage similarly leads not to self-centeredness, but "takes the form of fellowship and makes the imagination tender" (16: 215). He yearns towards rescuing others, towards "telling upon their lives with some sort of redeeming influence," towards saintliness (28: 369). This very yearning and his constant meditations paralyze his "Active Power (*Thatkraft*)" (SR: 98).

His imagination had so wrought itself to the habit of seeing things as they probably appeared to others, that a strong partisanship, unless it were against an immediate oppression, had become an insincerity for him . . . Few men were able to keep themselves clearer of vices than he; yet he hated vices mildly . . . (32: 412)

The yearning towards rescue and the love it brings has been for Deronda a way of escaping that isolated because unrooted self which has been his birthright.

His own face in the glass had during many years been associated for him with thoughts of some one whom he must be like . . . He was forgetting everything else in a half-speculative, half-involuntary identification of himself with the objects he was looking at, thinking how far it might be possible habitually to shift his centre till his own personality would be no less outside him than the landscape . . . (17: 226, 229)

It is at one of those moments of gazing on the blank which is himself that he finds Mirah beside the river. And his subsequent reference to himself as "Orestes or Rinaldo" (19: 245) is doubly telling. Through these namings, even as they are one more way of dealing with his sense of having no identity, he makes his own actions a part of that flow of time from past to present; the allusions insert him into the heroic frame of significant actions which he constantly seeks.

George Eliot keeps the romance analogies close to Deronda because he does indeed, and consciously, have "something of the knight-errant in his disposition" (28: 370); and because, after Mirah's rescue, she wants the readers to share the experience with those who know Daniel. She wants us to feel ourselves like Mab and the others, "in the first volume of a delightful romance" (20: 249). By involving us so determinedly and allusively in romance, George Eliot for the last time examines the myths that sensitive men and women must have if the dead weight of present-day life is not to crush them. Teufelsdröckh falls into the abyss. Deronda avoids it by ascending consciously into heroic romance (and he significantly lacks the rational education that was part of Teufelsdröckh's undoing). His romance we may not find so interesting, but it tells why we miss the "shadow" in his life which we find in most romances – and in Gwendolen's story (35: 484). Deronda deals with those demons of the self by distancing them; he understands their mythic analogues and thus retains his sanity.[26]

If "demons" do not invade his own psyche, they abound in the lives of the women he would rescue. The story of Mirah has all the characteristic images we have come to see in the Victorian spiritual biography: the child who feels an orphan because she is so ill-used by her father (who would sell her into bondage if he could) leaves him only to find the world still a "hell" (20: 257), and herself a "poor wanderer" (47: 644) in it. Though she, a young Jewess, remembers her "People . . . driven from land to land and . . . afflicted," she finds hope gone and her mind "into war with itself." And then: "Faith came to me again: I was not forsaken" – Deronda saves her (20: 263–4). The last song we hear her sing summarizes her history:

Lascia ch'io pianga	[Let me lament
mia cruda sorte,	My cruel destiny,
e che sospiri	Let me sigh
la libertà.	For freedom;
Il duolo infranga	Let grief sunder
queste ritorte	The chains that bind me,
de' miei martiri	If only out of pity
sol per pietà.	For my anguish.]

(61: 796)[27]

It is Almirena's aria from *Rinaldo*, sung when the heroine is imprisoned in the fortress of the sorceress Armida. The song tells the reader something of Mirah's feelings, of course; she sings just after Hans Meyrick has given his "romance" of "the Vandyke Duchess," complete with the baritone's death and her marriage to Deronda, "with [his] fine head of hair, and glances that will melt instead of freezing her" (61: 794–5; Hans is borrowing Tasso's words for his description of the glance: *Gerusalemme liberata*, XVI: lxvii – Armida seducing Rinaldo). Mirah, not knowing Gwendolen's case, as the readers do, quite naturally and jealously sees her as some sorceress–queen enchanting Daniel.

But her song underlines what the reader has been experiencing from the novel's opening paragraph – albeit only consciously when

Deronda's history has been juxtaposed to Gwendolen's. The readers know that Gwendolen's story is also summarized by "Lascia ch'io pianga":

> Il duolo infranga
> queste ritorte . . .

Gwendolen herself has announced early-on that she has "read and learned by heart at school" the *Gerusalemme liberata* (5: 76). But not until she meets Deronda does her real education begin. And it will indeed involve her getting the Tasso "by heart." Only grief will, finally, sever the chains binding her.

The novel begins, literally, when Deronda discovers in the gambling Gwendolen "something of the demon" (32: 408):

> Was the good or the evil genius dominant in those beams? Probably the evil; else why was the effect that of unrest rather than of undisturbed charm? (1: 35)

Though he will come to see in her not some "vulgar" enchantress "setting snares" for him but rather one more of "the Hagars and Ishmaels" for whom he has such pity (36: 489), he will discover that in her case a Rinaldo's rescue is not so easily effected. And in that, as George Eliot tells us, "some education was being prepared for Deronda" (35: 485). It is an education which will show the limits of romantic action.

George Eliot introduces Gwendolen at the first point in her life when she becomes aware, however glibly, that the world does not necessarily order itself to her desires. It is indeed a "break in consciousness" (as Frye calls the beginning of romance),[28] for it is the point where Gwendolen is asking "What can I do?"

> And even in this beginning of troubles, while for lack of anything else to do she sat gazing at her image in the growing light, her face gathered a complacency gradual as the cheerfulness of the morning. Her beautiful lips curled into a more and more decided smile, till at last she took off her hat, leaned forward and kissed the cold glass which had looked so warm. How could she believe in sorrow? If it attacked her, she felt the force to crush it, to defy it, or run away from it, as she had done already. Anything seemed more possible than that she could go on bearing miseries, great or small. (2: 47)

But the burden on her will only increase.

Gwendolen's kissing of her mirrored image is a gesture perfectly appropriate to this "princess in exile" who has never had roots anywhere ("A human life," George Eliot writes of Gwendolen, "should be well rooted in some spot of a native land" – 3: 50) – and whose roots will be in "romance" in its most demonic sense (the mirror-kiss reminds us that Tasso's Armida has a mirror about her when she seduces Rinaldo). George Eliot throughout her fiction has used the mirror as the emblem of self-absorption: Hetty Sorrel, Rosamond Vincy, Mrs Transome, Gwendolen – all these women define themselves iconographically by their adoration of their mirrored images, a self-worship which places them amongst the Romantic egoists whose lives comprise, finally, a "Satanic masquerade, . . . entered on with an intoxicated belief in its disguises" (64: 831). Except for one moment Rosamond certainly never loses the intoxication. Hetty does so only when confronted with death. Gwendolen Harleth alone successfully goes through a fire-baptism. Her story, at its beginning a conventional "Sorrows of Gwendolen" tale, full of wanderings and ennui, becomes by its end a *Sartor Resartus*: very unRomantic and very full of romance. It introduces Gwendolen to a world of "fellowship" and "movements of awe and tenderness" (see above, p. 172) undreamt of in her experience – even if they are in that *Gerusalemme liberata* she has "by heart."

Like Charlotte Brontë, George Eliot will find the vanity-mirror emblem the perfect embodiment of the kind of egoism that controls her men and women. It is an emblem for her, as for Quarles and Bunyan and for the Romantics, of being bound to and within the surface of self:

> Believe her not, her glass diffuses
>   False portraitures: . . . she abuses
> Her misinform'd beholder's eye . . .

In vain he lifteth up the eye of his heart to behold his God, who is not first rightly advised to behold himself: . . . for if thou canst not apprehend the things within thee, thou canst not comprehend the things above thee; the best looking-glass, wherein to see thy God, is perfectly to see thyself. (Emblem II: 6; see fig. 2, p. 54)

Know "the things within thee" first.[29] But any world within hardly interests Hetty, or Rosamond, or Gwendolen as they gaze into their mirrors. They see nothing beyond their surfaces; they feel nothing beyond their desires. They are actresses, "representing" themselves according to Mrs Lemon or "genteel romance" (6: 83), imagining themselves in dramas or romantic ballads, avoiding – if it threatens at all – any hint of demon-empires within the self. "I am not talking about reality, mamma," Gwendolen says when Mrs Davilow reminds her that she is afraid of the dark (6: 85). These egoists are what René Girard calls "romantic *vaniteux*"; living completely on their surfaces, they are perfect solipsists and have no sense of anything transcending themselves.[30] To the narrator's constant urging that each see "que la terre tourne autour du soleil," the reply is: "Je vous jure que je ne m'en estime pas moins" (6: epigraph, p. 82). Convinced that they are utterly original and determined to be no one's disciples they intend to follow what Gwendolen calls "her favourite key of life – doing as she liked" (13: 173). Nothing, not religion, not romance, displaces them from their own self-esteem:

the religious nomenclature belonging to this world was no more identified for [Gwendolen] with those uneasy impressions of awe than her uncle's surplices seen out of use at the rectory . . . Church was not markedly distinguished in her mind from other forms of self-presentation, for marriage had included no instruction that enabled her to connect liturgy and sermon with any larger order of the world than that of unexplained and perhaps inexplicable social fashions.   (6: 95; 48: 666)

Gwendolen may avow she has Tasso "by heart," but her fear of solitude and the dark and "the vastness in which she seemed an exile" (6: 95) tells us how little she understands his words. She thinks herself completely immune to Christian's need for journeying or to the quests in Tasso (reduced by her to "genteel romance"). And yet, as much as she would ignore the "unmapped country within," her unease upon first seeing Deronda and her fear of the picture of the dead head tell us that she is not – like Hetty – dead to any world above or below; the very fears show us that she is not a solipsist like Grandcourt. Gwendolen's increasingly terrifying isolation, always imaged by the mirror and finally climaxed by her mirrored entrapment on Grandcourt's boat, is the result of that impulse to exalt the self and obliterate all sense of anything beyond it. Her sighting of the novel's Rinaldo forces on her the encounter with, and conquest of, her own "Demon-Empire" (as it begins Armida's salvation process in Tasso). "You began it, you know, when you rebuked me," she tells Deronda (36: 509), referring to her trouble. And he defines for her the "refuge" that will save:

"We should have a poor life of it if we were reduced for all our pleasure to our own performances. A little private imitation of what is good is a sort of private devotion to it . . . The refuge you are needing from personal trouble is the higher, the religious life, which holds an enthusiasm for something more than our own appetites and vanities."   (36: 491, 507–8)

It is indeed an answer to her question, repeated more and more as the glass's image becomes less fetching, "Why shouldn't I do as I like, and not mind?" (36: 501).

The language George Eliot employs as Gwendolen faces that "uncertain shadow [which] dogged her" (35: 484) and seeks help from her "priest" (35: 485) is baldly the language of religious romance, the language of an Armida losing control over her demon servants. The drugged air of the gambling halls that Gwendolen had chosen for "escape" follows her into marriage with Grandcourt, whose "sort of lotos-eater's stupor . . . was taking possession of her" (13: 172). She tries desperately for "new excitements that would make life go by without much thinking" (35: 477). Thus, the "demonic force" that Deronda witnessed at the gaming table seems to him even more at work within her after the marriage (35: 459). And, as the readers know, "Furies" have entered her life (31: 407) because she violated that "question of right or wrong" which Lydia Glasher's existence forced her to see, and which "rouse[d] her terror" (28: 355). Thereafter life has become the "labyrinth" (24: 317) she had feared, and those mirrors she had worshipped become part of her "painted gilded prison" (48: 651). The "many shadowy powers" that haunt her (44: 616) force her to *see* what she will call the "two creatures" of her self (56: 756), two creatures she sees objectified by Deronda and Grandcourt. The husband is the "monster" (48: 649), the total egoist who is the "immovable obstruction in her life, like the nightmare of beholding a single form that serves to arrest all passage though the wide country lies open" (54: 744); he is her "worst self" personified (54: 740), and the more terrible because he is connected in Gwendolen's mind with Lydia Glasher, a woman "who had the poisoning skill of a sorceress" (44: 616). Standing quite opposite to and above all of this, as in Tasso or any epic romance, is the savior, Deronda. Like Rinaldo, he is there to bring "that change of mental poise which has been fitly named conversion"; his "peculiar influence" will make of "heaven and earth" a "revelation" for Gwendolen, will arouse the godborn within her (35: 484–5). He is her "recovered faith," kept "with a more anxious tenacity, as a Protestant of old kept his Bible hidden or a Catholic his crucifix" (48: 655). In the course of her story he becomes "a part of her conscience," precisely as Rinaldo becomes part of Armida's in the Tasso (35: 468):

> My dear (she said), that blesseth with thy sight
>   Even blessed angels, turn thine eyes to me,
> For painted in my heart and portray'd right,

Thy worth, thy beauties, and perfections be;
Of which the form, the shape, and fashion best,
Not in this glass is seen, but in my breast.
. . .
O let the skies thy worthy mirror be.

(Gerusalemme liberata, XVI: xxi)

The religious language that begins to accompany and color this demon-world in which the "princess" lives tells us what George Eliot is doing: Gwendolen is being dragged against her will into a life where "vision" – the word appears even more than in *Felix Holt* – either feeds life, or else destroys it. Such vision shows us the difference between heaven and earth, and gives us the possibility of escaping the hells of our own making. And it demands recognition of the demons of the inner self: "for if thou canst not apprehend the things within thee, thou canst not comprehend the things above thee," noted Quarles; "the best looking-glass, wherein to see thy God, is perfectly to see thyself." Standing between Grandcourt and Deronda, Gwendolen is poised between a hell of her own choice (she put the ring on too! – 28: 358) and a world of possible rescue if she can "escape from herself" and "the evil within" (54: 746). She learns "to see all her acts through the impression they would make on Deronda" (54: 737), and learns too (in his words) "more of the way in which your life presses on others, and their life on yours" (36: 508). And then: not healing, but its beginning – "the process of purgatory . . . on the green earth" (54: 733), "the awakening of a new life within her" (56: 762).

Deronda could not utter one word to diminish that sacred aversion to her worst self – that thorn-pressure which must come with the crowning of the sorrowful Better, suffering because of the Worse.   (56: 762)

This returns us to Mirah's aria: "Il duolo infranga queste ritorte." For Gwendolen, as for Teufelsdröckh, the "'*Divine Depth of Sorrow*' lies disclosed," and with it renunciation, where "Life, properly speaking, can be said to begin" (SR: 189, 191). "You have had a vision of injurious, selfish action – a vision of possible degradation," Daniel tells Gwendolen; "think that a severe angel, seeing you along the road of error, grasped you by the wrist, and showed you the horror of the life you must avoid . . . Think of it as a preparation" (65: 839–40). Gwendolen's regeneration is not cast in Carlyle's triumphantly apocalyptic tones, but the *fact* is there, in her appreciation of going home:

All that brief experience of a quiet home which had once seemed a dulness to be fled from, now came back to her as a restful escape, a station where she found the breath of morning and the unreproaching voice of birds, after following a lure through a long Satanic masquerade, which she . . . had seen the end of in shrieking fear lest she herself become one of the evil spirits who were dropping their human mummery and hissing around her with serpent tongues. (64: 831)

She has been to the center of her own inferno. Emerging, she can see the world with new eyes, see its specialness apart from herself, see its "natural supernaturalism." And she will see what "a Minnow is man" (SR: 258):

The world seemed getting larger round poor Gwendolen, and she more solitary and helpless in the midst . . . she felt herself reduced to a mere speck . . . she was for the first time feeling the pressure of a vast mysterious movement, for the first time being dislodged from her supremacy in her own world, and getting a sense that her horizon was but a dipping onward of an existence with which her own was revolving. (69: 875–6).

George Eliot, then, in the harsh light of her portrayal of Philistia, gives us as much of the language and situations of romance *within* Gwendolen's "unmapped" self as she does on the surface of Deronda's history. And yet this Rinaldo can not finally liberate the woman who will teach him so much. Like Tasso's Rinaldo, he can feel pity but cannot offer the love she craves (see *Gerusalemme liberata*, XVI: li; XX: cxxxiv–cxxxvi). The man whose "rescue" impulses have been so constantly rewarded must be separated from this "sorceress" whose demons have entered his life. It is a separation that *shows* the reader the limits of romantic action – *except*, as Deronda says to Gwendolen, *in the mind*: "Now we can perhaps never see each other again. But our minds may get nearer" (69: 878). Daniel's mind was the locus of the novel's opening; his statement at its end recalls us to his titular position. As in Bunyan's dream, the mind has been the place of Deronda's spiritual education through the agency of Gwendolen's sufferings. His historical yearnings, his need to participate in a significant action, both would be naive if he had only Mordecai's "visions"; Gwendolen's "visions" show the other – and more real – kind of visions in this world. Her case is as necessary for Deronda as his "romance" is for her: each exposes the other to worlds never before encountered, each gives leaven and needed pattern to the other's experience. Each redefines for the other – and for us – what "romance" is. "We *are* such stuff as dreams are made of." And

Gwendolen's nightmare world of demons is *real* in a way that even Mirah's history can not be. It takes the two histories together to make the emphasis (and how alike Gwendolen and Mirah are is emphasized by Gwendolen's appropriating for herself a term Mirah applied to herself during their one interview: Gwendolen too will see herself as a "beggar by the wayside" when Deronda saves her, and both women have been seeking "deliverance" from their oppression – 48: 653; 56: 758, 760). But Mirah, though once near to suicide, has had the sustaining thought of her people, and she has never seen herself as the center of all life.[31]

Compared to her, Gwendolen's case is so strong because it forces Deronda into a life where sympathy is not so easily extended (we remember his early repugnance to the demon-filled gambler); her case and Grandcourt's will not allow him to "hate vices mildly." George Eliot tells us that what Deronda "most longed for was either some external event, or some inward light, that would urge him into a definite line of action, and compress his wandering energy" (32: 413). Gwendolen supplies both, as surely as Mordecai and Mirah, and she provides Deronda's *real* "education"; she makes him an "organic part of social life" rather than some "yearning disembodied spirit." His rescue of Gwendolen is not easy, is not even certain. But it keeps Deronda *alive* to the terrors of that unrooted self (he too is rootless) which has neither myths nor visions to keep hold of. It gives this man who "had never had a confidant" (37: 526) a vision of a world of inner darkness and isolation which he must acknowledge his if he is to *see* the "skies" of Mordecai's world. Daniel has in Gwendolen's experience an answer to his implicit question, that one which Bunyan asked himself: "whether we were of the Israelites, or no?" (B: 11). Gwendolen's suffering gives the triumphant answer; it is the "inward light" to the life Mordecai has envisioned. Their tears at the end signify this *shared* vision:

At last she succeeded in saying brokenly –
"I said . . . I said . . . it should be better . . . better with me . . . for having known you."
His eyes too were larger with tears.   (69: 878)

It is also the final vision of Rinaldo in Tasso: "From his pure fount ran two streams likewise,/Wherein chaste pity and mild ruth appears" (*Gerusalemme liberata*, XX: cxxxiv).

Lest we miss the way in which Gwendolen gives *life* to the Zionist visions of Mordecai, George Eliot parallels Daniel's efforts to help her at Grandcourt's death with his meeting of his mother. This woman, a princess who had been a great singer, is a Jew. Her suffering counterpoints Gwendolen's in extraordinary ways. Indeed, in this most operatic of novels, Alcharisi's words are yet one more capitulation – *da capo* – of Mirah's "Lascia ch'io pianga," a lament of her cruel destiny. And Daniel, whose "own face in the glass had during many years been associated for him with thoughts of some one whom he must be like" (17: 226), finds that likeness "amidst more striking differences": his mother seems part demon, "a Melusina, who had ties with some world which is independent of ours," a "sorceress," "like a dreamed visitant from some region of departed mortals" (51: 688; 53: 723, 730). He finds one of the sources of himself a woman who loathes everything he believes in, who finds such visionary Jews as Mordecai jailers, and who sees in the myth of the Hebrews the way towards imprisonment. And as she tells her story, she recapitulates Gwendolen's life history: she has no "talent to love" (53: 730; Gwendolen: "I can't love people" – 7: 115); she feels that marriage stifles (51: 688; 53: 744), she has never wanted to be "hampered with other lives" but to enjoy the "freedom to do what everyone else did, and be carried along in a great current, and not obliged to care" (51: 693). Unlike the young Englishwoman, Alcharisi has never been afraid of "the wide world"; it has been her passage to living a "large life." But her vision of being an artist has been smashed by her origins:

"You may try – but you can never imagine what it is to have a man's force of genius in you, and yet to suffer the slavery of being a girl. To have *a pattern cut out* – 'this is the Jewish woman, this is what you must be . . .' That was what my father wanted . . . He hated that Jewish women should be thought of by the Christian world as a sort of ware to make public singers and actresses of. As if we were not the more enviable for that! That is a chance of escaping from bondage." (p. 694)

To her the "great current" was a life of choice. The Judaism of her father patterned everything to bondage. To free her unwanted son from the "bondage" of that heritage was for her the only act of "love" she was capable of: "I delivered you from the pelting contempt that pursues Jewish separateness" (p. 698). For her the deliverance is a triumph – even if the result has been her "poor, solitary, forsaken remains of self" and "ghosts upon the daylight" (p. 699).

In this we see Gwendolen's story without its end: Alcharisi's immense physical pain leaves her "alone in spots of memory" ("and

I can't get away") – not the memory of the opera diva but of the daughter who denied her heritage and of the mother who denied the heritage of her son. Like Gwendolen, Alcharisi feels a kind of "retributive calamity [hanging] about her life" (35: 481) – and thus she makes her revelation to Deronda. Yet hers is a suffering no one – and certainly not her son – can comfort. His words to this determined woman – who demands that he "acknowledge" her right to be an artist, to be free of her father's "pattern" – are inadequate; they ring hollow in the face of her will. Although she "would bend . . . all to the satisfaction of self" (53: 727), we cannot help sympathizing with her need. Deronda's words will sustain Gwendolen, but he can not see round his mother. There is a Brontëan intensity in her anger and bitterness, in her sense that her history off the stage has been one long death-in-life, in her hatred of being a woman and a Jew, and it is an intensity that makes her case one which utterly negates Daniel's usual formulas. He has only the language that Gwendolen's life has been educating him to feel – and it is not enough. He is affronted by the fact that this "symbol of sacredness" does not conform to his imagined image, will not be comforted, can not be rescued and cared for. There is a force in her speech – in those "chest tones" – that wellnigh shatters the novel.

George Eliot makes no comment. The dangers of the very myths that animate *her* vision are exposed by Alcharisi, for whom they have been binding chains on her very nature. The "great current" the novel celebrates has been for her a drowning. And the paradox is not resolved by the "Judaism with a difference" that will be Deronda's messianic theme. It is the paradox involved in the very need of myths. (George Eliot's women constantly feel the entrapment of being female: Maggie notes how it hinders significant action for her, Mrs Transome curses it, even Gwendolen early on jokes about it: "We women can't go in search of adventures . . . We must stay where we grow, or where the gardeners like to transplant us" – (13: 171). Perhaps one of the problems in *Deronda* is that Daniel never seems to register significantly Alcharisi's indictment.)

Deronda would be a modern Moses – in the middle of his mother's monologue Mordecai is heard telling Mirah that Daniel is "an accomplished Egyptian" (52: 721) – but he cannot be that for his mother. The Moses reference calls our attention to the "Egyptian's" efforts to free the Jews from two kinds of bondage – to the Egyptians, and to their own slave mentality (that mentality which for Mordecai is a "darkness" blocking "vision" – 42: 591).

Daniel will be able to help Gwendolen get free of such bondage, but for his mother nothing is possible. She remains the unrescued and unredeemed soul. She remains that part of vision which is ghastly, and which opposes Mordecai's "vision" of "action, choice, resolved memory" with its ugly demonic side. More importantly, she remains that part of Deronda – that likeness of him, that source of him – that can not be altered, that will not fit into Mordecai's vision unless its historical basis, the suffering Jews, serves to animate it. In Daniel's interview with her, he sees that part of himself that no "romance" has ever suggested to him. It prepares him for his coming meeting with Gwendolen; it indeed makes their final encounters the keystone of the "education" his experience of her has been. Alcharisi's case highlights Gwendolen's "victory" – the word is too strong, and yet is right for her – but emphatically underlines the limitations of Mordecai's vision without the animation of the human (and a human that is not defined by gender), without a profoundly felt sense of "natural supernaturalism."

"Whether we were of the Israelites, or no?" Bunyan asked, as did Carlyle. George Eliot echoes both in her last novel. Alcharisi is, literally, while Gwendolen is not. And yet this young English-woman is an Israelite in the most urgent way imaginable: in her suffering. Daniel Deronda must give his name to the novel because that name emphasizes its parable: Daniel – "God is my judge." In George Eliot's last "experiment in life" God may be, as Mordecai defines Israel, no more than "the core of affection which binds a race and its families in dutiful love, and the reverence for the human body which lifts the needs of our animal life into religion, and the tenderness which is merciful to the poor and weak and to the dumb creature that wears the yoke for us" (42: 590). But the idea of something beyond the self that enlarges our lives and gives us the power to acknowledge and then to reconcile the ideal and the demonic within ourselves must be acknowledged if the world is not to become our hell, a mirrored palace containing only Grandcourts.

The sufferings in *Daniel Deronda* recall the novel's motto – "Let thy chief terror be of thine own soul" – and recall its emblematic mirrors. Deronda, like Gwendolen, must see himself before he can finally know what he is capable of, before he can believe – not consider intellectually – Mordecai's visions. Gwendolen's case gives substance to Alcharisi's reported sufferings, and to Mirah's. And it educates Deronda to the "covenant of reconciliation": "The sons of Judah have to choose that God may again choose them . . .

The divine principle of our race is action, choice, resolved memory" (42: 598).

And for George Eliot such a vision must be Jewish. Like Carlyle, she has no other "language" but the "nomenclature" of the Judeo-Christian religion to assert the paramount duty of fellow-feeling, and to illustrate the "pathway" towards freedom from slavery to the self and from the idolatry of a world which is alien to any better self and cares not to choose between right and wrong or anything beyond satisfying itself. In her final novel George Eliot ceases to be the historian or remembrancer we have known; memory and history have not been enough to keep vision free, unconstricted. In *Daniel Deronda* she is the sacred romancer, and baldly so. Tasso (with Handel) gives her the double plot structure to express the novel's key idea: "separateness and communication." And it gives her demons a-plenty to explore the inner life. The telling changes – indeed, reversals – she makes place the "Christians" of mid-Victorian England in the guise of Tasso's heathens, worshippers of self and of this world; and Tasso's saving Christians become in the modern retelling two Jews and one "Egyptian" whose words – "like the touch of a miraculous hand" (65: 840) – have something of Christ's power of love about them. The "sorceress," in both romance and novel, is converted; but beyond that we know nothing for both endings are alike. The sorceress' new life inscribes a tangent to the larger myth. Tasso's romance and Judaism show men a higher and a lower rather than a constant image of what lies about them in history's time. Romance originates in polarity, in the separation of the Hebrew from the heathen, the wheat from the chaff, the better self from the demon-empire. The Tasso and the history of the Jews together give life a vertical dimension, and man the possibility of transcendence.[32]

The novel is called "Daniel Deronda" because finally it is the history of the development of his consciousness. Israel's history and Tasso's romance express in 1876 the path towards the natural supernaturalism possible to non-epic man. The Sterne epigraph to chapter 19, where Deronda's story is given, has told us this:

I pity the man who can travel from Dan to Beersheba, and say, "'Tis all barren;" and so it is: and so is all the world to him who will not cultivate the fruits it offers. (19: 245)

For George Eliot the only source of vision for a nineteenth century that has been travelling from Dan to Beersheba and finding all barren is in Jerusalem liberated – politically or, in the heathen case, psychologically. We are *all* Israelites.[33]

"George Eliot's I don't rank as Novels but as second Bibles . . . You never think or feel you are reading fiction, but biography . . . and biography of people into whose minds and hearts you can enter with the intensest sympathy" (GEL: VI: 340). This letter, from John Brown (one of Blackwood's readers) in 1877, places precisely the effect George Eliot wanted her words to exert. She had insisted at the publication of *Silas Marner* that "the word *story*" be avoided in all announcements (GEL: III: 384). In her first novels she had assertively been the remembrancer who has known Adam Bede and Mr Tulliver. Even earlier, in "Janet's Repentance," she had insisted on her narrative position as not "the bird's eye glance of a critic" but one "on the level and in the press" with her protagonist as "he struggles his way along the stony road, through the crowd of unloving fellow-men" (*Scenes*: I: 322). By the time of *Daniel Deronda* the knowing omniscient eye dominates; but it is not the eye of a Dickens narrator looking on the Dedlock world of Chesney Wold, nor that of a Carlyle sitting in judgment on the French Revolution. It is more Virgil's shade, leading us towards the vision which will allow us to say, "There is a lower and a higher!" For George Eliot only the world of romance joined to the world of mythic history can bring us into this vision (and within this text she does not hesitate to call her work a "story"). Daniel Deronda himself may never satisfy; he gazes too calmly on the demons of life, and they do not gnaw at his "bowels" as they do at the innards of Bunyan or the Old Testament Hebrews. But the reader who can not feel Gwendolen's leaving the world of despair behind has missed her strong terrible vision. Her final repetition of "it shall be better with me because I have known you" (510, 878, 882) is cathartic. We must share it if we have paid attention to George Eliot's guiding voice.

We all – narrator, characters, readers – engage in constructing this book of life, "trying to make character clear before [us], and looking into the ways of destiny." For Gwendolen Harleth's inner life, as for Daniel Deronda's more outwardly connected story, we have seen that "tragic mark of kinship . . . such as has raised the pity and terror of men ever since they began to discern between will and destiny." For George Eliot, rewriting her book for the last time, only one structure was available in 1876 that she hoped would still give meaning to action and choice: that of the *Commedia*, *Pilgrim's Progress*, Israel in Egypt – epic, allegory, history: biblical romance. We discover our spiritual and better self only by seeing it in relation to a world larger than our own, only by breaking out of ourselves into that larger world, "above and below." As novelist – historian, seer, romancer – she offers us the parchment roll.

So she moved on, and we move on behind her.

Conclusion

The novel as book of life

Pliable: And do you think that the words of your Book are certainly true?
Christian: Yes verily, for it was made by Him that cannot lie. (B:149)

"It is a very ancient story, that of the lost sheep – but it comes up afresh every day."
     "That is a way of speaking – it is not acted on, it is not real," said Gwendolen, bitterly. (DD: 36: 494)

I began this study by suggesting Blake's "Behemoth and Leviathan" as the perfect emblem for the determination of Carlyle and the Victorian novelists to expose both the traps of Vanity Fair and the "Demon-Empires" within. That drawing suggests the Romantic internalization of the quest without its dangers of solipsism; Behemoth and Leviathan are, after all, God's creatures and not simply man's psychic projections. The drawing suggests too, as Northrop Frye has pointed out, that for Blake "taking the order of nature to be the circumference or horizon of all human effort" is joining Satan's party.[1] There *is* a world elsewhere, a power beyond the self leading human beings to assert the godlike within.

The progress of Carlyle's work and that of those Victorian novelists who took the same path seem to me suggested in Blake's reading of Job. In *Sartor Resartus* there is the temptation felt by Teufelsdröckh to name nature God; there is the assertion that "the GOD'S-PRESENCE" is manifested "in our fellow-man" (SR: 66), and there is the vision of nature and man as inextricably interconnected: "Yes, truly, if Nature is one, and a living indivisible whole, much more is Mankind, the Image that reflects and creates Nature, without which Nature were not" (SR: 246–7). But by the time of the *Latter-Day Pamphlets* this nature has degenerated into a demon-occupied dunghill and thus into "nature" as Bunyan defined it, a nature which was indeed the imprisoning circumference of a Godless world. Carlyle's typical man in 1850 is not Diogenes Teufelsdröckh but a man "enchanted," quite content with this "natural" world as long as he has money and food; he has become a pig: "Hrumph!" And the prophet who *sees* another world thus finds himself thundering to the "deaf and dumb" through "extinct Hebrew" language.

The novelists who work in Carlyle's path – who believe in "natural supernaturalism" and who are determined that their words be read as more than "mere *words*" – do not give in to Carlyle's despair in the face of a nature dis-godded and a language desacralized. None ever gives up the kind of journey Teufelsdröckh made: in Lucy Snowe and Eugene Wrayburn and Gwendolen Harleth, as in Jane Eyre, Florence Dombey, and Silas Marner, these novelists insist to the end of their careers on the possibility of a redemption whose agent is the "still small voice," the godlike, within another human being. The progresses of their protagonists towards "natural supernaturalism" are a *sine qua non* in all the novels they write, their sign of belief in the power of language to alter human lives, to connect the reader with the godlike. What Gwendolen Harleth learns these novelists want their readers to *see*: words – emblematic words, not "mere *words*" – are "acted upon," are "real."

Thus the traditional language of the Bible and Bunyan and the physical and psychological landscapes it offers kept alive the "sacred" way of words in a very secular literature and urged the "sacred" relationship of authors and readers.

Yet was our relation a kind of sacred one; doubt not that! For whatsoever once sacred things become hollow jargons, yet while the Voice of Man speaks with Man, hast thou not there the living fountain out of which all sacrednesses sprang, and will yet spring? Man, by the nature of him, is definable as "an incarnated Word." Ill stands it with me if I have spoken falsely: thine also it was to hear truly. (FR: IV: 323)

Words could create a world of pilgrims "in friendly company." Even the more pessimistic Thackeray, closing his *Pendennis* (in 1850) with a comment on the "Ordainer of the lottery" under whose dispensation "the false and worthless live and prosper," yet adds:

and, knowing how mean the best of us is, let us give a hand of charity to Arthur Pendennis, with all his faults and shortcomings, who does not claim to be a hero, but only a man and a brother.[2]

The emphasis on charity to a man and brother marks precisely what Carlyle and the novelists were about. They wanted their work to be a *scola cordis* so that men might say spontaneously "thou *art* my Brother" (SR: 245). They wanted their words to be a "secular scripture," a sacred romance bringing the old scripture up to date by showing man that "the great twins of divine creation and human recreation have merged into one" (in Frye's words),[3] into "natural supernaturalism." Their faith was that by schooling the heart of man, he would discover within some remnant of the godlike which would enable him to find a way out of the circumscribing prison of the "natural" world.

Yet Thackeray's ironic note about the lack of poetic justice in a world governed by chance suggests how embattled this tradition of sacred romance was in mid-century Victorian England. Charlotte Brontë's constant interruptions of her narratives with comments about her "romantic readers" and their dislike of the "unvarnished truth" point to the breakdown of the "sacred" reading of words. Similarly, Dickens' experiments with tenses and his increasing tendency to literalize the old emblems testify to his sense that his readers took everything as "entertainment." George Eliot's turn in *Daniel Deronda* towards the epic romance of Tasso and towards Dante as a way of illuminating truth offers a comment indeed on the power of quotidian reality to obliterate the "unseen but not unreal world" that Carlyle and all the novelists took as their "reality."

Thackeray himself offers the best illustration of the state of the tradition of writing that has been my focus. He constantly satirizes the fictional conventions – the "sacred scriptures" – of his age and refuses to do more than "play" the role of sage–hero (though the "play" is very serious). He does not share Carlyle's belief in the possibility of creating "vision" through words. The critical outrage against his fictions, interestingly similar to the later outrage against Hardy, stems, I suspect, from the public's intuition that Thackeray would not offer the myths of order – and of humanity – they desperately needed, and which their most popular novelists gave them; they *felt* he did not believe. Thackeray agrees certainly with Carlyle and Dickens and George Eliot that fiction must be an "illustrative garment of Fact." His novel, he wrote in the preface to *Pendennis,* may "fail in art," but "it at least has the advantage of a certain truth and honesty . . . If there is not that, there is nothing." Furthermore, the tradition that author and reader are in "constant communication" is axiomatic with him (and not merely because of serial publication): his novel, he adds, "is a sort of confidential talk between writer and reader." The problem comes in the nature of that talk, and in the nature of the definition of "truth and honesty." Thackeray does not believe in changes of heart; he gives us no

Rochesters or Wrayburns or Gwendolens:

> We alter very little. When we talk of this man or that woman being no longer the same person whom we remember in youth, and remark (of course to deplore) changes in our friends, we don't, perhaps, calculate that circumstance only brings out the latent defect or quality, and does not create it . . . Are you not awe-stricken, you, friendly reader, who, taking the page up for a moment's light reading, lay it down, perchance, for a graver reflection – . . . to think how you are the same *You*, whom in childhood you remember, before the voyage of life began! (59: 621–2)

And as for the possibility of breaking out of our isolation through fellow-feeling:

> How lonely we are in the world! how selfish and secret, everybody! . . . Ah, sir – a distinct universe walks about under your hat and under mine – all things in nature are different to each –. . . you and I are but a pair of infinite isolations, with some fellow-islands a little more or less near to us. (16: 177–8)

There is no comfort, no aspiration, in this prose, no belief that "where two or three are gathered together" real fellowship is possible, and with it some sense of "natural supernaturalism." There is no "incarnated Word" here. Isolation is the natural condition of Thackeray's Major Dobbin, and of his Everyman. The battles and the pilgrimages, the orphans and the prisons, are the stock devices of his fictions as they are of the fictions of his fellow Victorians. But for Thackeray these images do not call up remembrances of God's grace or man's goodness. They reflect Vanity Fair, not sacred romance. They are mirrors of reality, not emblems speaking *sub specie aeternitatis*.[4]

And Hardy? His fiction is the great anti-type for the novels of this study. He does not question if we can know God or nature or the godlike, or man's relationship to them; he *knows* man cannot achieve such visions. Although he structures his fiction around pilgrimages, it is simply to parody the effort: paradises await no one, only more intense awarenesses of hell and cataclysm. Jude Fawley (1895) may resemble Christian – and Teufelsdröckh – in that "internal warfare between flesh and spirit." But his journey, ending at the Christminster that had been his youthful dream, mocks all idea of progress. Death comes as he hears "the Remembrance games" – all reminding him that he has no saving memories, neither the Word nor the voice of a human being. Not Amy Dorrit's voice; not Daniel Deronda's Jewish heritage; not Lucy Snowe's Bible. Only Job's curse: "Why died I not from the womb? . . . I should have slept: then had I been at rest! . . . There the prisoners rest together; they hear not the voice of the oppressor."[5] The natural world has triumphed. Hardy separates himself from the Victorians because he refuses to share – or to reinforce – their belief that fiction will "make a traveller of thee," will be a *scola cordis*. For him Puritan allegory and Romantic quests and the life of Diogenes Teufelsdröckh come together in a prison full of deluded men who have insisted on envisioning nature as good, time as a seedfield, life as a progress. The very clumsiness of the voices of his narrators makes grisly fun of his predecessors. A real mirror shows man dying – nothing else. Words are simply "mere *words*."

It is Lawrence's rejection of the premise that modern man need be a "dead man in life," and his adoption of the role of the novelist as hero, which mark his relationship to the English *de te fabula* tradition of Carlyle and the novelists whom I have discussed. Lawrence knew the English Sunday, he knew Bunyan and the emblem tradition, he knew the Romantics, he felt Carlyle's analysis of the Age of Machinery. He also knew the cataclysms that put a final end to the Victorians' visions, but he was determined to maintain their sacred romances. And he believed that the novel could show man a rainbow and offer the promise of a path onward out of the muck. "It is rather hard work," he said at the beginning of *Lady Chatterley's Lover*, "there is now no smooth road into the future: but we go round, or scramble over the obstacles."[6] No wonder he wrote his own *Apocalypse*. He differs immensely but not essentially from Carlyle and the Victorian sacred romancers. Like them he would have his men and women find "the water, namely, of Knowledge and of Life" (SR: 234). He believed in the English tradition of words that were not "mere *words*," that would and did make travellers of their readers as they schooled their hearts.[7]

In all this wild welter, we need some sort of guide. It's no good inventing Thou Shalt Nots! What then? Turn truly, honourably to the novel, and see wherein you are man alive, and wherein you are dead man in life . . . To be alive, to be man alive, to be whole man alive: that is the point. And at its best, the novel, and the novel supremely, can help you.

His call is a restatement of the faith the Victorian novelists felt in their words as an "illustrative garment of Fact," a source of "doctrine," "healing," and "guidance." For them, as for Lawrence, "The novel is the one bright book of life."[8]

Notes

Preface

1 Carlyle's letter is reprinted in the C. F. Harrold edition of *Sartor Resartus*, pp. 303–4.
2 From Bulwer Lytton, "On certain principles of art in works of imagination," in *Caxtoniana: A Series of Essays on Life, Literature, and Manners* (New York: Harper and Brothers, 1864), pp. 317–19.
3 Bulwer Lytton, *Zanoni*, 3 vols. (London: Saunders & Otley, 1842), I: xviii.
4 Bulwer Lytton, "On the normal clairvoyance of the imagination," in *Caxtoniana*, p. 37.
5 The phrase is George Levine's in his discussion of author–reader relationships in *The Realistic Imagination: English Fiction from Frankenstein to Lady Chatterley* (Chicago: Univ. of Chicago Press, 1981), p. 22.
6 *John Bunyan* (London: Thomas Nelson and Sons, [1905]), pp. 169–70.

Introduction. The WORD made novel

1 *Scola Cordis* is by Christopher Harvey, but it was attributed to Quarles in the nineteenth century and published in the same volume with the *Emblems* and *Hieroglyphs*; see Rosemary Freeman, *English Emblem Books* (1946; rpt. New York: Octagon Books, 1978), pp. 232–3. The Dickens line is the epigraph he proposed for *Martin Chuzzlewit*, quoted by John Forster, *The Life of Charles Dickens*, ed. J. W. T. Ley (London: Cecil Palmer, 1928), p. 311.
2 U. Milo Kaufmann, *The Pilgrim's Progress and Traditions in Puritan Meditation* (New Haven: Yale, 1966), p. 200, discusses Bunyan's sense of the pilgrimage as connecting past and future.
3 Ibid., p. 201. See too William Haller, *The Rise of Puritanism* (1938; rpt. Philadelphia: Univ. of Pennsylvania Press, 1972), chapter 3, for a discussion of how books yielded "a new version of the sacred epic of the fall and regeneration of man." For a discussion of this tradition as it flourished among evangelicals in Victorian England, see Elisabeth Jay, *The Religion of the Heart: Anglican Evangelicalism and the Nineteenth-Century Novel* (Oxford: Clarendon, 1979), p. 148.
4 Sacvan Bercovitch, *The Puritan Origins of the American Self* (New Haven: Yale, 1975), pp. 30–1.
5 Ian Watt, *The Rise of the Novel* (Berkeley: Univ. of California Press, 1957), pp. 74–80. G. A. Starr, *Defoe and Spiritual Autobiography* (Princeton: Princeton Univ. Press, 1965), chapter 1, and J. Paul Hunter, *The Reluctant Pilgrim* (Baltimore: Johns Hopkins, 1966),

chapters 4–5, discuss the origins and development of Puritan auto-biography and biography and Defoe's transfer of their structures and languages into fiction. Frank Kermode, *The Sense of an Ending* (London: Oxford, 1966), p. 67, suggests that "the rise of what we call literary fiction happened at a time when the revealed, authenticated account of the beginning was losing its authority."

6 M. H. Abrams, *Natural Supernaturalism* (New York: Norton, 1971), p. 13. The metaphorical rather than literal reading of scripture is of course a significant part of Christian thought, as Jacob Boehme and the Inner Light Protestants illustrate.

7 Geoffrey Hartman, "Romanticism and anti-self-consciousness," in *Romanticism and Consciousness*, ed. Harold Bloom (New York: Norton, 1970), p. 54.

8 Peter Coveney's splendid *The Image of Childhood* (1957; rpt. Baltimore: Penguin, 1967), reminds us that Wordsworth is not the first to stress the original innocence of the child; Blake, Rousseau, and even some Hebrew and Christian writers had given the idea currency. But for the Victorians Wordsworth is identified with the idea, as the novels of George Eliot and Dickens attest.

9 *The Complete Works of Hannah More* (New York: Harper and Row, 1835), VI: 36–7. Elisabeth Jay, *Religion of the Heart*, pp. 55–6, focuses on the conflict in Victorian fiction between these two conceptions of the child.

10 U. C. Knoepflmacher, "Mutations of the Wordsworthian child of nature," in *Nature and the Victorian Imagination*, ed. Knoepflmacher and G. B. Tennyson (Berkeley: Univ. of California Press, 1977), p. 394, notes that the Victorians felt at once nostalgia for and skepticism about the Wordsworthian child. "The criticism . . . arises out of skepticism and doubt that have their roots in empirical observation." See articles by Andrew Griffin and George Levine in the same volume for discussions of the de-emphasis of actual nature in Victorian literature (Ruskin always excepted). Griffin notes, pp. 172–3, that the Victorians essentially "invert Wordsworth" by internalizing the Romantic relationship with the natural world.

11 Eric Vogelin, "Postscript: on paradise and revolution," *The Southern Review*, 7, n.s. (January 1971), pp. 27 and 39, suggests that the prevalence of prison imagery in nineteenth- and twentieth-century literature is an expression of the "consciousness of having lost the freedom of movement in the open cosmos, of being closed up within oneself." He connects this sense of entrapment with the deformation of traditional symbols: "As the process gains momentum, the symbols of open existence – God, man, the divine origin of the cosmos, and the divine logos permeating its order – lose the vitality of their truth and are eclipsed by the imagery of a self-creative, self-realizing, self-expressing, self-ordering, and self-saving ego that is thrown into, and confronted with, an immanently closed world."

12 Alexander Welsh, *The City of Dickens* (Oxford: Clarendon, 1971), p. 130. Masao Miyoshi, *The Divided Self: A Perspective on the Literature of the Victorians* (New York: New York Univ. Press, 1969), p. xv, notes

that throughout the nineteenth century "it was 'unrealistic' romance that suggested new ways of exploring the unconscious and the irrational, the other self, within the framework of the novel." See too the important discussions of the romance and realistic traditions of nineteenth-century fiction by Edwin M. Eigner, *The Metaphysical Novel in England and America: Dickens, Bulwer, Melville, and Hawthorne* (Berkeley: Univ. of California Press, 1978) and George Levine, *The Realistic Imagination.* Eigner, pp. 73–5, notes how the *Doppelgänger* figures of German Romantic fiction and the Victorian novel derive from the allegorical tradition.

13 Bulwer Lytton, *Ernest Maltravers* (London: George Routledge and Sons, n.d.), p. viii.

14 Herbert L. Sussman, *Fact into Figure: Typology in Carlyle, Ruskin, and Pre-Raphaelite Brotherhood* (Columbus: Ohio State Univ. Press, 1979), p. 15, defines the "chief, but unacknowledged, formal principle" of Carlyle, Ruskin and the Pre-Raphaelite Brotherhood as "the shaping of fact into formal parallels with traditional iconography."

15 Bulwer Lytton, *A Strange Story* (New York: J. F. Taylor, 1897), p. xiv.

16 Quoted by Valentine Cunningham, *Everywhere Spoken Against: Dissent in the Victorian Novel* (Oxford: Clarendon, 1975), p. 52. See too Elisabeth Jay, *Religion of the Heart,* pp. 195–6, for discussion of evangelical attitudes towards the novel. E. P. Thompson, *The Making of the English Working Classes* (1963; rpt. New York: Vintage, 1966), p. 365, discusses the relation of Methodism and Utilitarianism. Throughout this study "evangelical" means both non-conformists and the evangelicals within the established Anglican church.

17 Wesley quoted by Richard D. Altick, *The English Common Reader* (Chicago: Univ. of Chicago Press, 1957), p. 35.

18 G. B. Tennyson, "The *Bildungsroman* in nineteenth-century English literature," in *Medieval Epic to the "Epic Theatre" of Brecht* (Los Angeles: Univ. of California Press, 1968), p. 141.

19 Jerome Buckley, *Seasons of Youth: The Bildungsroman from Dickens to Golding* (Cambridge: Harvard, 1974), p. 19. Susanne Howe's *Wilhelm Meister and His English Kinsmen* (New York: Columbia, 1930), is the essential study of the *Bildungsroman* as the English developed it. She notes the relation of the central figure of these novels to the figures in the early moral allegories.

20 Bulwer Lytton, *England and the English,* ed. Standish Meacham (1833; rpt. Chicago: Univ. of Chicago Press, 1970), p. 282.

21 Quoted in Susanne Howe, *Wilhelm Meister,* p. 222. Howe discusses Lewes' *Ranthorpe* and his novel fragment *The Apprenticeship of Life* in her survey.

22 Martin Swales, *The German Bildungsroman from Wieland to Hesse* (Princeton: Princeton Univ. Press, 1978), pp. 34–5, 164.

23 Tennyson, "The *Bildungsroman,*" p. 143, calls *Sartor* "that handbook of the Victorian *Bildungsroman.*" Alan Mintz, *George Eliot and the Novel of Vocation* (Cambridge: Harvard, 1978), p. 21, suggests that the secularized version of the Puritan ideas of Calling and work gave George Eliot, Carlyle, and Newman, as well as many other Victorians, "a serviceable principle of biographical design."

24 Mrs Sarah Ellis, *Pictures of Private Life* (1837; rpt. New York: J. & H. G. Langley, 1844), p. iv.
25 George Landow, *Victorian Types and Shadows: Biblical Typology in Victorian Literature, Art and Thought* (Boston: Routledge & Kegan Paul, 1980), p. 3. Landow finds "a great, almost astonishing, revival of biblical typology" in the first two-thirds of the century.
26 Rosemary Freeman, *English Emblem Books*, p. 13.
27 See introductory chapters: Sussman, *Fact into Figure*, and Landow, *Victorian Types*.
28 Ruskin notes how as a child he "got through the evening" on Sundays "over the Pilgrim's Progress, Bunyan's Holy War, Quarles's Emblems, Foxe's Book of Martyrs, Mrs. Sherwood's Lady of the Manor" and other such evangelically approved texts; see *Praeterita*, in *Works*, ed. E. T. Cook and Alexander Wedderburn (London: George Allen, 1903–12), XXXV: 72–3, 128. For considerations of the *force* of the religious tradition in Victorian England, see Elisabeth Jay, *Religion of the Heart*; and also Donald Davie, *A Gathered Church: The Literature of the English Dissenting Interest, 1700–1930* (New York: Oxford, 1978). John R. Reed, *Victorian Conventions* (Athens: Ohio Univ. Press, 1975), pp. 20–4, suggests that "interpreting existence in emblematic terms was a customary approach for the nineteenth-century mind." Rosemary Freeman (*English Emblem Books*) notes the continued popularity of Quarles into the nineteenth century.
29 Hugh Witemeyer, *George Eliot and the Visual Arts* (New Haven: Yale, 1979), p. 75. Sussman, in his chapter on "Victorian figuralism" in *Fact into Figure*, offers a similar thesis, focusing on Carlyle and Ruskin.
30 William Buckler, *The Victorian Imagination: Essays in Aesthetic Exploration* (New York: New York Univ. Press, 1980), pp. 31 and 18.
31 Joan Webber, *The Eloquent "I": Style and Self in Seventeenth-Century Prose* (Madison: Univ. of Wisconsin Press, 1968), pp. 14, 22–4, discusses, with Bunyan as illustration, the Puritan author's habit of speaking directly to the reader, thus emphasizing the reader's own participation in the author's experiences; the "I" of the narrative is an exemplum, an instrument towards the reader's own salvation. Samuel Pickering, Jr, *The Moral Tradition in English Fiction, 1785–1850* (Hanover, N. H.: Univ. Press of New England, 1976), p. 58, locates as one source of the convention of authorial intrusion the religious writers of the late eighteenth century who "intruded themselves into their narratives . . . to underline the didacticism of their stories . . . Positing a student–teacher relationship between the author and reader, narrative intrusions focused attention not on the art of, but on the didacticism of, the novel." Eigner, *Metaphysical Novel*, p. 64, and Levine, *The Realistic Imagination*, p. 22, also discuss this reader–author relationship, as does U. C. Knoepflmacher in his Preface to *Laughter and Despair* (Berkeley: Univ. of California Press, 1971).
32 Northrop Frye, *The Secular Scripture: A Study of the Structure of Romance* (Cambridge: Harvard, 1976), p. 186.
33 Bulwer Lytton, *The Caxtons* (London: George Routledge and Sons, n.d.), p. iii.
34 Quoted in *Novelists on the Novel*, ed. Miriam Allott (New York:

Columbia, 1959), pp. 49–50. But see George Levine's discussion of Scott in *The Realistic Imagination*, chapter 4.

35 George Levine, *The Boundaries of Fiction: Carlyle, Macaulay, Newman* (Princeton: Princeton Univ. Press, 1968), p. 15. Levine also notes that the "tradition of realistic anti-romance is . . . related very clearly to the novelists' keen sense of audience," to the writers' efforts to establish a "personal relation" with the reader (see p. 10 and entire introductory chapter). In "Realism reconsidered," in *The Theory of the Novel*, ed. John Halperin (New York: Oxford, 1974), p. 239, Levine writes: "Although novels may aspire to create the illusion of reality and to tell the truth, the most fruitful direct approach to fiction is through a focus on romance elements, the romance being the generator of form."

36 Robert Langbaum, "The art of Victorian literature," in *The Mind and Art of Victorian England*, ed. Josef Altholz (Minneapolis: Univ. of Minnesota Press, 1976), p. 31, suggests that the barely tolerable plots of Victorian novels are "an anachronistic hangover from an earlier time when belief in a publicly objective moral order made revelation through action possible." Alexander Welsh, *The City of Dickens*, p. vi, connects the breakdown of faith with the "Victorian readiness to make a heaven of hearth and home, and the ambition of the novel virtually to impose its own religious construction of reality." The emphases of Bulwer, Dickens, George Eliot, Mrs Ellis and a thousand others on "scenes of every-day life" offer ample support to this thesis.

37 Levine, *The Boundaries of Fiction*, p. 15. Northrop Frye, *Anatomy of Criticism* (1957; rpt. New York: Atheneum, 1966), p. 304, notes, in considering the differences between novel and romance, that in the latter "a suggestion of allegory is constantly creeping in around its fringes."

38 Frye, *The Secular Scripture*, p. 15.

39 Langbaum, "Art of Victorian literature," p. 32, writes of the Victorians' use of the omniscient narrator: "It is . . . in Victorian fiction that the omniscient narrator first becomes an *issue*, just because the omniscient voice has lost authority, no longer knows the story as God would know it. The omniscient narrator becomes conspicuous because the Victorian novelist is so nervously self-conscious about speaking with such a voice." For discussion of the breakdown of the novel's "paternal" authority, see Edward Said, *Beginnings* (New York: Basic Books, 1975), especially chapter 3.

40 Last Carlyle quotation from *Reminiscences*, ed. James A. Froude (London: Longmans, 1881), I: 322. Kathleen Tillotson, *Novels of the Eighteen-Forties* (1954; rpt. London: Oxford, 1961), pp. 150–6, discusses the general impact Carlyle had on the mid-century novel. Donald Stone, *The Romantic Impulse in Victorian Fiction* (Cambridge: Harvard, 1980), p. 11, notes of Carlyle's place in "transmuting Romanticism into Victorian themes and values": "It was Scott and Carlyle, above all others, who conditioned the Victorian attitude, positively and negatively, toward Romanticism and romance." My focus is on Carlyle because for the Victorians Scott's province was never the "inward world." Bulwer noted "how sparingly Scott dissects

the mechanism of the human mind; how little the inclinations of his genius dispose him either toward the metaphysical treatment or the poetical utterance of conflicting passions." See "On some authors in whose writings knowledge of the world is eminently displayed," in *Caxtoniana*, pp. 407–9.

1. Carlyle in "Doubting Castle"

1 Owen Barfield's discussion in *Saving the Appearances: A Study in Idolatry* (New York: Harcourt Brace, n.d.), of the dis-godding of the natural world, of the elimination of "spiritual substance" from the external world, offers significant commentary on the kind of insights Carlyle was developing in his work up through the *Heroes* lectures. And Linda Nochlin's discussion of realism in the visual arts (*Realism* (Harmondsworth: Penguin, 1971), p. 45) helps focus the problems Carlyle and the novelists faced: "it was not until the nineteenth century that contemporary ideology came to equate belief in facts with the total content of belief itself: it is in this that the crucial difference lies between nineteenth-century Realism and its predecessors"; earlier artists "were looking through eyes, feeling and thinking with hearts and brains, and painting with brushes, steeped in a context of belief in the reality of something other and beyond that of the mere external, tangible facts they beheld before them."

2 For the Puritan conception of Calling, see William Haller, *Rise of Puritanism*, pp. 124–7, and Bercovitch, *Puritan Origins*, pp. 15–16.

3 George Levine, *The Boundaries of Fiction*, pp. 68–71, discusses Carlyle's relation to Romanticism, noting: "Despite his occasional fits of pantheism in *Sartor*, [Carlyle] found it difficult to perceive the harmony between man and nature which was indispensable to the Romantic affirmation."

4 G. B. Tennyson discusses Carlyle's use of the *Märchen* in *"Sartor" Called "Resartus"* (Princeton: Princeton Univ. Press, 1965), pp. 76–81, 95–8, 190–3. Carlyle, Tennyson notes, "customarily translated the term *Märchen* by 'Fabulous Tale'" and found it "the proper vehicle for contemporary allegorical symbolism." Needless to add, my discussion of *Sartor* is immensely indebted to Tennyson's book.

5 Tennyson, *"Sartor" Called "Resartus"*, p. 175, calls the Editor "the protagonist of *Sartor* as a novel" and notes, p. 169, that this figure controls nearly one-half of the statements in the book.

6 Ibid., pp. 256–7.

7 On the Editor-reader, see Janet R. Edwards, "Carlyle and the fictions of belief: *Sartor Resartus* to *Past and Present*," in *Carlyle and His Contemporaries*, ed. John Clubbe (Durham, N. C.: Duke Univ. Press, 1976), p. 98, where Carlyle's method is compared with Thackeray's in *Vanity Fair*.

8 J. H. Van den Berg, "The subject and his landscape," in *Romanticism and Consciousness*, ed. Harold Bloom (New York: Norton, 1970), pp. 57–65, offers a contrast between Rousseau and Augustine as they approach nature which is instructive in showing us what Carlyle is

doing in this section of *Sartor*: "The inner self became necessary when contacts between man and the world about him were devalued . . . Augustine, believing that the approach to himself is an aspect of his relation to God, wishes to speak of God and not himself; Rousseau means to speak of the self of the individual, the 'self' which is of significance because of itself. Augustine has no knowledge of this self, he does not know the self of this self-satisfied individualism."

9 Steven Marcus, *Dickens from Pickwick to Dombey* (New York: Simon and Schuster, 1965), pp. 54–91, discusses *Oliver Twist* in the context of Bunyan and the Romantics. Marcus suggests, p. 80, n. 1, that "the remarks about clothes all through the novel lead one to surmise that Dickens may recently have read *Sartor Resartus*."

10 The way Victorians "read" texts and remembered them is extremely important in any effort to generalize about their ideas and beliefs: i.e., *their* "Wordsworth" is not necessarily Wordsworth "as he really is" or as we may read him; this is especially true when such "loaded" issues as the child or nature are being considered. Even George Eliot, thinking about *Sartor* in 1859, singled out "little Diogenes eating his porridge on the wall in sight of the sunset, and gaining deep wisdom from the contemplation of the pigs and other 'higher animals' of Entepfuhl" to describe the "pleasure" Carlyle's book had given her (GEL: III: 23)!

11 Quoted in Bercovitch, *Puritan Origins*, p. 16.

12 Quoted ibid., p. 17.

13 Frye's discussion in *The Secular Scripture*, p. 142, of the shadow-device in Christian writings is significant for suggesting what Carlyle is doing with Teufelsdröckh: "Such devices in Christian stories reflect the revolutionary and dialectical element in Christian belief, which is constantly polarizing its truth against the falsehoods of the heathen, but, like other revolutionary doctrines, feels most secure when the dark side takes the form of a heresy that closely resembles itself."

14 Bercovitch, *Puritan Origins*, pp. 17–18: "The way of the soul, [the Puritans] maintained, starts 'with a holy despair in ourselves' and proceeds 'with a holy kind of violence' back to Christ; it means acknowledging the primacy of that which is Another's, and *receiving* the ability to respond. Hence the advantage of self-knowledge: the terror it brings may exorcise our individuality. It may drive us to 'desire to be found, not in ourselves.' It may teach us that to love our neighbors as ourselves is to realize how drastically 'self is against the good of our neighbours.'" Alan Mintz, *George Eliot and the Novel of Vocation*, notes that in Carlyle, Newman, Mill, and George Eliot "a life begins when the passion for a certain calling is first discovered, and it ends when that passion is consummated or spent, and between there are moments of apprenticeship, trial, and production"; see chapter 2, "The shape of a life in biography and autobiography," pp. 21–51.

15 Sterling's comments are reprinted in Harrold's edition of *Sartor*, p. 315. George Landow, in *Victorian Types*, pp. 168–9, agrees, noting that Carlyle, "accustomed . . . to conceiving human life in biblical terms," used typology "to spiritualize" secular forces; his typical allusions "are entirely subjective and internal." For commentary on Christian's

breaking away from this world, see Welsh, *The City of Dickens*, p. 59, and Mintz, *George Eliot and the Novel of Vocation*, p. 13.

16 George Levine discusses Ruskin's connecting of nature and the human in "High and low: Ruskin and the novelists," in *Nature and the Victorian Imagination*, ed. Knoepflmacher and Tennyson, p. 149: "To compensate for the loss of the mountain spirit, Ruskin must look down to that staple of Victorian virtue and fiction, the humble English cottage."

17 Miyoshi, *The Divided Self*, pp. 145–6, discusses what prevents the experience described in *Sartor* from becoming solipsism.

18 See Kaufmann, *The Pilgrim's Progress*, pp. 61–79, for a discussion of Bunyan's presentation of Christian's experience in the House of the Interpreter, of how the pilgrim "closed with the Word."

19 Albert J. LaValley, *Carlyle and the Idea of the Modern* (New Haven: Yale, 1968), pp. 62–5 and 127–9, considers Carlyle's presentation of the madness and the unconscious throughout *Sartor* and the other writings. Jonathan Arac, *Commissioned Spirits* (New Brunswick, N. J.: Rutgers Univ. Press, 1979), pp. 114–38, focuses on this issue of madness in Carlyle's history and in Dickens' *Bleak House*.

20 Tennyson, *"Sartor" Called "Resartus"*, pp. 256–7, discusses the present tense in *Sartor*. See too Arac, *Commissioned Spirits*, pp. 119 and 122, and Vernon Lee, *The Handling of Words* (1923; rpt. Lincoln: Univ. of Nebraska Press, 1968), p. 181.

21 See Barfield's discussion of this process in history, *Saving the Appearances*, pp. 86, 123–4: in terms of nature, pagan and medieval philosophers had felt phenomena and their names as both representatives of the godlike and had believed that "to learn about the true nature of words was at the same time to learn about the true nature of things"; "modern man" perceives words to be as unrelated to the things named as he himself is unrelated to nature. In *Natural Supernaturalism*, pp. 307–8, Abrams discusses Carlyle's consideration of "consciousness" in "Characteristics": "'consciousness,' because it strikes a division between the knowing self and its fragmented objects and between the thinking self and its activities, is equatable to evil and disease; and the replacement of 'unconsciousness' by these modes of self-consciousness, in the first stages of philosophy and science, is the historical truth embodied in the fable of Adam's loss of paradise." See my article, "Idolatry for the English: Carlyle's lecture on paganism," in *Interspace and the Inward Sphere*, ed. Norman Anderson and Margene Weiss (Macomb, Il.: Essays in Literature, 1978), 75–86.

22 See Barfield, *Saving the Appearances*, p. 108. Kaufmann, *The Pilgrim's Progress*, pp. 165–74, discusses the Puritans' expressions of interest in nature.

23 David L. DeLaura, "Ishmael as prophet: *Heroes and Hero Worship* and the self-expressive basis of Carlyle's art," *Texas Studies in Literature and Language*, 1 (Spring 1969), 718–21.

24 LaValley, *Carlyle and the Idea of the Modern*, p. 216. See also Mintz, *George Eliot and the Novel of Vocation*, pp. 25–41.

2. The terrible beauty of Charlotte Brontë's "Natural Supernaturalism"

1 *Christian Remembrancer*, April 1848; reprinted in *The Brontës: The Critical Heritage*, ed. Miriam Allott (London: Routledge, 1974), p. 91.

2 Both Valentine Cunningham, *Everywhere Spoken Against*, and Elisabeth Jay, *Religion of the Heart*, offer significant discussions of Brontë's relation to the religious traditions in which she was raised. We have little certain information on her reading of Carlyle. A reference in a letter written to W. S. Williams, 15 June 1848, comments on Carlyle's style and indicates knowledge of his works. She was reading his *Miscellanies* in April 1849 ("I like Carlyle better and better"), though she noted that she had not read *The French Revolution*. See *The Brontës: Life and Letters*, ed. Clement Shorter (London: Hodder and Stoughton, 1908), I: 424; II: 40, 44. *Fraser's Magazine*, where *Sartor* began appearing in 1833, came to the parsonage beginning in 1831; see Shorter, I: 83–4, for Brontë's welcome of the journal to "the little wild, moorland village where we reside."

3 *Life and Letters*, I: 363.

4 *Revue des deux mondes*, 31 October 1848; reprinted in *Critical Heritage*, ed. Allott, pp. 101–2. Brontë's comment, in *Life and Letters*, I: 462–3.

5 Albany Fonblanque, in the *Examiner*, 3 November 1849 (reprinted in *Critical Heritage*, ed. Allott, p. 127), applauded Brontë's "irresistible grasp of reality." She much admired this review (see *Life and Letters*, II: 81).

6 Quoted in Abrams, *Natural Supernaturalism*, p. 211.

7 Alan Mintz's discussion of vocation, *George Eliot and the Novel of Vocation*, p. 6, applies with special force to Charlotte Brontë because her characters, like George Eliot's, are usually women: "This spiritualization of work is a secularized version of the Puritan belief that a man is called by God to a specific worldly vocation and that his success in it is a token of salvation."

8 *Jane Eyre*, Penguin edition (Harmondsworth, 1966), p. 481.

9 *Life and Letters*, II: 31.

10 Brontë's concern, while reading Mrs Gaskell's *Mary Barton*, about *Shirley*'s resemblance to it "in subject and incident" is important, particularly since Mrs Gaskell uses Carlyle by name so often in her novel. See *Life and Letters*, II: 23.

11 Robert Bernard Martin, *Charlotte Bronte's Novels: The Accents of Persuasion* (New York: Norton, 1966), p. 138.

12 E. P. Thompson's discussion of the early nineteenth-century's use of religious language to justify industrial labor practices should be noted here: "The factory system demands a transformation of human nature, the 'working paroxysms' of the artisan or outworker must be methodised until the man is adapted to the discipline of the machine." Thompson quotes from Dr Andrew Ure's *Philosophy of the Machine* (1835) to show how moral and religious issues were constantly discussed in the language of machinery: Ure described a factory as "a vast automaton, composed of various mechanical and intellectual

organs . . . all of them being subordinated to a self-regulated moving force"; and urged "every mill-owner *to organize his moral machinery on equally sound principles with his mechanical*" (see *Making of the English Working Classes*, pp. 359–62; Thompson's italics). Brontë's novels register the growing use of this kind of language to talk about the "inward world."

13 Lawrence Jay Dessner, *The Homely Web of Truth: A Study of Charlotte Brontë's Novels* (The Hague: Mouton, 1975), pp. 72 and 79, calls *Jane Eyre* "a religious 'tale,' a spiritual autobiography," and adds: "[Charlotte Brontë's] disdain of contemporary fiction had led her in *Jane Eyre* to the older form of moral *exemplum*, to the fiction in her Aunt's 'mad Methodist Magazines full of miracles and apparitions, and preternatural warnings, ominous dreams, and frenzied fanaticism'" (quotation from Mrs Gaskell). Michael Wheeler, *The Art of Allusion in Victorian Fiction* (New York: Barnes and Noble, 1979), pp. 36–43, gives close attention to allusions in *Jane Eyre* to *Pilgrim's Progress* and *Paradise Lost*, and suggests that "the allusions indicate that *Jane Eyre* . . . is to be read as a *spiritual* autobiography." Sandra M. Gilbert and Susan Gubar, *The Madwoman in the Attic: The Woman Writer and the Nineteenth-Century Literary Imagination* (New Haven: Yale, 1979), pp. 342–3 and 370, note the similarity of *Jane Eyre* to *Pilgrim's Progress* and assert that Brontë makes her novel "an 'irreligious' redefinition, almost a parody, of John Bunyan's vision." I would argue that Brontë offers a very serious *religious* redefinition of Bunyan, and intends absolutely no parody.

14 *Church of England Quarterly Review*, January 1850; reprinted in *Critical Heritage*, ed. Allott, p. 156.

15 For the affinities of Puritan and Romantic explorations of the self, see James N. Morris, *Versions of the Self* (New York: Basic Books, 1966), pp. 5–6. For a description of Methodist autobiography, see T. B. Shepherd, *Methodism and the Literature of the Eighteenth Century* (1940; rpt. New York: Haskell House, 1966), pp. 143–62.

16 David Lodge, *The Language of Fiction* (New York: Columbia, 1966), pp. 134–5.

17 Kaufmann, *The Pilgrim's Progress*, pp. 200–1.

18 Bercovitch, *Puritan Origins*, pp. 14–15, discusses the Puritan sense of the mirror: "For Baxter, Dell, and Richard Mather, the mirror radiated the divine image. They never sought their own reflection in it, as did Montaigne and his literary descendants through Rousseau. They sought Christ, 'the mirror of election' and 'Prospective-Glass for Saints' . . . The Puritans felt the less one saw of oneself in the mirror, the better; and best of all was to cast no reflection at all, to disappear. Their mirror was scriptural: 'We all with open face beholding, as in a glass, the glory of the Lord, are changed into the same image' (2 Cor. 3: 18)." For a discussion of the Romantics' handling of the mirror – particularly the mirror of "nature" – see Stephen J. Spector, "Wordsworth's mirror imagery and the picturesque tradition," *ELH*, 44 (1977), 85–107. In *The Divided Self*, Miyoshi notes the prevalence of mirror imagery throughout the nineteenth century.

19 In having Helen Burns read *Rasselas*, Brontë underlines her attachment to the old Mythus of religion and ethics.

20 Adrienne Rich, "Jane Eyre: the temptations of a motherless woman," *Ms.*, October 1973, calls Bertha "Jane's alter ego." See also Gilbert and Gubar, *Madwoman in the Attic*, p. 360, for an extended discussion of the function of Bertha Mason.

21 Kaufmann, *The Pilgrim's Progress*, p. 201.

22 Barfield, *Saving the Appearances*, pp. 177–8.

23 Harold Bloom, "The internalization of quest-romance," in *Romanticism and Consciousness*, ed. Bloom, p. 6.

24 Vogelin, "Postscript: on paradise and revolution," pp. 32–4.

25 Kaufmann, *The Pilgrim's Progress*, p. 236.

26 I am grateful to my colleague Thomas Shea for pointing out to me the significance of this passage.

27 Richard Dunn, "The natural heart: Jane Eyre's Romanticism," *Wordsworth Circle*, 10 (Spring 1979), 197–204; and Ruth B. Yeazell, "More true than real: Jane Eyre's 'Mysterious Summons,'" *Nineteenth-Century Fiction*, 29 (1974), 127–43, discuss this call in the context of Brontë's use of Romantic ideas in her novel.

28 Lodge, *Language of Fiction*, p. 140.

29 Bloom, "The internalization of quest-romance," p. 10, notes that "Romantic or internalized romance, especially in its purest version of the quest form, the poems of symbolic voyaging that move in a continuous tradition from Shelley's *Alastor* to Yeats's *The Wanderings of Oisin*, tends to see the context of nature as a trap for the mature imagination."

30 Frye, in *The Secular Scripture*, pp. 181–4, contrasts the sexual creation myth (with its earth-mother focus) and the artificial creation myth (with its sky father), and suggests that the artificial myth became the chief one for Western religion because "it emphasizes the uniqueness, the once-for-all quality, in the creative act, and helps to deliver us, if not from death or Mallarmé's 'chance,' at least from the facile ironies of an endlessly turning cycle." In the Old Testament, Ecclesiastes is desperately poised between these two myths.

31 S. Kierkegaard, *Fear and Trembling, and The Sickness Unto Death*, trans. Walter Lowie (Garden City, N. Y.: Doubleday, 1954), pp. 159–60.

32 Abrams' discussion of apocalyptic marriages is relevant here, *Natural Supernaturalism*, pp. 37–46. His comment that in *Pilgrim's Progress* "the land and city which is the goal is represented in a bluff rendering of the language of sexual desire" (p. 168) directs us to a source, along with Methodist hymns, of Brontë's very sexually charged language. Both Cunningham (*Everywhere Spoken Against*) and Jay (*Religion of the Heart*) discuss Brontë's use of "the language of religious devotion." See also note 40 below.

33 See Jay's account of the language of conversion as applied by Brontë to both Rochester and St John Rivers, *Religion of the Heart*, pp. 256–7. I do not agree with Jay, p. 258, that Jane's "final tribute . . . to St. John seems . . . strangely out of keeping with her previous critical attitude."

34 See Gilbert and Gubar's discussion of this problem, *Madwoman in the Attic*, pp. 395–8.

35 For a reading of *Villette* which places the novel "in the context of its contemporary tradition, the art of autobiography at the Victorian midcentury," see Janice Carlisle, "The face in the mirror: *Villette* and the conventions of autobiography," *ELH*, 46 (1979), 262–89. The author discusses Brontë's work in the context of the work of the Romantics and early Victorians.

36 Andrew Hook, "Charlotte Brontë, the imagination and *Villette*," in *The Brontës: A Collection of Critical Essays*, ed. Ian Gregor (Englewood Cliffs, N.J.: Prentice Hall, 1970), p. 143.

37 Robert Colby, *Fiction with a Purpose* (Bloomington: Indiana Univ. Press, 1967), p. 203.

38 Bercovitch, *Puritan Origins*, pp. 30–1. Terry Eagleton, *Myths of Power: A Marxist Study of the Brontës* (London: Macmillan, 1975), p. 67, notes how the "Evangelical discipline . . . [was] useful in curbing the libertine, over-assertive self."

39 George Levine's suggestion, *The Boundaries of Fiction*, p. 68, that *Sartòr Resartus* "marks the transition from the Romantics to the Victorians because it adds one quality to the Romantic vision which had not yet become dominant – desperation" applies with equal force to the Brontë of *Villette*. See too Hillis Miller's discussion of Romantic–Victorian differences in *The Disappearance of God* (1963; rpt. New York: Schocken, 1965), pp. 13–15.

40 George Landow's comment, in *Victorian Types and Shadows*, p. 168, that Carlyle's "pillars of fire and cloud are entirely subjective and internal," applies with equal force to Brontë's biblical allusions. She uses them for Lucy Snowe's narrative to suggest the psychological desolation of her protagonist; the very fact that they are associated with a Providential plan, with divine order, makes them appeal to Lucy as reins on any hopeful dreaming. At one point Lucy imagines some "imperious rules . . . commanding a patient journeying through the wilderness of the present, enjoining a reliance on faith – a watching of the cloud and pillar which subdue while they guide, and awe while they illumine – hushing the impulse of fond idolatry, checking the longing out-look for a far-off promised land" (II: 21: 309). Lucy's scriptural correspondences promise deprivation, never rest and peace – never the "reality" of Christian salvation (she sees herself as among the Israelites who never get to the Promised Land).

41 Robert Langbaum, *The Poetry of Experience* (New York: Norton, 1963), p. 16.

42 Terrifying too because of the images employed to suggest Lucy's efforts to conquer feeling: "I invoked Conviction to nail upon me the certainty, abhorred while embraced, to fix it with the strongest spikes her strongest strokes could drive; and when the iron had entered well my soul, I stood up, as I thought, renovated" (III: 39: 566). See Gilbert and Gubar, *Madwoman in the Attic*, pp. 411–12, and E. P. Thompson, *Making of the English Working Classes*, pp. 40–1, 369–72, for a discussion of the sources and significance of such language.

3. Transmutations of Dickens' emblematic art

1 *The Letters of Charles Dickens*, ed. Walter Dexter (Bloomsbury: Nonesuch Press, 1938), III: 348.
2 There are two book-length studies of Carlyle's influence on Dickens: William Oddie, *Dickens and Carlyle* (London: The Centenary Press, 1972), and Michael Goldberg, *Carlyle and Dickens* (Athens: Univ. of Georgia Press, 1972). Q. D. Leavis, in F. R. Leavis and Q. D. Leavis, *Dickens the Novelist* (London: Chatto and Windus, 1970), p. 125, suggests in her study of *Bleak House* that the "contemporary parts of *Past and Present* seem to me to have been second only to Shakespeare in influencing Dickens."
3 Quoted by John Forster, *The Life of Charles Dickens*, pp. 727–8.
4 Alexander Welsh, *The City of Dickens*, especially part II, "The earthly city," offers a richly suggestive discussion of the Bunyanesque tradition in Dickens' work. See too Steven Marcus, *Dickens from Pickwick to Dombey*, pp. 73–87, for a discussion of the Puritan background of *Oliver Twist*.
5 Leavis and Leavis, *Dickens the Novelist*, p. 335. J. R. Harvey, *Victorian Novelists and Their Illustrators* (London: Sidgwick and Jackson, 1970), gives careful attention to Dickens' relation to his illustrators, and notes, p. 74: "The vision of the old moral prints was still alive in his imagination, fused with the world he saw around him."
6 Michael Steig, *Dickens and Phiz* (Bloomington: Indiana Univ. Press, 1978), pp. 4–5.
7 Pickering, *The Moral Tradition in English Fiction*, pp. 107–12; see also Jay, *Religion of the Heart*, pp. 154–62, for discussion of these deathbed scenes; and Joseph W. Reed, Jr, *English Autobiography in the Early Nineteenth Century, 1801–1838* (New Haven: Yale, 1966), p. 35.
8 Freeman, *English Emblem Books*, p. 119.
9 The birdcage emblem is central to *Little Dorrit*, from the literal use in the opening number to its psychological notation in the cases of Amy Dorrit and Clennam, and to its social commentary in the case of Mrs Merdle's uncaged parrot. Charlotte Brontë gives the emblem the traditional meaning in *Jane Eyre* (see III: 1: 405–6; 10: 539; 11: 572), including the common use of the prison experience of Paul and Silas to underline the idea; again, however, Jane – freed by feeling from the "soul's cell" – finds her salvation in this world.
10 Both Teufelsdröckh's and Pip's life journeys are associated with water throughout. Jerome Buckley, *The Victorian Temper* (1951; rpt. New York: Vintage, 1964), pp. 97–105, discusses the frequent use the Victorians gave this image when writing of conversions.
11 Quoted words from M. H. Abrams, *Natural Supernaturalism*, p. 13.
12 George Landow, "'Swim or drown': Carlyle's world of shipwrecks, castaways, and stranded voyagers," *Studies in English Literature*, 15 (Autumn 1975), 647.
13 Coveney, *The Image of Childhood*, p. 140.
14 For a discussion of this focus on death, see Welsh, *City of Dickens*, pp. 119 and 170–1; and Jay, *Religion of the Heart*, pp. 163–5.

15 George Levine, "High and low: Ruskin and the novelists," in *Nature and the Victorian Imagination*, pp. 137–52, discusses this image of Blandois before the Alps.

16 Leavis and Leavis, *Dickens the Novelist*, pp. 148–50. Mrs Leavis discusses throughout her essay the ways Dickens uses and exposes "the clichés of Romanticism."

17 J. Hillis Miller, *Charles Dickens: The World of His Novels* (1958; rpt. Bloomington: Indiana Univ. Press, 1969), pp. 232–4, discusses Dickens' use of the labyrinth.

18 Stanley E. Fish, *Self-Consuming Artifacts* (Berkeley: Univ. of California Press, 1972), pp. 250–60, comments on Bunyan's use of memory in *Pilgrim's Progress*, and helps us to see more clearly what differences Dickens introduces in his appeals to remembrance: "Memory is the repository of the master's rule, the source of the inner light, the pulpit that the Holy Ghost preaches in. It is only memory that enables us to impose the correcting perspective of what is distant on what is near. Only by remembering can we resist the temptation to read causality into the mere sequence of events. Only memory can affirm against both the appeal and the fear of things present by bringing to mind the promise of things to come." In Dickens, memory serves more to bring to mind the promise of things that might have been.

19 Michael Timko, "The Victorianism of Victorian literature," *New Literary History*, 6 (Spring 1975), 615. Northrop Frye, "Dickens and the comedy of humors," in *The Victorian Novel: Modern Essays in Criticism*, ed. Ian Watt (New York: Oxford, 1971), p. 68, writes of the "hidden world" to which Dickens' heroes and heroines turn for renewal: "The victorious hidden world is not the world of nature in the Rousseauistic context of that word. The people who talk about this kind of nature in Dickens are such people as Mrs. Merdle . . . For all its domestic and sentimental Victorian setting, there is a revolutionary and subversive, almost a nihilistic, quality in Dickens's melodrama that is post-Romantic, has inherited the experience of the French Revolution, and looks forward to the world of Freud, Marx, and the existential thriller."

20 The reviewer quoted is John Forster, the *Examiner*, 8 October 1853; reprinted in *Dickens: The Critical Heritage*, ed. Philip Collins (New York: Barnes and Noble, 1971), p. 292.

21 Bercovitch, *Puritan Origins*, pp. 17–18. Mrs Leavis' analysis of Esther Summerson's "fully human" characterization, in *Dickens the Novelist*, pp. 155–60, is the most judicious defense of Esther in modern Dickens criticism.

22 The quoted words are Frye's, *The Secular Scripture*, p. 157: "The secular scripture tells us that we are the creators; other scriptures tell us that we are actors in a drama of divine creation and redemption . . . Identity and self-recognition begin when we realize that this is not an either–or question, when the great twins of divine creation and human recreation have merged into one, and we can see that the same shape is upon both."

23 Dickens' emblematic use of the mirror throughout *Bleak House* draws

attention to the spiritual and psychological condition of his men and women. Lady Dedlock's entrapment within a demonic world is thus indicated: ". . . until she sees her brooding face, in the opposite glass, and a pair of black eyes curiously observing her." The eyes belong to Hortense.

24 Two facts from the text should keep us from any temptation to name Rouncewell Carlyle's ideal Captain of Industry: (1) On his first appearance in the novel, he implicitly proclaims as outmoded the "strong bond" – "of love, and attachment, and fidelity" – which his mother has advocated before the Dedlocks; it had been his idea, he reports, to "sever" that bond (28: 352–3). (2) Trooper George resists his brother's plan to give him a position with the statement, as he turns towards "the green country" of Chesney Wold, that "there's more room for a Weed than there is here" (63: 746–8). Chesney Wold is not the ideal; indeed, in their closed atmospheres, the Dedlocks and the Rouncewells are not markedly different. But, as the narrator notes early on, "There is much good in" Chesney Wold (2: 11), mainly a delicacy of feeling that is anything but prevalent elsewhere.

25 [Dickens], Nonesuch *Letters*, II: 335.

26 Lee, *The Handling of Words*, p. 181. Lee compares Dickens' use of the present tense in *Bleak House* with Carlyle's in the history, and finds in the novelist simply melodrama. Eigner's discussion, in *Metaphysical Novel*, pp. 192 ff., of parallel plots is particularly illuminating. Of *Bleak House* he writes, pp. 205–6, that the omniscient narrator offers us "the despairing, unimaginative vision, characteristic of a materialistic century, from which Dickens is trying to convert us by the juxtaposition of his parallel plots"; Esther Summerson, in her narrative, "supplies the missing imagination." I disagree: Esther and the omniscient narrator *together* see the Romance within reality – one perceives the godlike, one the demonic; each offers confutation of the material view.

27 Leavis and Leavis, *Dickens the Novelist*, p. 252.

28 John Lucas, *The Melancholy Man* (London: Methuen, 1970), p. 328.

29 Dickens stresses that Headstone's moral nature has been developed at a school which taught "that you were to do good, not because it *was* good, but because you were to make a good thing of it" (II: 1: 264).

30 John Lucas, *The Melancholy Man*, pp. 336–7, discusses the infection of the pastoral landscape in *Our Mutual Friend*, and points out that it is outside the city where Betty Higden dies, Wrayburn nearly drowns, and Riderhood and Headstone drown together. The inversion of all traditional images is Dickens' point.

31 See Barbara Hardy's analysis of this confrontation scene, in "The complexity of Dickens," in *Dickens 1970*, ed. Michael Slater (New York: Stein and Day, 1970), pp. 32–3.

32 Robert Garis, *The Dickens Theatre* (Oxford: Clarendon, 1965), p. 230, sees in this marriage "social prophecy," Dickens' intimation that "the condition of England can be saved only by a new and deep amalgamation of the classes."

33 Deirdre David, *Fictions of Resolution in Three Victorian Novels* (New

York: Columbia, 1981), p. 203, defines this ending as a form of a "retreat from the world in which most of *Our Mutual Friend* is situated to a West End fairyland where [Dickens' extended family] devotes itself to innocent play, and to the dispensation of money made from rubbish collection to all the worthy characters who are enfolded within the circle of magical domesticity."

34 Freeman, *English Emblem Books*, pp. 135 and 232; Steig, *Dickens and Phiz*, chapter 1.
35 January 1845; reprinted in *Dickens: The Critical Heritage*, ed. Collins, pp. 160–1.
36 January 1854, and January 1862; reprinted in *Dickens: The Critical Heritage*, pp. 296–7, 437 (Philip Collins notes that Lord Acton is responsible for the comments in the later passage).
37 [Dickens], Nonesuch *Letters*, III: 125.

4. Speaking through parable: George Eliot

1 Barbara Hardy, *The Novels of George Eliot* (1959; rpt. New York: Oxford, 1967), p. 137; hereafter cited parenthetically in the text.
2 Reprinted in *Essays of George Eliot*, ed. Thomas Pinney (New York: Columbia, 1963), p. 288.
3 Ibid., p. 287. George Eliot's reading of Carlyle was intense from as early as 1841, during the period of her religious upheaval. In December 1841 she wrote to a schoolfriend urging her to read *Sartor*; she noted Carlyle's "devotion to the Author of all things" even though he was "not 'orthodox.'" Although in later years she would not have called him a "grand favourite," as she does here, her essays on his *Life of Sterling* and on an anthology of his writings indicate her abiding appreciation. See GEL: I: 122.
4 John Paterson, in his Introduction to the Riverside edition (Boston: Houghton Mifflin, 1968), p. xxvii, notes that George Eliot gives "actual and historical" names to the places through which Hetty passes on her journey, while "the other place-names of the novel are fictitious and semi-allegorical."
5 Christopher Herbert, "Preachers and the schemes of nature in *Adam Bede*," *Nineteenth-Century Fiction*, 29 (March 1975), 419. Donald Stone's chapter on George Eliot, in his *Romantic Impulse*, is the most comprehensive consideration of George Eliot's relation to Romanticism.
6 Cunningham, *Everywhere Spoken Against*, p. 167.
7 Herbert, "Preachers and the schemes of nature," p. 425. Donald Stone, *Romantic Impulse*, p. 208, suggests that George Eliot's obvious hatred of Hetty "betrays a sense of insecurity as to exactly how desirable or plausible the Loamshire way of life really is."
8 Chapter 15 – with Hetty gazing into her mirror and Dinah gazing out the window – has striking affinities with Quarles' emblem of "Flesh and Spirit" (see fig. 9, page 99), as David Leon Higdon has shown (see note 29, below).

9 Introduction to the Penguin edition (Harmondsworth, 1967), p. 14.

10 Brian Swann, "*Silas Marner* and the new mythus," *Criticism*, 18 (Spring 1976), 106–13, discusses the novel's response to Carlyle and to Victorian mythographers.

11 See David R. Carroll's discussions of this paralleling of Marner and Cass in "*Silas Marner*: reversing the oracles of religion," *Literary Monographs*, I, ed. Eric Rothstein and Thomas K. Dunseath (Madison: Univ. of Wisconsin Press, 1967), pp. 178, 197–8.

12 Ibid., pp. 196–9.

13 Frye, *Anatomy*, p. 198, has commented on *Silas Marner* and romance, as has Carroll, "*Silas Marner*: reversing the oracles of religion."

14 In *Essays of George Eliot*, ed. Pinney, pp. 270–1. Alan Mintz, *George Eliot and the Novel of Vocation*, p. 70, connects George Eliot's sense of her vocation with Milton's "spirituali[zation of] his calling"; and he notes, p. 21: "George Eliot's way of seeing character has its most conspicuous parallels among the great biographies and autobiographies of the mid-Victorian era."

15 See Samuel Pickering's discussion of the religious writers' use of narrative intrusion "to underline the didacticism of their stories" and dispel any idea that their writing was "art"; in *The Moral Tradition in English Fiction*, p. 58. See also Jay, *Religion of the Heart*, pp. 216–19, for a discussion of the evangelical background of George Eliot's realism.

16 Herbert, "Preachers and the schemes of nature," p. 422, discusses "the prominence given significantly in *Adam Bede* to the matter of education": "The long description in chapter 21 of the three workmen toiling over their lessons has unmistakably the quality of an allegorical panel and makes a powerful comment on the large question of man's relation to Nature . . . Such a passage, with its implications that uneducated peasants are less than fully human, makes a conspicuous break with Wordsworthian praise of mankind in the humblest, most natural, most instinctive state. To train and uplift the mind, George Eliot suggests, is to rescue human beings from brutish animality."

17 U. C. Knoepflmacher, *George Eliot's Early Novels* (Berkeley: Univ. of California Press, 1968), p. 217, notes this. Barbara Hardy, *Tellers and Listeners: The Narrative Imagination* (London: Athlone Press, 1975), pp. 76–8, discusses George Eliot's handling of memory in *The Mill*, and adds that "Mr. Tulliver's traditions and rituals are not as simple as George Eliot's natural imagery suggests." See too Donald Stone's discussion of George Eliot's use of memory and its relation to her Romantic sources (*Romantic Impulse*, pp. 212–17). Stone argues, p. 213, that "Eliot's Wordsworthian sensibility . . . directs, and finally mars, the development of *The Mill on the Floss*."

18 Raymond Williams, *The Country and the City* (New York: Oxford, 1973), p. 169, locates the "break in the texture of the novel" in the "disconnection" between the idiom of the author and that of her characters, between "an analytically conscious observer of conduct with a developed analytic vocabulary" and a "people represented as living and speaking in mainly customary ways."

19 Peter Coveney discusses this Introduction in detail in his commentary

to the Penguin edition of the novel (Harmondsworth, 1972).

20 Trans. Dorothy L. Sayers (Harmondsworth: Penguin, 1949), p. 71.

21 U. C. Knoepflmacher, "Fusing fact and myth: the new reality of *Middlemarch*," in *This Particular Web*, ed. Ian Adam (Toronto: Univ. of Toronto Press, 1975), p. 58. Frank Kermode, *The Sense of an Ending*, p. 56, discusses history's relationship to fiction in terms that particularly illuminate George Eliot's alignment of history and art: "'The thread of historical continuity,' as Hannah Arendt notices, 'was the first substitute for tradition; by means of it the overwhelming mass of the most divergent values, the most contradictory thoughts and conflicting authorities . . . we reduced to a unilinear, dialectically consistent development.' History, so considered, is a fictive substitute for authority and tradition, a maker of concords between past, present, and future, a provider of significance to mere chronicity."

22 David Carroll "*Middlemarch* and the externality of fact," in *This Particular Web*, ed. Ian Adam, p. 78.

23 David Carroll, ibid., pp. 82–4, noticing "the perfectly complementary nature" of Bulstrode and Raffles, focuses on the demonic imagery, "monsters, vampires, and assorted succubi (the stock in trade of Gothic fiction) who live a subterranean metaphoric life beneath the provincial surface of the novel." His discussion calls our attention to how often George Eliot uses the trappings of romance, no matter what "real" picture she is presenting.

24 Matthew Arnold, *God and the Bible*, ed. R. H. Super (Ann Arbor: Univ. of Michigan Press, 1970), p. 378.

25 Quotations from Tasso, included in the text, are from the translation by Edward Fairfax in 1600 (New York: Capricorn, n.d.). I can find no record of any performance of *Rinaldo* in the nineteenth century. But George Eliot, who loved opera (except Wagner), quotes one of the most familiar (and most often programmed) arias of Handel's opera, and plots her "romance" so similarly to the plotting of *Rinaldo* that coincidence seems unlikely.

26 Leon Gottfried, "Structure and genre in *Daniel Deronda*," in *The English Novel in the Nineteenth Century: Essays on the Literary Mediation of Values*, ed. George Goodin (Urbana: Univ. of Illinois Press, 1972), pp. 164–75, discusses George Eliot's refusal to allow "real" wickedness in her world of romance. For a disagreement and an interesting commentary on George Eliot's turning to "the motifs of folklore" in her last novel, see Mintz, *George Eliot and the Novel of Vocation*, pp. 153–4.

27 Handel-Rossi lyric translated by Dale McAdoo for the Handel Society recording (RCA Victor ARL1–0084). The song is essentially Armida's lament in Tasso after Rinaldo deserts her.

28 Frye, *The Secular Scripture*, p. 102: "Such a catastrophe, which is what it normally is, may be internalized as a break in memory, or externalized as a change in fortunes or social context." Frye notes too, p. 109, that mirror images traditionally "turn up near the beginning of a romance to indicate the threshold of a romance world."

29 See David Leon Higdon's discussion of George Eliot's use of emblems,

"The iconographic backgrounds of *Adam Bede*, chapter 15," *Nineteenth-Century Fiction*, 27 (September 1972), 155–70. Hugh Witemeyer, *George Eliot and the Visual Arts*, pp. 91 and 211–12, n. 67, finds suggestions of emblem book influence dubious.

30 René Girard, *Deceit, Desire, and the Novel: Self and Other in Literary Structure*, trans. Yvonne Freccero (Baltimore: Johns Hopkins, 1966), p. 15. See too Bercovitch, *Puritan Origins*, pp. 14–15, and Spector, "Wordsworth's mirror imagery," pp. 85–107. George Levine, in *The Realistic Imagination*, pp. 266–73, notes that "the character of the 'highest' (i.e., most 'altruistic') beings in Eliot's novels is increasingly defined by the absence of what we traditionally think of as character." This exaltation of selflessness, as her mirrors attest, comes out of George Eliot's reverence for the religious tradition's assertions of the need to destroy self in order to find the soul – Quarles hoped to "be no longer I" (*Emblems*, "Invocation").

31 Deirdre David, *Fictions of Resolution*, p. 168, offers an illuminating comparison of Mirah and Gwendolen as autobiographers: Mirah "presents a perfectly coherent narrative," "tells her own story without self-consciousness," while Gwendolen "cannot tell her own story" and needs an interpreter to make sense of it for her. Selflessness allows psychological – and narrative – order.

32 Deirdre David, ibid., p. 204, writes of the end of *Deronda*: "the fact that Eliot displaces her critical imagination right out of English society seems to reveal an implicit belief that the novel itself can no longer create resolutions of social tension . . . *Daniel Deronda* seems to refute the implicit suppositions of [*North and South* and *Our Mutual Friend*] that fiction can offer moral lessons, or alleviate social uneasiness, and it takes itself, as a novel that can perform these functions, right out of society."

33 See George Levine's important discussion of "George Eliot's hypothesis of reality," *Nineteenth-Century Fiction*, 35 (June 1980), 1–28, for commentary on the inextricable connection of the two parts of *Deronda*. Levine notes the statement in George Eliot's notebooks about the biblical Daniel – "The unknown teacher . . . is entitled to the praise that he was the first who grasped the history of the world, so far as he knew it, as one great whole, as a drama which moves onward at the will of the Eternal One" – and adds: "*Daniel Deronda* attempts once more, in the new language of science, to confirm the ideal hypothesis of the Old Testament."

Conclusion. The novel as book of life.

1 Northrop Frye, *Spiritus Mundi: Essays on Literature, Myth, and Society* (Bloomington: Indiana Univ. Press, 1976), pp. 238–9.

2 William Makepeace Thackeray, *Pendennis*, ed. Donald Hewes (Harmondsworth: Penguin, 1972), 75: 785. References hereafter given parenthetically in the text.

3 Frye, *The Secular Scripture*, p. 157.

4 George Levine's chapters on Thackeray in *The Realistic Imagination* are

especially important to seeing Thackeray "whole." Levine writes of the "unbridgeable" gap between fable-land and reality as Thackeray draws them, and notes that for Thackeray, emblematic language has become "chatter," mere words indeed.

5 Thomas Hardy, *Jude the Obscure*, ed. C. H. Sisson (Harmondsworth: Penguin, 1978), III: 10: 251; VI: 11: 485–6.

6 D. H. Lawrence, *Lady Chatterley's Lover* (1928; rpt. New York: Bantam, 1968), p. 1.

7 In *Lady Chatterley's Lover*, Connie registers Lawrence's fear of what has happened to language: "All the great words, it seemed to Connie, were cancelled for her generation: love, joy, happiness, home, mother, father, husband, all these great, dynamic words were half dead now, and dying from day to day . . . It was as if the very material you were made of was cheap stuff, and was fraying out to nothing" (pp. 63–4). Levine, *The Realistic Imagination*, p. 326, associates Lawrence's work with that of the Victorian sages, and adds that for Lawrence "the language of realism has become only the language of gossip."

8 D. H. Lawrence, "Why the novel matters," in *Selected Literary Criticism*, ed. Anthony Beal (New York: Viking, 1966), pp. 105–7.

Index

Index

Index

Index